On the Boundaries of American Evangelicalism

On the Boundaries of American Evangelicalism

The Postwar Evangelical Coalition

Jon R. Stone

St. Martin's Press
New York

Library of Congress Cataloging-in-Publication Data
Stone, Jon R., 1959-
  On the boundaries of American Evangelicalism : the postwar
  Evangelical coalition / Jon R. Stone.
      p. cm.
  Based on the author's thesis (doctoral)—University of California,
  Santa Barbara, 1990.
  Includes bibliographical references and index.
  ISBN 0-312-17342-3
  1. Evangelicalism—United States—History—20th century.
  2. United States—Church history—20th century.   I. Title.
  BR1642.U5S76 1997
  280'.4'097309045—dc21   97-10593
                                                                          CIP

Design by Acme Art,Inc.

First edition: November, 1997
10 9   8   7   6   5   4   3   2   1

For my Parents,
Robert H. and Bobbie Jean Stone,
whose lifelong love and sacrifice have made all
my achievements possible

Contents

Religious Periodical Abbreviations. .viii

Acknowledgments ix

CHAPTER ONE: Defining Evangelical Diversity 1

CHAPTER TWO: A Boundary Approach to the Study
of American Evangelical Protestantism 23

CHAPTER THREE: The Liberal and Conservative
Divide in American Protestantism, 1880–1930 51

CHAPTER FOUR: The Emergence of a "New" Evangelicalism,
1940–1960 73

CHAPTER FIVE: The Evangelical Boundary Dilemma:
Checking the Drift toward Liberalism, 1940–1965 117

CHAPTER SIX: The End of the New Evangelical Coalition,
1965–1990 159

Notes 185

References and Sources 203

List of Referenced Christian Periodicals 220

Index 221

Religious Periodical Abbreviations

CC:	*Christian Century*
CL:	*Christian Life (and Times)*
CT:	*Christianity Today*
KB:	*King's Business*
SST:	*Sunday School Times*
UEA:	*United Evangelical Action*

Acknowledgments

It is often noted that books are collaborative efforts. This saying proves no less true in the case of this present study on the social structural dynamics of postwar American evangelicalism. Beginning as a doctoral dissertation written in 1990 under the direction of Phillip E. Hammond, Catherine L. Albanese, and Birger A. Pearson, and focusing on secularization and related socio-historical themes in American evangelicalism from 1940 to 1965, this book has evolved into a much more complex (and readable) work.

Over the past several years, this study has been shaped by and has benefited greatly from conversations with a number of gracious individuals willing to listen to a young scholar opine about a subject on which even angels fear to speak. These include Eileen Barker, Michael A. Burdick, Walter H. Capps, Jonathan Cordero, Craig J. Hazen, Benton Johnson, Leeba Lessin, Phillip C. Lucas, Martin E. Marty, Eric Mazur, J. Gordon Melton, Wade Clark Roof, Richard J. Severson, Michael Shott, Mark A. Shibley, Ninian Smart, Jerome Soneson, Rodney Stark, Bryan R. Wilson, and a great number of unnamed reviewers.

Along the way, this research project received several boosts in the form of two travel grants from The Institute for the Study of American Evangelicals and three research grants from the University of California at Santa Barbara, one of these from its Interdisciplinary Humanities Center and two from the Department of Religious Studies. I would also like to thank the reference librarians and interlibrary loan personnel from the University of California at Santa Barbara and librarians from the University of California at Berkeley, the Graduate Theological Union, Westmont College, Fuller Theological Seminary, Biola University, Wheaton College, and the Billy Graham Center Archives. A special thanks to Steve Jolley, a minister of the Santa Barbara Community Church, for helping me confirm an obscure but crucial reference.

I also received invaluable advice and editorial support from Maura E. Burnett at St. Martin's Press, which I gratefully acknowledge. I would also like to thank Richard Taylor for his great help in compiling the index.

The most valuable support has been from my extended network of family and friends. I would like to express my appreciation to the following people: to my lovely grandparents, Irene Timme and Curtis and Lois Stone; to my brothers and their wives, Richard and Dawn Stone and David and Mary Stone; to my nieces and nephews, Lauren, Shawna, Bethany, Christopher, Brenton, and Zachary; to some of my many friends, Mark Adams, Brian and Maria Allen, Katherine Baker, John and Carrie Birmingham, Thomas and Karin Bryan, R. Bruce Evans, Bill and Sharon Francis, Michael Graczyk, Helen Harrington, Daniel B. Listoe, Casey and Kathy Roberts, young Tristan and Matthew Roberts, Clyde and Betty Taylor, Scott and Annelie Williams, Brian and Cybelle Wilson, and Roy Zyla; and lastly, to the members of my J.V. Water Polo and J.V. Boys Swimming teams at Santa Barbara High School, whom I coached, in season and out, from 1994 until my removal to Berkeley in 1997 (most notably, Landon Hess, John Kelty, Jason Argyropoulos, Luke Trower, Arjun McAvoy, Greg Snyder, Clinton Kitson, John Barron, Devon Charlton, James Hatsedakis, and Trey Evans). I will forever remain their most loyal fan.

Without question, my greatest love and warmest affections go to my parents, Robert H. and Bobbie Jean Stone, to whom this book is dedicated (sorry about the topic).

Scribere Jussit Amor.

—Jon R. Stone
University of California, Berkeley

CHAPTER ONE

Defining Evangelical Diversity

Only that which has no history is definable.
—Nietzsche

FROM THE ARRIVAL OF THE PILGRIMS AT PLYMOUTH plantation as a beacon of hope in the New World, to the satellite broadcasts of televangelists beaming the light of the Christian Gospel, evangelical Protestant religion has been a visible and defining presence in the history of the American people. Indeed, despite its many debates and divisions, its manifold organizational forms, and the foibles of its various representative leaders, to read the story of American evangelicalism is, in a great way, to read about the vitality of the Protestant spirit in the New World. Protestantism, especially its evangelical form, has been and still remains an influential force in shaping the history of the United States. Not surprisingly, the Protestant presence has been a subject of enduring interest to social scientists, historians, and journalists. Their works chart the diverging conservative, moderate, and liberal paths and record the changing fortunes of its right and left wings.

But as Protestantism's expressions have changed and its fortunes have fluctuated, so also have the interests of scholars who have sought to document and analyze those various transformations. In more recent times, some researchers have been intrigued by the declining influence of the once-powerful liberal mainline.[1] Still others have been captivated by the strong resurgence of Protestant conservatism—evangelicalism in the 1970s and fundamentalism in the 1980s—and especially its present incursion into America's social and political arenas.[2]

Over the past decade an amazing amount of attention has been focused on conservative Protestantism, with studies examining everything from its origins and numerical growth (Liebman and Wuthnow 1983; Bromley and Shupe 1984) to its social and political activism (Jorstad 1987; Bruce 1988; Moen 1989; Smidt 1989; Provenzo 1990; Jelen 1991; Jorstad 1993; Bruce, *et al.* 1995) and mass media evangelism (Hadden and Swann 1981; Hoover 1988; Bruce 1990; Jorstad 1993; Melton, *et al.* 1997). But even using the precision of social science, with attempts both to quantify evangelicalism (Hunter 1982) and to clear away some of the theoretical misconceptions surrounding it (Warner 1979), scholars have nevertheless found evangelicalism an elusive phenomenon that, more often than not, defies comprehension and confounds precise explication. By all accounts, to use a familiar cliche, evangelicalism has been a difficult nut to crack.

Interestingly, the self-professed evangelical scholars who have weighed in have been less concerned with measuring conservative Protestantism's organizational strengths and effectiveness. Instead, their analyses have tended to focus more generally on much more fundamental concerns, such as laying out an agenda for evangelical effectiveness in a society they see as indifferent, sometimes hostile, to biblical Christianity.[3] Even their historical treatments have tended to conceal an underlying apologetic or oblique evangelistic agenda. What is more, upon closer examination of these evangelical writings, one comes away with a vague sense that evangelicals are a little uneasy, even anxious, about who they are and how to define their community. In reading their works, one detects recurrent allusions to "evangelical identity" that suggest to the outside observer that evangelicals themselves are not entirely certain about their own identity. What, then, is one to make of this one all-inclusive "evangelicalism" of which many evangelicals write but cannot seem to define? Does such an "ism" exist, or is it merely a fiction, an ideal envisaged by evangelicalism's more hopeful and visionary spokespersons? It is the argument of this study that evangelicalism *is* a fiction. The cohesiveness that the observer perceives from a distance does not bear out when one takes a closer and more studied look. What one discovers is that evangelicals themselves are deeply divided over who they are and even over what in fact constitutes evangelicalism.

THE BOUNDARIES OF EVANGELICALISM

Traditionally, evangelicalism has been identified with the more popular forms of Protestantism in America. From the frontier churches, spawned through revivalism, to the splinter groups, formed through doctrinal disagreements, evangelicalism has grown increasingly in numbers as well as in kinds. Though evangelicalism's individual institutional histories have varied, its constituents have all, in one way or another, claimed some connection to a type of Protestantism that looked to the authority of the Bible to anchor its beliefs as well as to orient the lives of its adherents in this world.[4]

Over the past fifty years, evangelical spokespersons have taken up the problem of defining the boundaries of evangelicalism with unequalled interest, searching for clues to understanding their broad and broadening "community"—its characteristics and vastly diverse and ever-changing constituency. One has only to glance at the titles of books and articles by these spokespersons to see that something is definitely amiss in the evangelical camp.[5] When one considers that these spokespersons are the more highly visible representatives of mainstream evangelicalism, their uncertainty over who is and who is not an evangelical becomes all the more intriguing. Should not evangelicals know where to draw the boundaries of their own community?

How, then, might we account for the confusion evangelicals display over what it means to be an evangelical and over the limits of evangelical diversity? One answer can be found by looking at the boundaries themselves, that is, by the way evangelicals have sought to delimit the evangelical "community" and the social structural dynamics this definitional process entails. Accordingly, this study on the boundaries of American evangelicalism will examine the emerging evangelical definitional crisis as seen through the books, articles, editorials, and printed speeches of its reputed leaders published since the early 1940s and its continuing impact on evangelicalism into the early 1990s. The thoughts and initiatives put forth by representative spokespersons will be a clue to the social structural dynamics that underlie this persistent definitional dilemma.

In this introductory chapter, I will first consider the problems evangelical scholars have faced in their own attempts to account for evangelicalism's growing diversity. Second, I will outline an explanation for what I call the "evangelical boundary dilemma," a dilemma having its roots in the immediate postwar period. Third, I will note a number of earlier studies that, while making some allusions to the evangelical boundary dilemma, give little attention to the critical role the shifting boundary has played in defining evangelical self-understanding and in contributing to the evangelical definitional crisis. In the final section of this chapter I will sketch out the direction the argument of this study will take in the chapters to follow.

DESCRIBING EVANGELICAL DIVERSITY

When evangelical scholars talk about the diversity of evangelicalism—its broadening boundaries—they typically employ metaphors to help them picture the variety they see before them. But, far from clarifying that diversity, their reliance on metaphors seems only to compound the problem of understanding. One reason for this is that metaphors are descriptions, not explanations.

One example of this reliance on metaphorical images to describe evangelical diversity is found in the work of Timothy L. Smith. Over the past two decades, Smith has put forth two metaphors that evangelicals have embraced with uncritical approval.[6] In the 1970s, Smith spoke of evangelical diversity in terms of a "mosaic." However, more recently he exchanged "mosaic" for what he believed to be a more descriptive image of evangelicalism, that of a "kaleidoscope." As Smith related, "my favorite metaphor for the history of American evangelical movements is that of a kaleidoscope—a more *dynamic image,* certainly, than the one with which I began ten years ago, the mosaic" (Smith 1986:128, emphasis added). The picture that "kaleidoscope" presents, said Smith, is one of change and is therefore an apt metaphor to describe evangelical history. As Smith explained: "In virtually every successive decade since the year 1700, the emergence of new spiritual movements, the regrouping of old alliances, and the effort to respond biblically to current moral and political challenges have produced significant changes in the pattern of North American Protestantism" (Smith 1986:128). Thus, the kaleidoscope metaphor, Smith argued, presents the best picture of these changes.

To be sure, the kaleidoscope metaphor suggests ever new, unrepeatable patterns unfolding before the observer. Every moment is new, yet some moments are similar enough to other moments that a person can detect patterns that are analyzable or can be set into larger theoretical models for analysis. But Smith did not offer his kaleidoscope metaphor for the purpose of analysis, but merely as a description of the diversity of his tradition. While Smith's observations were certainly accurate, his analysis stopped well short of explanation. His endeavor to describe the dynamic as a "kaleidoscope" failed to explain why a changing configuration of Protestant types exists and persists. While metaphors help us answer the question, "What is it like?," at the same time, they are not capable of answering the more analytical questions, "What is it?" and "Why is it like that?" Sociologist Rodney Stark was correct when he asserted that "The problem with metaphors is not that they are false, but that they are empty" (1986:315). They are empty in the sense that they leave us with no better understanding of a phenomenon than when we started. "Concepts are *names* not *explanations,*" Stark reminded us reprovingly; "To name some objects or phenomena tells us nothing about why they occur or what they influence" (1986:315). Metaphors are helpful if one aims simply to point out the relationship or resemblance of two or more phenomena. Metaphorical language may certainly open the eyes of the observer to one or more features of a phenomenon, but often this comes at the expense of obscuring the functions of those features as a whole.

In the past few years, evangelicals have begun to describe evangelicalism in terms of "family resemblances" (after Wittgenstein). Robert K. Johnston offered this metaphor as "a new model for describing American evangelicalism" that is both "useful and illuminating" (Dayton & Johnston 1991: 255, 258). Evangelical scholars appear to be excited by its prospects for descriptive clarity. "The notion of family resemblance," said Johnston, ". . . is a helpful one in coming to understand American evangelicalism. Rather than seek exclusive categories, it is useful to recognize the familial nature of

American evangelicalism" (1991:256). While Johnston's adaptation of Wittgenstein represents a creative attempt to solve a persistent definitional dilemma, one clear problem with this metaphor is that it offers little more explanation than previous ones. To say, with Johnston, that "evangelicals have similar traits" does not strike me as particularly useful or analytically illuminating. To call evangelicalism a "family"—even an "extended family"—explains little and takes us no further down the path of understanding than "mosaic" or "kaleidoscope" does.[7] While it is true that the notion of "family resemblances" creates a typology of sorts against which various types of groups are compared and classified, this heuristic strategy is self-defeating in that one has to determine which "type" is normative, that is, the one "ideal" against which all forms are to be measured. If one seeks to define and to know the cause of these phenomena—why such diversity occurred, for example—then one will find descriptive metaphors hopelessly inadequate.[8]

An obvious problem with all these efforts to define evangelicalism is that scholars' use of descriptive metaphors is analytically empty. Metaphors such as "kaleidoscope," "mosaic," "spirit," "mood," "family resemblances" are far too vague. To be sure, concepts such as "tradition", "movement", "denomination", "community" are much more helpful in that one can at least compare evangelical phenomena to these sociological categories to see if they aptly apply, but these particular terms are likewise imprecise. What do we gain if we call evangelicalism a "denomination," "movement," or "tradition" that cannot already be inferred from the term "evangelical-*ism?*" To define a movement as a "movement" is an inexcusable tautology.

While Smith may have had too great a fondness for the "kaleidoscope" metaphor, he at least nudged his evangelical colleagues to point their gaze in a more analytical direction when he alluded to evangelicalism as an ever-changing coalition of Protestants centered around core beliefs. Indeed, considering evangelicalism as a "coalition" is precisely the direction analysis should take. "Coalition" is a concept that moves beyond merely descriptive metaphors in that one can use it to analyze and explain. As Rousseau observed over two centuries ago, coalitions result from goal-directed activity, yet endure only until the goal is either obtained or abandoned (1984:111). "Coalition" implies a dynamic alignment of individuals or groups with common interests or goals.[9] For this reason, therefore, "coalition" appears to be a more analytically useful concept to apply to such a dynamic and diverse phenomenon as American evangelicalism.

THE EVANGELICAL "COALITION"

As one peruses the history of Protestant Christianity in America, one gains the impression that its evangelical wing has largely been a collection of changing constituencies. It has been a "collection" in the sense that evangelicals have always worked together toward larger goals. It has also been a "changing constituency" in that while evangelicals have often gathered into coalitions of interests and common causes, those coalitions have often been short-lived, almost always separating over some theological or ecclesiological disagreement too fundamental for them to ignore. This recurring dynamic has tended to work against evangelicalism's periodic attempts to effect and maintain unity. Put in more theoretical terms, while the members of evangelicalism's various and competing coalitions have often changed over time, the process of coalition building, and even the coalitions themselves, presents a similar dynamic pattern from which one can construct an analytical model.

What is more, a fundamental problem every coalition must solve is the problem of defining the extent of its alliances. That is, in order to bring together a coalition, individuals or groups of individuals are compelled to decide how comprehensive the coalition will be: which ideologies to include and which to exclude. Implicit in this definitional dynamic is the process of aggregation and separation, or what Plato referred to as "collection" and "division"—the gathering together of similar phenomena and the sifting and sorting of those phenomena into specific related forms.[10] This recurring process of collection and division results in a coalition of changing constituents, a process that tends ultimately to work against coalitional unity.

The postwar new evangelicals, on whom this study focuses, faced this very definitional quandary. In order to form their coalition, moderates found it necessary to define who the "true" evangelicals were. But in order for their coalition to encompass an ever-larger constituency of evangelicals, they began to allow for a broader definition of "evangelical." As a result of this broadening of the boundaries of the evangelical coalition, "evangelicalism" became so comprehensive that by the 1970s it began to lose almost all of its definitional precision. If collection and division is the central coalitional dynamic of postwar American evangelicalism, then in order to understand better the diversity of American evangelicalism—and explain it—one must understand how this boundary dynamic shaped and shapes evangelical self-understanding and, with it, "evangelicalism" more generally.

It must be stressed that this study is not concerned with finding *the* definition of evangelicalism. Instead, the specific intention here is to examine the dynamics of postwar American evangelicalism's definitional difficulties, that is, its continuous attempts to define the extent of its coalitional boundaries, especially the boundaries between evangelical and non-evangelical. Because this study will take as its point of reference the postwar evangelical coalition known as the new evangelicalism, it is necessary to introduce the conditions under which the new evangelical coalition was formed. This will be done by briefly tracing the story line this study will follow, beginning just after the denominational ruptures caused by the theological and ideological battles that took place early in the twentieth century.

AN HISTORICAL OVERVIEW

By the end of the fundamentalist-modernist controversy of the 1920s, two opposing theological groups within American Protestantism had clearly differentiated themselves from one another: fundamentalists and liberal Protestants. While fundamentalists effectively lost control of the mainline denominations during this time and all but disappeared from the religious landscape, during the 1930s, fundamentalism, which had become a culturally marginal movement, began to transform itself into a vast and highly diversified religious subculture. Joel Carpenter (1980 and 1984c) has traced the development of this extensive organizational network through which fundamentalist groups were able to shore up their defenses against modernism.[11]

Similarly, David Harrington Watt has argued that conservative Protestantism's strength, or its resolve to fight modernism, did not evaporate as a result of the heated controversies of the 1920s. As Watt wrote, "It had, rather, raised the question that would dominate much of the history of conservative Protestants in twentieth-century America: now that evangelicalism was clearly a subculture, how should evangelicals orient themselves toward America's dominant culture" (1991:42). As a subculture, the struggle to define the Christian's relationship to secular society continued into the Depression years, "producing nearly as many individual responses to the new situation as there were individual Fundamentalists" (1991:42).

But there were those within the fundamentalist movement who looked forward to another day. While some waited for Armageddon, other, more moderate, fundamentalists worked tirelessly for what they anticipated as a coming revival of "biblical" Christianity in Depression-era America.[12] As Carpenter pointed out, "rather than persisting in their public antimodernist crusading, fundamentalists during the 1930s were strengthening their own institutional base. Within this network, they believed, they could maintain their conservative doctrines and lifestyles, and on [conservatism's] renewed strength launch out in an enlarged program of evangelism" (1984c:33).

David Watt concurred with Carpenter's assessment of fundamentalism's strength and vitality as a religious subculture. Said Watt, "Subsequent developments reveal how misleading it is to describe the fundamentalist controversies as simple fundamentalist defeats. The controversies were followed by a string of impressive evangelical accomplishments" (1991:34). Indeed, scholarship during the 1980s and early 1990s, especially that of Carpenter and George Marsden, has shown that whatever decline occurred within fundamentalism, it was a decline primarily in influence and not in organizational and membership strength. Wrote Marsden, "Despite defeats in the denominations, the intrafundamentalist battles of the 1930s, and the impact of the depression, fundamentalist institutions had been growing" (1987:47). Watt corroborated Marsden's observation: "the pattern is rather one of sustained steady growth. And in each decade since the fundamentalist controversies conservative Protestants displayed considerable strength" (1991:35). Far from being a decade of defeat, then, "the 1930s were years of effervescence rather than of decline" (1991:35).[13] Fundamentalism appeared poised to take full advantage of a long-awaited revival of religion.

But fundamentalists were not all of one mind about themselves and their relation to secular society. To many, fundamentalism represented the last remnant of orthodox Protestant religion in a godless world. However, an increasingly sizable minority of moderate fundamentalists was not content to wait for the apocalyptic end of the world to make things right again. These moderates began to express their dissent with greater frequency and with greater verve. Sometime in the 1940s this group began to emerge as a distinct challenge to fundamentalism itself, especially fundamentalism's orientation to secular culture. Several components made up the ambitious program of these younger, better educated, and more socially minded church leaders and theologians. First, these renegade fundamentalists and other moderate conservatives sought to reclaim the nineteenth-century evangelical tradition, from which they believed the churches had departed during the denominational wars of the 1920s. Second, these moderates were not content to remain on the margins of American religious life but attempted to return orthodox Protestantism to the cultural center and regain the influence it had lost (Hedstrom 1982). Third, in order to accomplish their revival of nineteenth-century evangelical Protestantism and recover its cultural influence, these postwar evangelicals worked tirelessly to forge a coalition of orthodox Protestants that cut across the spectrum of American evangelical Christianity.

By laying down an ambitious and socially relevant agenda, this broad coalition of moderate fundamentalists and conservative evangelicals was directly challenging the pessimistic separatism and religious and cultural marginalization that came to characterize the fundamentalist movement of the 1920s and 1930s. In so doing, this "new breed" of fundamentalists made it clear that they were determined to wrest control of the helm of orthodoxy and direct a course toward theological and cultural respectability for conservative Protestantism, a respectability that had been severely undermined by the previous generation's overzealous ecclesiastical inquisitions as well as its embarrassing theological obscurantism.[14] With a sense of optimism, the new evangelicals began to draw together an interdenominational coalition of moderate to conservative Protestants through which the spirit of nineteenth-century American evangelical Protestantism might be revived. But they did not stop there, for these new evangelicals also challenged the legitimacy of the "left-leaning" agenda of the mainline Protestant establishment.

The move toward a more moderate position did not come without its complications, however. Though the new evangelicals sought to build a coalition that would include moderates and conservatives, the animosity that both liberal Protestants and fundamentalists historically felt toward each other had been at times so intense that when the new evangelicals emerged to challenge the effectiveness of these opposing forms of Protestantism, they were viciously attacked by both sides. The liberals cast a jaundiced eye toward this new-style evangelicalism, regarding it as little more than a slight variation of fundamentalism. The fundamentalists, for their part, were equally suspicious of this "neo" evangelicalism, believing that its proponents sought to make peace with liberals rather than continue the valiant fight against the evils of modernism. The very idea of a "progressive" fundamentalism was as inconceivable to liberals as it was unpalatable to fundamentalists.

As a result of being neither liberals nor fundamentalists, the new evangelicals found themselves in a difficult position, in a peculiar boundary quandary. While the new evangelicals strove to be both orthodox and progressive, the strong distinction already established between fundamentalists and liberals during the early decades of the twentieth century militated against achieving an inclusive, let alone clearly defined, middle position. The new evangelicals could not effect the reconciliation between the two poles within Protestantism that they had hoped to achieve. Try as they might, the new evangelicals simply could not please both groups, which continually called on the new evangelicals to declare unequivocally their allegiance to either one side or the other.

Thus, having situated themselves precariously between the sharp boundary that defined liberals and fundamentalists—a boundary that both groups vigilantly guarded and dared not cross or blur—the new evangelicals gained for themselves the opprobrium of both and the approbation of neither. By the mid-1950s, when the suspicions of the fundamentalists and the apprehensions of the liberals (not to mention ambivalence of the evangelicals) failed to bring about cooperative dialogue, the new evangelicals denounced both fundamentalists and liberals as illegitimate evangelicals and began to move in their own direction. Though the new evangelicals believed the coalition they were establishing would revive nineteenth-century evangelical Protestantism and would bring with it an outpouring of evangelistic fervor and a long-awaited national spiritual renewal, in reality, two unintended consequences resulted: first, evangelicals spent most of their energies differentiating themselves from fundamentalists and liberals; second, the postwar evangelical coalition grew so broad that the boundary between themselves and other Protestants became increasing difficult, if not impossible, to draw.[15]

What is interesting to observe is that while postwar evangelicals claimed to be theologically orthodox, the friction between new evangelical and fundamentalist spokespersons consistently centered on their conflicting responses to secular society. Evangelical and fundamentalist responses to modern culture differed in that evangelicals have traditionally sought to engage the world and transform it from within, while fundamentalists have more typically resisted contact with secular culture, seeking not to transform secular society but to rescue individuals from its damning influence. During the 1950s, separatist fundamentalists condemned the new evangelical strategy of influencing society from within as "selling out" to worldliness for the sake of evangelistic expedience. By contrast, fundamentalists sought to "witness" to secular society by denouncing its evils and calling people to "come out" of secular culture and join them "outside" the world of sin and godlessness. The result of this divided response to secular society has been bitter division within the ranks of postwar conservative Protestantism—a breach that still distinguishes fundamentalists from evangelicals.[16]

But evangelical acceptance of society did not come without some reservations. Evangelicals were cautious not to cross the line between the church and the world, lest they fall prey to the iron grip of secularism. This noticeably ambivalent stance toward participation in secular society is rooted in the Protestant conservative belief that such participation in modern cultural life is erosive to a Christian's spiritual life. This dualistic separation of life into sacred and secular spheres presents the believer with the predicament of how he or she can live in secular society and participate in its cultural and intellectual life without losing his or her religious faith. Such a predicament makes the line between "the Church" and "the world" a critical matter for the believer to distinguish. The point at which an individual crosses the line or blurs the boundary between what is "of Christ" and what is "of the world" is therefore of greatest concern to those wishing to maintain their orthodoxy so as to save their souls.

While evangelical adjustment to and fundamentalist retrenchment against modern society typified conservative Protestantism's dual response to the "crisis of secularity" during the immediate postwar years,[17] this divided response has persisted, threatening as before to rend orthodoxy from within. Fundamentalists such as Harold Lindsell and Carl McIntire have pointed to evangelical "concessions" to secular society as the defining differences between themselves and the new evangelicals, a gauge evangelicals have likewise used in drawing a distinction between themselves and fundamentalists.[18] Although their quarrel has been over where to draw the line between religious faith and secular society, to say that their fight is merely a theological one is to overlook both the social structural adjustments and organizational rigidification that is at the root of their division.[19]

INTEREST IN THE BOUNDARIES OF EVANGELICALISM

The concern evangelicals display over defining their community boundaries is not novel. Indeed, evangelicalism's attention to the integrity of its boundaries has occasionally been pointed out by both historians and sociologists. But while scholars have noted the existence of the evangelical boundaries, no one has, as yet, examined in detail the importance of postwar evangelical boundary concern as a key to understanding the dynamics of evangelical diversity. When the boundaries of evangelicalism are discussed by scholars, their analyses tend to focus on the *theological* differences between rival Protestant groups, not on the social structural dynamics at the heart of these concerns. To demonstrate this analytical oversight, I will briefly highlight both this underdeveloped interest in evangelical boundary consciousness and the overemphasis on theological concerns that characterize most scholarly analyses of American evangelical Protestant diversity.

Martin E. Marty, an ever-astute observer of American religious culture, discussed the tensions within contemporary American evangelicalism as tensions that all systems of orthodoxy face. This dynamic tension is especially evident in pluralistic societies in which a number of rival orthodoxies compete for control over the same tradition. American evangelicalism exemplifies this dynamic aptly. As Marty explained, "most of the energies expended recently by evangelicals have been directed chiefly to the cause of demarcating or delineating boundaries between themselves and American Protestant liberals on the one hand or fundamentalists on the other" (Marty 1977:190). The boundary preoccupation of modern evangelicalism relates closely to the question of continuity with or connectedness to nineteenth-century evangelical Protestantism. As Marty put it, "Nineteenth-century Protestantism serves as such an ideology in the eyes of most twentieth-century American Protestants, and thus the controversy as to who are the best custodians of its lore has religious and social consequences" (1977:191). Thus, conservative evangelicals regard nineteenth-century Protestantism as the best expression of Protestantism, a Protestantism that held fast to the verities of the Reformation before it was "perverted" by the theological deviations of liberals and modernists and "subverted" by the ecclesiastical divisiveness of fundamentalists (1977:190-191).[20] It is against this romanticized version of nineteenth-century Protestantism that evangelicals measure themselves and their relationship to other Protestant groups. Thus, by claiming nineteenth-century evangelicalism as their true heritage, the postwar new evangelicals saw themselves in the role of reformers of a tradition from which they believed fundamentalism, as well as liberalism, had sharply departed.

James Davison Hunter, whose study focused on evangelicalism's "coming generation" and "the cultural costs and consequences of [evangelicalism's] survival in the modern world," also noticed the evangelical preoccupation with boundaries to the right and left (1987:ix). But, as with Marty's analysis, Hunter likewise identified evangelicalism's interests as primarily theological. For instance, the activity he discerned as "redrawing the boundaries of faith" restricted itself to the dimensions of religious belief (e.g., faith) and behavior (e.g., personal ethics, the family, political activism). Hunter argued that "Evangelicalism shares with the larger Protestant phenomenon a fixation with theology. Yet its concern is far more intense." Moreover, stressed Hunter, "not only do Evangelicals distinguish themselves from other religions this way, but they distinguish themselves from liberal Protestantism this way as well" (1987:19).

In Hunter's analysis, then, theological orthodoxy and religious orthopraxy appear to delimit the boundaries of evangelical Protestantism. As Hunter suggested, "the history of conservative Protestantism in twentieth-century America has, in large measure, been the history of the effort to maintain the purity and integrity of its theology." To this end, Protestants regularly stake out "the theological criteria determining the range and the limits of acceptability. Such criteria provide a test for group membership: those who adhere belong; those who do not adhere entirely or on particular points do not belong" (1987:19). Though Hunter did not address the new evangelicalism's separation from the fundamentalist movement, his discussion on evangelical concern over its boundary with secular society nonetheless underscores the cognitive consequences of the evangelical desire to abandon fundamentalist cultural and ideological separation in favor of greater participation in modern American culture.

Hunter's discussion differs from Marty's in that Hunter centered his analysis on evangelical (and fundamentalist) preoccupation with the problem of maintaining ideological purity in the face of modernity. Additionally, Hunter sought to learn how the doctrinal beliefs and ethical behaviors of the conservative evangelical community were shaped and continue to be shaped by modern secular life.[21] Indeed, to a great extent, the issue is survival. Hunter's observation affirms at least one of the underlying assumptions that this study seeks to correct, namely, that scholars tend to identify "theology" as the defining characteristic of evangelical Protestantism and the engine of its differentiation from its rivals to the right and the left. As this study will make clear, "theology" is a symbol marking the boundary between groups, not the boundary itself.

Other scholars, typically evangelical ones, have likewise examined the split within postwar conservative Protestantism, noting the separation between the fundamentalists and the new evangelicals. However, in their analyses of this split within the old fundamentalist coalition, they have tended to restrict their discussions to the theological issues that informed the division. Aside from personal and institutional histories, they have given scant attention to the social structural or group boundary dimensions of this in-house conflict.

For example, in his groundbreaking study, Farley P. Butler explored "the process whereby conservative evangelicalism became divided into evangelicalism and fundamentalism," but only within its theological context. Though noting the coalitional dynamics, such as "the softening of the distinctives of conservative evangelicalism by the new evangelicals in an attempt to gain wider acceptance" and the "desire for de-alienation from the broader American culture" (1976:261), in the final analysis, theological explanations prevail. As Butler related, in the decades before 1940, fundamentalism had been a broad coalition of theologically and ecclesiologically diverse groups. While throughout the 1920s and 1930s a number of differences of opinion on theology and polity characterized the fundamentalist movement, these differences "had remained submerged and evangelicals and fundamentalists had worked together in a great many organizations." The advent of Billy Graham in the late 1940s, Butler argued, brought these differences to the surface. "The emergence of Billy Graham in 1949 and his rapid rise to national prominence had set the stage for the division within conservative evangelicalism" (1976:8).[22] Both Billy Graham and his inclusive evangelistic program were enthusiastically embraced by the new evangelicals, who saw cooperative evangelism as a means to a national revival and a possible reunification of divided American Protestantism.[23] But although Billy Graham became a symbol of the new evangelical revolt—the main "theological" catalyst that created the two competing forces within the ranks of conservative Protestantism—Butler maintained that the controversies that swirled around Graham were primarily theological in nature. Indeed, Butler strongly insisted that "any view which fails to see the struggle primarily in religious terms will be essentially faulty" (1976:250).

Both William Abraham and George M. Marsden saw the new evangelicalism as a theological reform movement within fundamentalism. As Abraham put it, "contemporary evangelical orthodoxy should be seen as a *theological* reaction against fundamentalism. At its best, it should be viewed as a deliberate, well-planned attempt to reform fundamentalism and purge it of its more bizarre and obnoxious features. . . . [I]ts very use of the term 'evangelical' was adopted to further this goal" (1984:15, emphasis added). The evangelicals, while discarding these "bizarre and obnoxious features," still "kept the basic five points of the fundamentalist creed" and even "took great pride in their theological orthodoxy" (1984:22).[24] At the same time, as Abraham reminded us, the new evangelicals "were at great pains to distance themselves from liberalism and neo-orthodoxy" (1984:22).

Similarly, Marsden placed the new evangelicals in the precarious position of occupying something akin to a theological and ecclesiastical "no man's land" between two warring sides. As Marsden explained, "Not only were the new evangelicals attempting to reform fundamentalism, they at the same time remained loyal fundamentalists who viewed their more basic mission as the reform of degenerating Protestantism" (Marsden 1987:6). For Marsden, Fuller Theological Seminary in Pasadena, California, became the symbol as well as the center of the new evangelical program to recover theological orthodoxy. As Marsden wrote:

> Much of the plot that shaped the Fuller heritage centered around efforts to get rid of these more recent aspects of fundamentalism and yet retain its essential commitment to evangelical orthodoxy and antimodernism. Those at Fuller were not breaking away entirely from original fundamentalism since original fundamentalism included the defense of the very orthodoxy they were attempting to recover (1987:10).

Evangelicals, according to Marsden, initially set out not to break with fundamentalism but to reform it. But in their efforts to redefine the fundamentalist agenda (that is, to redraw the boundary between fundamentalism and secular society), the evangelicals found themselves (or perhaps consciously placed themselves) between the sharply defined positions of the liberals and their former fundamentalist colleagues. This middle position placed the new evangelicals in an ambiguous category: neither fundamentalist nor liberal nor modernist nor neo-orthodox. Even so, though informed by theological differences, I would argue that their middle position was not by nature ideological but social structural. While religious ideas may have created and informed the differences between these groups, they were not in themselves the differences.

A different view than those of the several studies touched on above was given in Louis Gasper's earlier treatment of the fundamentalist-evangelical division in his book *The Fundamentalist Movement,*

1930-1956 (1981). In this work, Gasper located the breach between fundamentalists and new evangelicals as appearing sometime between 1941 and 1942, when the ultraconservative American Council of Christian Churches and the more moderate National Association of Evangelicals were founded. Gasper referred to this separation within the fundamentalist movement as the "dual alignment" in fundamentalism. But the disagreement that split one orthodoxy into two rival orthodoxies went beyond theology. As Gasper argued, these "two fundamentalist groups agreed doctrinally, but they were divided in method" (1981:26).[25]

The difference in method had to do with the issue of ecclesiastical separation, a theological argument with social structural consequences. Put simply, the issue had to do with whether fundamentalist churches and associations should be inclusive or exclusive, whether they should include in fellowship individuals and churches associated with the Federal (later National) Council of Churches or exclude from fellowship all churches so associated. Separatist fundamentalists sought to exclude liberals as well as those whose denominations were sympathetic to liberals. Nonseparatist fundamentalists did not draw so fine a line of exclusion. The exclusivistic path sought to preserve a pure fundamentalism that was free from theological contamination from both the liberal "heretics" who embraced modernism and evangelical "moderates" not fervently opposed to modernism in word or deed. While Gasper examined the development of competing wings within the fundamentalist movement, this present study traces the emergence of the new evangelical coalition, its clear separation from the fundamentalist movement, and its deliberate and carefully intentioned attempts to define its boundaries as distinct from fundamentalism as well as liberalism.

ORGANIZATION OF THIS STUDY

This study, which focuses on the social structural boundaries that played a prominent role in defining the self-understanding of postwar American evangelicalism, is organized as follows:

The first section of Chapter Two details the efforts by evangelicals to define themselves through metaphors, discussing the frustrations they have thus far experienced. This section also examines the multiplicity of typologies that evangelical scholars have employed in their attempts to unravel and understand the complex diversity of modern evangelicalism. As with metaphors, typologies likewise fall short as analytical models, tending merely to describe the diversity already apparent rather than explain it.

But these oversights are characteristic not only of evangelical scholars but are also the case among scholars more generally, as the next part of this chapter shows. One assumption that seems to hinder clearer explication is the dualistic approach that many scholars bring to the study of American Protestantism—dividing phenomena into fixed opposing positions of liberal and conservative (what some have called the "two-party" model). What a person quickly discovers is that individuals and groups that claim evangelical roots cannot be so easily typed as either liberal or conservative. The social (and symbolic) boundaries that define and separate Protestant groups appear to play a greater role than either denominational preference or ideological bent traditionally suggests. As is the case with all social systems, community boundaries and the activities that define and redefine them underlie the activities of American evangelicalism. Chapter Two, therefore, focuses on the dynamics of group boundaries and amplifies some of the theoretical assumptions upon which this study is based. (Those less concerned with the theoretical underpinnings of this study and more interested in the historical narrative can easily skip ahead to Chapter Three.)

Chapter Three situates postwar tensions among the new evangelicals and fundamentalists and liberals within the context of the historic fundamentalist-modernist controversy, a debate that took place within the major Protestant denominations during the early decades of the twentieth century. This chapter underscores two consequences of the historic clash of traditional and modern worldviews: first, the sharp line that was erected between "liberals" and "fundamentalists" within the churches; and second, the fundamentalist loss of the center and subsequent movement to the margins of American religious and cultural life. The consequences of this controversy came to play an important role in shaping the perceptions of liberals, fundamentalists, and evangelicals during the postwar period. This background provides an explanation for the consistently negative attitudes that these groups have held toward one another since that time.

During the 1940s, moderate fundamentalists tried to move toward more theological and cultural respectability. To accomplish this, they needed to define a new basis for Protestant orthodoxy that would expand fundamentalism's narrowly constructed group boundaries. Through a process of redefinition, however, these new evangelicals gradually came to view themselves as different from their fundamentalist colleagues. Even so, because fundamentalism defined most of the issues that distinguished conservatives from liberals, the evangelicals were not altogether able to escape the fundamentalist orbit. Theoretically, the boundary tensions between fundamentalists and new evangelicals closely resembled a generalist/particularist pattern response in which one constituency seeks to expand the boundaries of the group while another seeks to restrict group boundaries. This social structural dynamic sheds light on one aspect of the conflict between these rival orthodoxies. With this dynamic in mind, therefore, Chapter Four considers the forging of the boundary between evangelicals and fundamentalists.

In their move toward a more religiously and culturally respectable position, the new evangelicals sought to form a new Protestant coalition. Though presented with several options, most especially Barthian neo-orthodoxy, the postwar evangelicals could not comfortably embrace liberal ecclesiastical, social, or theological concerns. Thus, Chapter Five examines the boundary between evangelicals and liberals with attention to the scrupulous efforts by evangelical leaders, first, to form a coalition that stopped short of liberal ecumenism, second, to define a social agenda that did not resemble liberalism's social gospel, and, third, to revive and reconstruct orthodox theology without following the problematic path of neo-orthodoxy.

The story does not end in the early 1960s, for the great efforts that the new evangelicals expended toward forming a cohesive coalition of Protestants that might effect a revival of orthodoxy failed to unite conservatives. Indeed, the social, ecclesiastical, and theological concerns that had defined the new evangelical agenda became the very issues that fostered diversity and growing division within the coalition from the 1960s to the 1990s. This unraveling of the new evangelical coalition is the focus of Chapter Six.

What is more, the new evangelicalism also spawned rival reform movements, each of these attempting to delimit the boundaries of the evangelical tradition and to define the acceptable limits of its diversity. As a consequence, since the 1970s American evangelicalism has been "in search of itself" (Henry 1976).[26] Evangelicals have been preoccupied with understanding the nature of their growing diversity by trying to answer the nagging question, "What is an evangelical?" Thus, in light of the boundary-defining activities explored in earlier chapters, Chapter Six looks at the current crisis of identity that evangelicals articulate and explains that that crisis is a consequence of the new evangelicalism's unresolved ambivalent relationship to modern culture. The concluding remarks in that chapter also consider a number of new directions in which the postwar evangelical coalition has been moving since the mid-1980s, especially its attempts to initiate dialogue with liberal Protestants and Jews and to forge moral and political alliances with American Catholics.

CHAPTER TWO

A Boundary Approach to the Study of American Evangelical Protestantism

FOR NEARLY HALF A CENTURY, evangelical Protestantism has been experiencing a crisis of identity. This "identity crisis" can be seen in the sustained concern evangelical spokespersons have shown over issues of self-definition that have appeared again and again in their many books and articles. The most salient of their definitional concerns centers around those beliefs and behaviors that mark the boundaries of acceptable diversity within the evangelical tradition. One need only to glance at a small portion of this literature to sense the uneasiness among evangelicals over the elasticity of the "evangelical" label and over the highly diverse types of Protestant Christianity that lay some claim to both this identity and its heritage.[1] This concern over who is and who is not truly evangelical and over the diversity of expression that Protestant evangelicalism has fought over as well as fostered should not be a surprise. Much of the Protestant experience in America has been one of dividing and coalition building, dynamics that inherently make for more complex social organizations with ever-expanding boundaries and increasingly vague group identities.[2]

For evangelicals, the trouble seems to stem from the frighteningly diverse forms of evangelicalism that have emerged since World War II. These forms present themselves in such varied ways as to make the term "evangelical" conceptually unwieldy. As Leonard Sweet observed, "the evangelical phenomena [sic] is a complex and challenging one" in that "[i]t looks as if everyone at times has either been drawn into the loosely twined evangelical camp or claimed the label, thereby stripping the concept of Evangelicalism of much analytic purchase" (1984:85). There is little doubt that this cluster of Protestants is both vast and varied. For instance, in his discussion of the "evangelical kaleidoscope," Timothy L. Smith (1986) mentioned a score of denominational groupings that at one time or another have been constituent parts of this complex coalitional form of Protestantism. These groupings include the following: Presbyterians, Baptists of all stripes, the Churches of Christ (both Independent and Non-Instrumental), Christian Reformed, Dutch Reformed, Brethren, Mennonites, Lutherans of one kind or another, Pentecostal and Holiness groups, Black Methodists, Free Methodists, Wesleyans, Nazarenes, Friends, and even Seventh-day Adventists, among many others.

What becomes troubling is that with so many groups identified as "evangelical," one begins to wonder aloud with Sweet, "Who is *not* evangelical?" Moreover, if nearly every Protestant denomination is, in one way or another, "evangelical," then how does one begin to talk about *an* evangelical tradition? If Sweet is correct, that the term has lost much of its precision, then one also begins to wonder whether scholars should not discontinue using the term altogether, as Donald Dayton has often urged. Indeed, if, as Dayton has told us, "the differences within [evangelicalism] are as great as the differences between it and the rest of the church world" (quoted in Sweet 1984:85; cf. Dayton and Johnston 1991), then a person might wonder what analytic usefulness there is in a word that distinguishes so little. Perhaps Sweet was not being hyperbolic when he likened the attempt to define modern American evangelicalism to kicking "a hornet's nest" (1984:86).

But while the religious denominations and communities that define themselves as part of the evangelical tradition have been great in number (perhaps 30-66 million adherents, according to Kantzer and Henry 1990:28)[3] and in kind, and while their institutional histories have been so diverse, almost altogether unique, as to make most efforts at generalization difficult, evangelical scholars remain undaunted in their efforts to classify evangelicals in order to clarify the use of the term. Evangelicals have a stake in defining their label, since by it they likewise define the boundaries of their own community.

Their preoccupation over this issue is especially intriguing, not simply because it troubles them, but because it consumes them. For evangelicals, it seems of first importance that the differences between themselves and non-evangelicals be clearly drawn in order to resolve this ever-increasing confusion over the boundaries of evangelicalism and the organizational problems that attend such confusion.

In this chapter I will first outline the efforts by evangelicals to define themselves, pointing out their frustrations over their own broadening boundaries. Second, I will consider some apparent shortcomings in analyses offered by scholars more generally. In this second section I will discuss the tendency of scholars to divide Protestantism into fixed liberal and conservative groupings (often called the "two-party" model), an imposition owing in large part to the strictly theological, psychological, sociological (that is, institutional), and historical assumptions scholars often make about religious phenomena. These two sections make two critical observations: first, that scholars tend, when examining modern evangelicalism, to describe its vast diversity rather than to explain it; and second, that scholars tend, when offering theories, to analyze evangelicalism in terms of rigid liberal/conservative typologies that often belie both its definitional struggles and its attempts to negotiate an intentional middle course between liberal and fundamentalist extremes. As an attempt to overcome this theoretical impasse, in the final section of this chapter I will offer a two-part model with which to analyze postwar American evangelicalism, a model that draws its insights from the inherent boundary dynamics of social groups and organizations.

EVANGELICAL SELF-UNDERSTANDING

Questions of identity precipitate a need for clearer definitions of the self and its relation to other selves. As with individuals, groups likewise search for clearer definition in relation to other groups. Typically, this search for clearer boundaries aims at striking a balance between inclusive and exclusive social structural definitions. Protestant evangelicalism exemplifies this dynamic no less characteristically than other social groupings. Unfortunately, most recent scholarship on American evangelicalism has directed much of its focus on the

ideological and ethical dimensions of religiosity. Models for categoriz-
ing evangelical phenomena are typically an analytic blend of theological, psychological, and sociological methods. This is most clearly
illustrated in the various typologies offered by scholars from the
evangelical tradition itself, such as James Davison Hunter, Nancy
Ammerman, Richard Quebedeaux, Robert E. Webber, William Abraham, and George Marsden. In this section I will outline in some detail
the various typologies these scholars offer. The aim of this discussion
is to give a sampling of the definitional debate among evangelical
scholars as well as to show the tendency among them to use typologies
to describe the diversity they see around them rather than offer
theoretical models to help explain it.

To answer the perplexing question, "What is an evangelical?,"
James Davison Hunter maintained that "the proper beginning for
social scientists is in the way Evangelicals define themselves"
(1981:368). Using this avowedly phenomenological approach,
Hunter attempted to isolate and describe "those core elements which
have withstood the vicissitudes of historical change, and upon which
present conservative Protestant unity is based" (1981:368). Hunter
then distinguished ideological and behavioral aspects in his interpretive scheme of evangelical Protestantism.[4] For quantitative purposes,
Hunter defined an evangelical as "a Protestant who believes in the
infallibility of the Bible, the divinity of Christ, and that salvation is
through faith in Jesus Christ (expressed in either a cognitive mode
or in a more experiential mode or in both)" (1981:369).[5] Hunter
recognized that by itself the belief dimension does not adequately
describe modern evangelicalism. As Hunter noted, contemporary
evangelicalism "is not a theological monolith defined solely by the
acceptance of these doctrines. Within it, there is a diversity of
religious traditions with differing doctrinal and behavioral emphases" (1981:369; cf., Abraham 1984:11). Elsewhere, Hunter (1983)
identified four specific traditions that constitute this diversity: the
Baptist, the Holiness-Pentecostal, the Reformed-Confessional, and
the Anabaptist. A brief description of each tradition will help clarify
his argument.[6]

According to Hunter, the most predominant of the four traditions
that make up modern evangelicalism has been the Baptist tradition
(1983:8). Revivalistic in nature, the Baptist tradition brings to evangel-

icalism its highly individuated emphasis on religious faith and salvation. This is seen clearly in its congregational or democratic form of church government. The Baptist stream also lends to evangelicalism its long and troublesome tradition of religious exclusivity with its tendency toward sectarian splits.

A second tradition Hunter identified is the Holiness-Pentecostal tradition. Although quite similar in theological and ecclesiastical structure to the Baptist heritage, its most prevalent feature is its stress on pietistic themes. An essential difference is its characteristic emphasis on the central role that the Holy Spirit plays in the processes of conversion and sanctification. "Perfectionist doctrines, moral and spiritual, distinguish the Holiness side of this tradition," wrote Hunter, "the 'second blessing' or the 'baptism of the Holy Spirit' with the attendant 'gifts of the Spirit' . . . are emphasized on the Pentecostal side" (1983:8). Both sides of this tradition underscore the personal and experiential dimension of religious faith.

Several features characterize the Anabaptist tradition, which, according to Hunter, represents a third stream making up modern evangelicalism. Originally a pejorative term calling attention to its insistence on adult or believers' baptism, Anabaptism brings to evangelicalism its emphasis on rational over experiential or emotional religion. It also lends to evangelicalism a tendency toward communitarian faith and an emphasis on social as well as religious reform. The most salient feature of evangelicalism's Anabaptist stream is perhaps its strong views on church/state relations. "Where the other traditions tend to be supportive of the government structure and the activities of the broader society," observed Hunter, "the Anabaptist tradition maintains more of a neutral, if not antagonistic, posture toward the state and a particular opposition to war and violence of any sort" (1983:8).

Similar to the Anabaptists, the fourth stream of the evangelical tradition, the Reformed-Confessional wing, likewise tends toward a rational view of individual conversion and religious faith. But there are notable differences as well. While only the Reformed side of the Reformed-Confessional tradition still holds to the Calvinist doctrines of predestination and election, both place strong emphasis on spiritual asceticism through separation of the believer from worldly amusements and the strict avoidance of sensual pleasure (Hunter 1983:8).

George Marsden, who, to be sure, was commenting upon an earlier phase of American evangelicalism, regarded the Reformed tradition as its central core, at least until evangelicalism was divided between separatists (fundamentalists) and non-separatists (new evangelicals) in the 1940s (see 1987:76).

While the differences might seem to preclude any natural coalition, what these four traditions have in common is their desire for "a purer, simpler, and more authentic form of religious experience, religious truth, and ecclesiastical authority," that is, "to recover the spirit and truth of the apostolic age of Christianity" (Hunter, 1983:9). In this way, evangelicals emphasize a primitivism similar to many nineteenth-century indigenous American religious sects and movements: they desire to recapture the vital faith of an earlier, less secularized time.[7] Thus, in a phrase, the common clarion call of these four streams is "Back to the Bible!" Interestingly, the theological and ecclesiastical differences evident in these four converging streams are easily overlooked by these differing types of "evangelicals" when they engage in common causes. Only when circumstances change and outside enemies no longer threaten do these fundamental differences resurface, and with them, tension, conflict, and further division.

These inherent tensions were especially evident during the fundamentalist-modernist controversy when issues were contraposed and evangelical Protestants—polarized into liberal and conservative camps—fought a protracted war over science and the inspiration and authority of the Bible. As Gregory Bolich pointed out, "Evangelicals found themselves espousing a common front of biblical inerrancy in order to unite on that issue. Gradually the matter became a highly visible point of battle." Those who led the battle were those most outspoken on the issue of biblical authority. "Eventually every wing of the fundamentalist coalition," wrote Bolich further, "found it necessary to affirm some understanding of the doctrine of biblical inerrancy, not only in the interest of evangelical unity, but because of pressures to avoid any false accusations of sympathy with the modernists who so vigorously ridiculed the ideas of inspiration and inerrancy" (1980:39-40). The fundamentalist coalition, with its common modernist enemy, allowed for a variety of orthodoxies so long as they opposed liberal compromise and apostasy. But, Bolich explained, "The diversified elements in fundamentalism had been controlled by union against a common foe. With the fall of modernism, the evangelicals came face to face with their internal problems. . . . The cause which had sustained their coalition for so long proved itself inadequate to effect a lasting union" (1980:42,43; cf., Gasper 1981:13-20).

Criticisms of Hunter's scheme have been aimed primarily at his interchangeable use of fundamentalism and evangelicalism, implying that these are one and the same phenomenon (Ammerman 1982). By some reckoning, of course, they are not. To regard fundamentalism as merely another type of evangelicalism is to ignore the careful attention both groups give to defining their differences on a range of social and theological issues. According to Hunter's schema, contemporary fundamentalists are but one side of the evangelical coin. While theologically this is perhaps undeniable, social structurally evangelicals and fundamentalists are quite concerned to point out and maintain their differences.

Nancy Ammerman (1982) put her finger on a distinction that is useful in understanding the division of conservative Protestantism into evangelical and fundamentalist camps. Though both fundamentalists and evangelicals were saddened by the fact that they were divided by disagreement in the 1950s, they nevertheless took every opportunity to amplify their differences, both theological and behavioral. For instance, Edward J. Carnell, president of Fuller Seminary during this period, lamented aloud, "It is too bad, in a way, that we have to use labels. In Antioch they were content to be called Christians. But all is not lost. By using carefully selected labels, we at least clarify our position in the theological spectrum" (1959b:971).[8] Indeed, Richard Quebedeaux has been critical of the way scholars and churchpersons "lump together with pejorative intent all theological conservatives into the worn Fundamentalist category." Generally, Quebedeaux explained, "Evangelicals resent being called Fundamentalists, and Fundamentalists likewise do not usually appreciate the Evangelical designation" (1974:19).[9] If we are to understand the one in relation to the other, then we must recognize that both traditions know who their friends and foes are and define themselves accordingly. Not all evangelicals are fundamentalists, and not all fundamentalists consider themselves evangelicals.

Though neither evangelicals nor fundamentalists appreciate being lumped together, it is not difficult for the non-evangelical to think of these two distinct groups as essentially dual expressions of the same orthodox religion. A researcher's work would be less complicated, however, if the distinctions were simply between what Carnell (1960) oppositionally called "cultic" and "classic" orthodoxy. Ironically, the more a person probes, the muddier the conceptual waters seem to become. This explains some of the confusion scholars experience and why definitions based on ideology fail to distinguish the differences that fundamentalists and evangelicals painstakingly underscore. It is also an important point to remember when exploring the labyrinth of conservative Protestantism: despite all their efforts, evangelicals have not been particularly successful in distancing themselves from their fundamentalist past or in defining themselves apart from it.[10]

In an effort to unravel the conceptual entanglements that modern evangelicalism presents, many of evangelicalism's own theologians and historians began to look to sociological categories. One example is found in the work of Richard Quebedeaux (1974, and 1978), who, as an interpreter and spokesperson for more socially conscious evangelicals, has spent much of his career sorting out the ideological diversity of conservative Protestantism. Quebedeaux pointed out that while the division between fundamentalist and evangelical in the 1950s created a confusing picture of the conservative Protestant landscape, our contemporary vision of it has grown even hazier, this because several separate yet ideologically related subgroups within both fundamentalist and evangelical schools of orthodoxy have emerged since that time. But, as Quebedeaux cautioned, the existence of these subgroups should not be taken to indicate a shift in the basic character of either evangelicalism or fundamentalism. To the contrary, these ideological "subsets" simply signal "that both varieties of Orthodox Christianity have undergone modification to some degree in the finer points of theology and, more profoundly, in their attitudes toward culture" (1974:19). Quebedeaux identified and labeled five subgroups on the Evangelical/ Fundamentalist continuum: Separatist Fundamentalism, Open Fundamentalism, Establishment Evangelicalism, the New Evangelicalism, and the Young Evangelicals. Because these several subgroupings will prove useful in the chapters to follow—particularly when dealing with new evangelical spokespersons who appear to move from one subgroup to another without seeming to change beliefs or theological emphases—it will be helpful to discuss where Quebedeaux drew his distinctions.

In Quebedeaux's typology, the Separatist Fundamentalists fall at the extreme conservative end of the spectrum. Described by Quebedeaux as personally and socially intemperate, Separatist Fundamentalists are undoubtedly the least theologically and ecclesiastically tolerant of orthodox Protestant groups. The Separatists are "the direct descendants of those individuals and groups in the Fundamentalist-Modernist controversy who felt it necessary to separate completely from any manifestation of Liberalism or Modernism they could discern" (1974:19-20). Separatists are usually distinguished from other groups by their complete separation from the "godless heresy" and apostasy they detect in other churches, their belief in the verbal inspiration and plenary inerrancy of the Bible, and their extreme premillennial dispensationalism (1974:20). Interestingly, the conflicts that defined evangelicals as different from fundamentalists—which will be examined in a later chapter—generally centered around these three concerns. Quebedeaux identified individuals such as Carl McIntire and Billy James Hargis and groups and institutions such as the American Council of Christian Churches and Bob Jones University as representative of Separatist Fundamentalism.

Open Fundamentalism, while almost as politically and religiously conservative as Separatist Fundamentalism, is not nearly as extreme and is certainly less vocal about its separation from discernible apostasy. Although Open Fundamentalism, to quote Quebedeaux, "sympathizes with the Evangelical desire to escape the odium surrounding the Fundamentalist designation, it sees no reason to abandon the term completely" (1974:26).[11] Quebedeaux regarded individuals such as John Walvoord of Dallas Theological Seminary and popular premillennialist author Hal Lindsey as the chief representatives of and spokespersons for this less strident wing of fundamentalism. What characterizes Open Fundamentalists as different from the Separatists is not so much their beliefs as their greater tolerance toward variance in belief. For the Separatists, all beliefs are either black or white; Open Fundamentalists allow for some theological shades of grey, albeit slight (cf., Hunter, 1983:9).

Along Quebedeaux's Evangelical/Fundamentalist spectrum, the Establishment Evangelicals are those most familiar to sociologists and historians. The Establishment Evangelicals differ at three significant ideological and behavioral points from both fundamentalists subgroups mentioned above. These points are: (1) the issue of separation from apostasy, (2) the inspiration and authority of the Bible, and (3) dispensational hermeneutics. As both fundamentalist groups charge, compromise by evangelicals on separation and dispensationalism has been at the expense of biblical authority.

Although Hunter listed "a belief in biblical inerrancy" (1981:368) as one of the hallmarks of an evangelical, Quebedeaux's analysis found problems with this indicator. Evangelicalism certainly does assert the inspiration and authority of the Bible, but, unlike fundamentalism, "it does not limit itself to the literal interpretation of Scripture at all points, nor does it revere any particular translation" (1974:28).[12] What we find instead is that along the evangelical end of Quebedeaux's continuum, "the whole question of the *nature* of biblical authority and inspiration has been reopened" (1974:28). This aspect of modern evangelicalism becomes even more evident as one moves "leftward" along the continuum. Among those representing the Establishment wing of evangelicalism, Quebedeaux identified individuals such as Billy Graham and Carl F. H. Henry. He also pointed to such institutions as the National Association of Evangelicals, Wheaton College, and Fuller Theological Seminary as symbols of Establishment Evangelicalism.

The New Evangelicals, maintained Quebedeaux, are the result of intellectual transformations or conversions that, as among Establishment Evangelicals, move the more intellectually respectable evangelicals further away from the extremes of fundamentalist orthodoxy.[13] The most significant of the alterations of traditional orthodoxy is the new evangelical acceptance of the historical-critical method of biblical interpretation. While New Evangelicals and Fundamentalists may both hold that the Bible is the divinely inspired Word of God, New Evangelicals part company with Fundamentalists over their further affirmation that the Bible is likewise the "word of man." Their acknowledgment that the Bible was written by persons bound by time and influenced by social and cultural circumstances moves New Evangelicals in a more liberal and neo-orthodox direction.[14] As Quebedeaux observed, "The old concepts of infallibility and inerrancy are being reinterpreted to the point that a number of Evangelical scholars are saying that the teaching of Scripture . . . rather than the text itself is without error" (1974:37-38). This conceptual shift places a greater emphasis on the interpretive role of the Holy Spirit in the life of the individual believer—a theme prevalent among the more experientially oriented charismatic and Pentecostal evangelicals.[15]

Unlike both Separatist and Open Fundamentalists, the New Evangelicals of Quebedeaux's schema embrace a definition of "evangelical" that includes many, if not most, Pentecostal and Holiness groups. This is consistent with Quebedeaux's observation that, theologically, "the New Evangelicals are again emphasizing the necessity of meaningful sanctification following regeneration . . ." (1974:38). While the New Evangelicals place greater emphasis on the action of the Holy Spirit in the individual believer's life, both Fundamentalists and Evangelicals, like their nineteenth-century forebears, hold up the "born again" experience as central to the Christian faith. Quebedeaux's New Evangelicals, however, stress moving beyond personal morality as the indicator of an authentic conversion (that is, as the test of true faith) toward a form of "social holiness" (that is, a faith in which the Christian ethic is lived out within a dying world; 1974:38).

Additionally, the New Evangelicals are distinguished from Establishment Evangelicals by their "marked aversion to Dispensationalism and its inherent apocalyptic speculations" (1974:38). By and large, these New Evangelicals eschew dispensational hermeneutics because they believe that the implications of its pessimistic views of secular society are socially stagnating. Their movement away from dispensational premillennial eschatology has enabled them to speak of the need for a biblical social ethic, an ethic that blends both liberal and conservative elements. Their emphasis, then, is not only on the conversion of sinful individuals, but also on the transformation of a sinful social order.[16] Yet, unlike liberalism, this ethic, while still "Christ-centered," does not extol the innate human ability to transform the world but exalts, instead, the transformative powers of Christ and the Holy Spirit working through fully converted individuals (that is, "born-agains").

Another characteristic that distinguishes New Evangelicalism from its more conservative brethren is its current rapprochement with mainstream liberal Protestantism[17] and its dialogues with both Roman Catholicism[18] and Judaism.[19] Conciliatory or ecumenical moves on the part of evangelicals during the 1950s and 1960s became a point of conflict between them and the stalwart fundamentalists. But even though Establishment Evangelicals, to use Quebedeaux's designation, sought to reduce their tension with both the mainline churches and secular society, many of them were made quite uncomfortable by this "left-leaning" direction. For example, E. J. Carnell's admission at a meeting with Karl Barth in 1962 that, like Barth, he too had problems with the traditional doctrine of biblical inspiration, did not sit well with many of his evangelical colleagues, not to mention with most of his fundamentalist detractors (Marsden 1987:194-195).[20] If one were to follow Quebedeaux's schema, it is these New Evangelicals who, by seeking to broaden the boundaries of evangelicalism, helped precipitate the end of the new evangelical coalition in the 1960s and 1970s.

From within the ranks of the New Evangelicals, Quebedeaux teased out a fifth group: the Young Evangelicals. It was with this group that Quebedeaux most identified. The Young Evangelicals, who came of age during the turbulent decade of the 1960s, adopted a mild form of the revolutionary anti-establishment spirit of their generation. Equally affected by the civil rights movement and the call for social reform, they could be characterized by their "fresh spirit of openness to all who seek to follow Jesus Christ and . . . [by] a profound desire to apply the Gospel to every dimension of life" (1974:40).

Quebedeaux's schematization is helpful in that he provided deeper insight into the "multiplexity" of modern conservative Protestantism—both fundamentalist and evangelical. But, because his typology is but only a snapshot, it is limited. To his credit, because he himself was one of the Young Evangelicals he profiled, Quebedeaux was able to expose the ideological nuances that non-evangelicals are often unable to detect. What is more, his ability to write fairly evenhandedly about each of these groups has made him a reliable guide to the labyrinthine world of conservative Protestant evangelical and fundamentalist subcultures.

One of the most elaborate and ambitious attempts to locate and type various evangelical groups was Robert Webber's categorization of evangelicalism into fourteen "subcultural" groups, each with its own theological emphasis and peculiar "sacred" symbols. Webber's work was an effort on the part of evangelicals themselves to mend the tearing evangelical fabric by calling on fellow evangelicals to remember their common heritage, or, to use Webber's more contemporary metaphor, their "common roots" (cf., Wells and Woodbridge 1977 and Ramm 1981). Because, for Webber, scholars who based their work upon historic or theological definitions have found it difficult to identify with precision what constitutes an evangelical, he therefore attempted to look beyond these methods and considered instead the social composition of evangelicalism.

According to Webber, the question, "Who are the evangelicals?" raises with it methodological problems that are not solved by the usual answer: evangelicals are Christians who believe in Jesus Christ and want to tell other people about it. To answer the "who" question of the evangelical phenomenon, one must also take its vast diversity into account and recognize that American evangelicalism "comprises a complex variety of subcultures within the larger evangelical culture" (1978:30). "All these groups," Webber explained, "reflect a theological unity at the center—in their confession of Christ and the doctrines which the Protestant Church has always believed. But because of their various historical origins and cultural shapes they reflect a diversity of expression in theological particulars and practice in areas where differences of opinion have been tolerated" (1978:31).

Webber's subcultural categorization divides American evangelicalism into fourteen ideal-typical expressions, summarized by Webber in Table One on page 36.

Though Webber's subcultural typology is conceptually helpful, there are, he admitted, "many smaller groups of varying shades of ethos within a single evangelical subculture" that defy precise classification and complicate even his elaborate scheme (1978:33). What becomes apparent from Webber's work, then, is that the changing nature and dynamic of evangelicalism makes difficult the task of organizing or operationalizing any expression of it into fixed categories or unmistakable types. As Dayton and Johnston (1991) further reminded us, the contemporary composition of evangelicalism in the 1980s and into the 1990s makes this task even more difficult.

William Abraham, who was not convinced that one should necessarily separate evangelicalism from fundamentalism, argued "that there are versions of the [evangelical] heritage that can be distinguished from modern fundamentalism and its recent offspring, conservative evangelicalism" (1984:ix).[21] The manner in which he

TABLE ONE

Webber's Fourteen Categories of Protestant Evangelicals

Subcultural Evangelical Group	Major Emphasis	Symbols
1. Fundamentalist Evangelicalism	Personal and ecclesiastical separationism; biblicism	Bob Jones University; American Council of Christian Churches; *Sword of the Lord*
2. Dispensational Evangelicalism	Dispensational hermeneutics; pretribulationalism and premillennarianism *[sic]*	Dallas Theological Seminary; Moody Bible Institute; *Moody Monthly*; Moody Press
3. Conservative Evangelicalism	Cooperative evangelism; inclusive of all evangelical groups; broad theological base	Wheaton College; Trinity Seminary; Gordon-Conwell Seminary; *Christianity Today*; Billy Graham; The Zondervan Corp.; National Association of Evangelicals
4. Nondenominational Evangelicalism	Unity of the Church; restoration of N. T. Christianity	Milligan College
5. Reformed Evangelicalism	Calvinism (some with a decidedly Puritan flavor); covenant theology and hermeneutics	Calvin College and Seminary; Westminster Seminary; Covenant Seminary; Reformed Seminary; Francis Schaeffer
6. Anabaptist Evangelicalism	Discipleship; poverty; the Peace movement; pacifism	Goshen College; Reba Place Fellowship; John Howard Yoder
7. Wesleyan Evangelicalism	Arminianism; sanctification	Asbury College and Seminary; Seattle Pacific College
8. Holiness Evangelicalism	The second work of grace	Lee College; Nazarene Church
9. Pentecostal Evangelicalism	Gift of tongues	Church of God; Assembly of God
10. Charismatic Evangelicalism	Gifts of the Holy Spirit	Oral Roberts University; Melodyland School of Theology
11. Black Evangelicalism	Black consciousness	National Association of Black Evangelicals
12. Progressive Evangelicalsim	Openness toward critical scholarship and ecumenical relations	Fuller Seminary
13. Radical Evangelicalism	Moral, social, and political consciousness	*Sojourners*; *The Other Side*; *Wittenburg Door*
14. Main-line Evangelicalism	Historic consciousness at least back to the Reformation	Movements in major denominations: Methodist, Lutheran, Presbyterian, Episcopal, Baptist

Source: Webber 1978: 32

identified those versions of Protestantism that are more evangelical than fundamentalistic accorded with behavioral qualities rather than simply doctrinal beliefs—though he by no means diminished the strict orthodoxy of the evangelicalism he included in his fundamentalism. What Abraham saw was that "despite differences of emphasis and expression, there is sufficient common appearance for both outsiders and insiders to identify a single evangelical tradition within the Christian tradition as a whole" (1984:9). Abraham, however, did not identify doctrinal agreement as the glue that holds the various types of evangelicalism together as one identifiable tradition, but he found instead a unity residing in "family resemblance" (cf., Dayton & Johnston 1991). Unfortunately, Abraham did not clearly identify what "resemblance" entails, so that, as with Quebedeaux and Hunter, the difference between "evangelical" and "fundamentalist" seems to be reduced to a matter of social etiquette. In the end, as Frank Spina has quipped, the best one can say is that "evangelicals are really 'fundamentalists with good manners'" (quoted in Abraham 1984:ix).

Abraham then pointed out that the problem in delimiting evangelicalism from fundamentalism stems from the intimate connection of modern evangelical orthodoxy, thus allowing for an interchangeable use of the two terms. This explains why many scholars tend to confuse the two phenomena. But this confusion is understandable, he said, given the historic setting of the rise of evangelical orthodoxy from fundamentalism after World War II (1984:11). As Abraham related it, the emergence of the evangelical contingent out of fundamentalism began when "a group of young, aggressive, well-educated, and talented fundamentalists, spearheaded by Billy Graham, quite deliberately used the word 'evangelical' to describe the new version of fundamentalism they sought to proclaim and defend in the fifties. Their innovation was so successful that the brand of evangelicalism that emerged has become the standard by which the content of evangelical theology is currently measured within self-confessed evangelical circles" (1984:11). As Abraham intimated, the evangelical "identity crisis" might not have occurred had not its contemporary spokespersons desired to gain a measure of theological and social sophistication as defined by mainline Protestantism, a sophistication they believed to be clearly lacking among fundamentalists. Thus, the postwar evangelicals sought to have the best of both worlds—to maintain a simultaneous "dialogue" with fundamentalists and with mainline liberals. As Abraham explained, "the new evangelicals had the unenviable task of holding to some of the core convictions of fundamentalism while discarding its more unpalatable ingredients" (1984:20). One consequence of this dynamic is reflected in the vast diversity that presently characterizes evangelical Protestantism.

As the foregoing discussion has attempted to illustrate, this determination to define the evangelical "community" has come to set the terms for much of evangelical scholarly discourse to date. If anything is clear from the abundance of scholarship on American evangelicalism, then whatever it is that constitutes the sine qua non of evangelicalism has thus far evaded the efforts by scholars to locate it— even those scholars within the tradition itself.[22] This difficulty in defining the character of evangelical religion and delimiting the extent of its "community" is likewise the case with researchers whose works explore the dynamics of American Protestantism more generally.

LIBERAL/CONSERVATIVE TYPOLOGIES

Scholars outside the evangelical orbit have tended to look at conservative Protestantism through different interpretive lenses, seeing far less diversity than insiders describe. For this reason, scholars outside the evangelical camp, though likewise offering typologies to describe Protestantism's divided house, tend to use broader brush strokes when portraying its variety. In fact, to change the metaphor, seldom do they seek clearer definition by differentiating the strands that weave themselves into a sort of evangelical tapestry. Because they see the tapestry as virtually an undifferentiated whole, the story most scholars of modern American Protestantism tell is often a tale of disagreements and divisions between two fairly distinguishable camps: the liberals and the conservatives.

What is more, most of the scholarship on the liberal and conservative impulses within Protestantism tends to distinguish American Protestants along ideological lines, focusing more generally on the theological contests between these warring factions. In addition to theological or doctrinal approaches, scholars have also employed psychological, sociological, and historical methods to examine the distinctions between religious "conservatism" and "liberalism."[23] While an extensive exposition of these methodologies would take one well beyond the purposes of this chapter, a brief sketch of each of these approaches is necessary to help underscore the analytical advantages of a boundary approach to the study of postwar American evangelicalism. In this way, I will define these approaches and then point out the shortcomings of each .

One approach to the study of American Protestantism is theological. Generally, this approach places liberals and conservatives on opposing sides of certain doctrinal issues. From the perspective of theological differences, liberals are usually identified as religiously rational and intellectually sophisticated in their theological reflection, inclined more toward "spiritualized" or moral interpretations of the Bible and Christian dogma. Conservatives, on the other hand, are typically portrayed as anti-intellectual and highly dogmatic. From a theological viewpoint, conservatives tend to be overly literal about the teachings of the Bible, reading the text as the inspired and inerrant word of God, sometimes to the point of absurdity.

One problem with theological models is their tendency to equate certain doctrinal positions with either a liberal or conservative theological stance. Often these models ignore the fact that groups sometimes hold doctrinal views that combine conservative and liberal tenants. The Evangelical Lutheran Church is one example of such a theological blend.

A second approach, psychological, typically examines the individual's responses to religious phenomena and how religious experiences affect the individual's psyche. In addition, psychological methods probe the depths of the souls of believers and unbelievers alike so as to understand both conversion and deconversion processes.[24] Scholars who seek to distinguish liberal and conservative religious experiences often contrapose "heart" and "head" in their models. Accordingly, liberals are characterized as experiencing religion rationally, while conservatives are generally thought to be more emotional, sometimes even ecstatic, in their responses to religious experiences.[25]

This perceived disjunction of heart and head, however compelling a typology, is both unfortunate and misleading. To equate conservative religion with "heart" (emotion) and liberal religion with "head" (intellect) inappropriately disjoins these complementary aspects of religious experience. As Rudolf Otto skillfully argued in *The Idea of the Holy* (1958), the religious, or numinous, experience is not only one of awesome dread (*mysterium tremendum*), but equally one of contemplative fascination (*mysterium fascinosum*). The numinous experience is an experience in which the individual apprehends the Holy through both the mind and the senses. One's total being—both "heart" and "head"—is affected. "These two qualities [of religious apprehension], the daunting and the fascinating," explained Otto, "now combine in a strange harmony of contrasts, and the resultant dual character of the numinous consciousness . . . is at once the strangest and most noteworthy phenomenon in the whole history of religion" (1958:30). Psychological models also tend to overlook the mystical encounters that even highly rational individuals may experience. In contrast to this either/or view, Otto recognized the necessary tension between rational and emotional aspects of religious experience, dual aspects that typify the experience of the human psyche before that which is "wholly other."

Sociological (or institutional) methods present a different analytical picture of liberal and conservative expressions than the preceding two approaches.[26] One of the earlier models of American Protestantism was presented by H. Richard Niebuhr in his classic 1929 study, *The Social Sources of Denominationalism* (1975). In this work, Niebuhr attempted to account for the varieties of institutional expression evident in the American religious landscape by considering certain social and economic forces. Applying the insights of Ernst Troeltsch and Max Weber to the American scene, Niebuhr elaborated a scheme through which one might explain the denominational character of American religion. Niebuhr identified three types of religious organizations: churches, denominations, and sects. The most prevalent and vital of these types in America has been the "denomination." Denominations, Niebuhr argued, are groups that, unlike sects, were accommodating to society, but, unlike churches, were unable or unwilling to dominate society.

The church/denomination/sect continuum that Niebuhr drew runs from liberal to conservative, based on the theological orientation of each grouping and the socio-economic profile of its constituents. According to Niebuhr's model, the lower an individual's economic status, the more conservative his or her religious preference and the more sectarian he or she is apt to become. Conversely, as an individual moves up the socio-economic ladder, he or she will, at the same time, shun sectarianism and begin to embrace more liberal or culture-affirming religions. Niebuhr identified the more socially sophisticated establishment churches with the upper classes and located the lower classes within the socially alienated churches, which he referred to as "the churches of the disinherited." Additionally, a sect's movement toward "denominational" status is effected by the tendency of the sect's second generation to move from world-rejecting to more world-affirming positions. The sect begins to "accommodate" to society and "compromise" its message as its members, who do not share the fervor of their fathers and mothers, begin to seek greater social acceptance.[27]

Niebuhr's distinction between church, denomination, and sect, and its subsequent refinements, have undoubtedly become the major model (or in Thomas Kuhn's now fashionable phrase, the "dominant paradigm") in the sociological analysis of liberal and conservative religious groups. Unfortunately, the church/denomination/sect paradigm, while an instructive model, has been freely and often uncritically applied by scholars to the "liberal establishment" and to the "disenfranchised fundamentalists." One unfortunate consequence has been the tendency among scholars to dismiss fundamentalists as socially, economically, and, by implication, religiously marginal. Indeed, critics of this typology rightly find fault with its less than neutral evaluation of the social dynamics of American Protestant diversity.

A fourth approach to the study of American Protestantism is historical. Among historical approaches, one interesting analysis of conservative and liberal impulses is the one offered by William McLoughlin. In his celebrated essay, "Is There a Third Force in Christendom?" (1967), McLoughlin set out to measure "conservatism" within the context of America's religio-cultural revivalistic tradition. McLoughlin took into account the role so-called "liberal" and "conservative" religious groups play in the process of religious and cultural reorientation or change—what he referred to as "awakenings."[28] McLoughlin did not regard either liberals or conservatives as in themselves instrumental agents of cultural innovation or stagnation. Indeed, to McLoughlin, "conservative" was not necessarily another word for narrow and defensive. Likewise, "liberal" was not

always synonymous with open-mindedness and innovation. Historically, he pointed out, liberals sometimes opposed religious and cultural innovation, and at other times conservatives were on the so-
called cutting edge of religious and cultural transformation. Finding
these traditional definitions inadequate, therefore, McLoughlin distinguished conservatism and liberalism in terms of the "Old Light versus
New Light" dynamic central to America's religious awakenings.

In McLoughlin's historical model, Old Light and New Light factions
have battled for control over society's norms and values, struggling
against one another until the New Lights eventually gained the upper-
hand in this religio-cultural contest. As McLoughlin related it, "after
perhaps a generation of furious polemical warfare, institutional infighting, and bitter schisms, the New Lights have emerged triumphant."
McLoughlin found this scenario to be the case in each of America's so-
called awakenings. The reason for New Light success, argued McLoughlin, is because its proponents "have produced a reformulation of the Old
Light orthodoxy into a new consensus that is able to maintain its claim
of orthodoxy and, at the same time, to adjust Christian doctrines and
practices to the new needs of a changing social order" (1967:47).[29]

The advantage of this "historical-context system of measure-
ment," argued McLoughlin, is that it "makes it easier to understand
why some of today's Conservatives are both Old Lights, because they
oppose the avant-garde of American theological and social reformulation, and New Lights because they have joined in the current Awakening as a revolt against the 'Liberal Protestant' consensus of the past fifty
years" (1967:50).

Several problems with this New Light/Old Light model are apparent. First, although this model perceptively identifies the changing
alliances throughout American religious history, McLoughlin's Old
Light/New Light configuration does not tell us why one "conservative"
group may be New Light, while at the same time another equally
"conservative" but opposing group may be Old Light. Indeed, what
defines both as "conservative" but not identically so? One might argue
that the changing alliances have at least as much to do with the
interrelationship of "conservative" and "liberal" groups as they do
with theological, psychological, and socio-economic differences.

A related problem with McLoughlin's approach is that the very
thing he touted as the advantage of his model undermines significantly

the conceptual clarity he proposed to offer. If conservatives can be both Old Lights and New Lights, and liberals can likewise be both Old Lights and New Lights, depending upon the positions they take, then what is the essential difference between conservative and liberal New Lights and conservative and liberal Old Lights? A more helpful question might be to ask, Why do New and Old Light positions and alliances apparently change with each issue? Instead, McLoughlin simply told us what we already knew: that things are as historically and religiously complicated and as conceptually foggy as they truly seem.

An additional problem with McLoughlin's analysis is his treatment of fundamentalism and new evangelicalism. He was not careful to discriminate fundamentalism from evangelicalism, often referring to new evangelicals as neofundamentalists, even after recognizing that they "prefer not to call themselves fundamentalists or neo-fundamentalists, adopting instead the term 'evangelicals' or 'Conservatives'" (1967:59). It can only be repeated that the boundaries that define evangelicalism and the lines that separate "true" evangelicals from all others seem to be an important aspect of evangelical self-understanding. As before, evangelicals appear to be quite sensitive to who is and who is not "evangelical," pointing to and even magnifying the differences among themselves rather than the family ties that bind them. Moreover, evangelicals and fundamentalists have been keenly aware of the distinction between themselves and have acted, and continue to act, to preserve this distinction. As a result, McLoughlin's insensitivity to the way in which groups identify themselves in relation and in opposition to other groups tends to distract from the thrust of his argument and to create greater conceptual confusion than necessary.

That said, I will now turn to a discussion of group boundary theories and derive from them a theoretical model for analysis of this social dynamic within postwar evangelical Protestantism that will guide the historical and interpretive narrative in the chapters to follow.

A BOUNDARY APPROACH
TO EXPLAINING EVANGELICAL DIVERSITY

The emergence of the "new evangelicalism" during the immediate postwar period and its subsequent separation from the fundamentalist movement serves to illustrate the coalitional nature of American evangelicalism more generally. To explain first its changing relation to historic fundamentalism, its ambivalent relation to modern culture, and then its diversification and present day definitional quandaries, it becomes necessary to construct a social structural model that takes into consideration the group boundaries "within" (which distinguish evangelical from fundamentalist) as well as the boundaries "without" (which mark the differences between evangelicalism and liberal Protestantism and neo-orthodoxy). Far from a metaphorical description of evangelical diversity, this kind of analytic model—which looks at evangelicalism in terms of its dual orientation to the demands of orthodox faith and the exigencies of modern life—provides a useful interpretive tool for explaining that diversity. For the purposes of this study, I will rely on the insights of anthropologists Fredrik Barth, Mary Douglas, and Anthony Cohen, especially as each touches on the importance of symbolic boundaries to a group's attempts to define itself in relation and in opposition to groups it perceives as its ideological rivals.

In his seminal study on "Ethnic Groups and Boundaries" (1969), Fredrik Barth sought to account for the persistence of ethnic groups and ethnic identity in pluralistic societies by shifting the focus of the study of ethnic phenomena from a group's cultural elements to its social boundaries.[30] In his ethnographic field studies, Barth noticed that groups within the same social system were clearly divided along respected social lines, indicating that a group's preservation did not depend on its cultural content (such as hats, masks, feathers, salutes) but on the maintenance of its distinct ethnic boundary. According to Barth, these symbolic boundaries, of which cultural content is a way of signaling their existence, function to differentiate one group from another. What is more, Barth argued, though it might vary characteristically from group to group, the boundary itself is simply the distinction between member and nonmember, insider and outsider. As Barth put it, though "the cultural features that signal the boundary may change, and the cultural characteristics of the members may likewise be transformed, indeed, even the organizational form of the group may change, . . . yet the fact of continuing dichotomization between members and outsiders allows us to specify the nature of continuity, and investigate the changing cultural form and content"

(1969:14). For Barth, then, the boundary is the group's sense of itself in relation to other groups and to outsiders. For the group's members, it is an identity based upon a sense of discrimination, separating "us from them." By functioning to preserve this fundamental distinction, the boundary therefore establishes the awareness and reinforces the understanding that "they are not us."

Furthermore, although ethnic groups are ascriptive by nature, Barth held that it is the social boundary that actually defines the group's distinctiveness more so than any physical or cultural characteristic. Since the boundary serves as the focal point of group distinctiveness, there exist symbolic markers that function to remind members of the boundary and to ward off outsiders who might encroach upon it. This does not mean, however, that social contact or social interaction cannot and does not occur. In fact, as James Dormon has observed, the boundary functions as the "structuring agent of social interaction" (1980:26). Although the symbolic nature of the boundary does allow interaction to take place, social interaction—or transboundary contact—does not occur without some restrictions. The boundary, in fact, places constraints on group members by prescribing what roles they are to play and with whom they may interact and transact business. In commenting on this point, Dormon noted that "Ethnic group functions in any society are *relative*, not absolute, and ethnic groups are best understood in terms of their interaction with other groups, not on the basis of their objectively manifested markers" (1980:27, emphasis added). The point here is that the boundary is not an object that defines differences but is an awareness of differences, differences that members strive to preserve. In reference to evangelical scholarship, this specific point is missed by researchers who look for metaphors to describe apparent organizational diversity or subtle kaleidoscopic changes.[31] The boundaries of evangelicalism persist despite the fact that the "content" by which evangelicals identify themselves and their allies—their beliefs and behaviors—changes.

Barth therefore offered two insights useful to this study on American evangelicalism. First, groups are keenly aware of their differences from other groups, even in the most subtle of symbolic ways. A second insight, implicit in Barth's work, is the correlation between the intensity of intergroup interaction and the strength of the group's boundary. While groups within a larger social system do interact with one another, interaction appears to strengthen group identity rather than weaken it. One reason for this is that when interaction threatens to weaken or blur group identity, group members reaffirm the symbols that mark their differences. Interaction, therefore, does not necessarily imply a weakened sense of identity but possibly, and conversely, enhanced group identification (cf., Hammond and Hunter 1984).

Operating from a different interpretive boundary model, anthropologist Mary Douglas, in her influential study, *Purity and Danger* (1984), found social experience rooted in and expressed through ritual symbolism. Douglas observed that pollution ideas and rituals of purification come to bear when community boundaries are threatened, weakened, or breached. For Douglas, rituals serve to protect a particular culture from contamination both internally and externally. But because social worlds touch and sometimes interpenetrate, groups are constantly on guard against the threat of contamination.[32] Moreover, because groups are ever aware of the precarious nature of their boundaries, they take great pains to guard themselves against wouldbe polluters. In these instances, boundaries are powerful structuring symbols. Indeed, Douglas further noted, individuals and communities "think of their own social environment as consisting of other people joined or separated by lines which must be respected" (1984:138).

Robert Wuthnow made a similar observation. Drawing on Douglas's analysis of group structures, Wuthnow pointed out that "social interaction always takes place within a matrix of lines and boundaries that define the perimeter of a given society or group and that draw internal distinctions within the group." Furthermore, "much of our behavior and much of our discourse is, in fact, guided by these boundaries—these structures—and is concerned with making sure that these boundaries are affirmed" (Wuthnow 1988:9). Not only do symbolic boundaries order a community's social experiences, they also provide meaning and purpose. As Wuthnow indicated, "symbolic boundaries are both powerful in their effects and are accorded power by the ways in which we act and think toward them" (1988:9). Similarly, Peter Berger and Thomas Luckmann hinted at the power symbolic boundaries exert over members who might otherwise stray from the security of the nomic or ordered constitution of community into anomy (see 1967:92-104). And, as sociologist Émile Durkheim observed, because individuals live in constant threat of anomy, ritual activities and symbolic concepts function "cohesively," thus reintegrating members and strengthening the community's collective identity. Or, to put it more succinctly, group boundaries are structural, normative, and purposive.

Douglas offered a unique insight into the way communities protect themselves against potentially polluting contact. To the observer, boundary concern and boundary-conserving behavior appear obsessive. Yet such behavior, however peculiar, has a certain logic within its own social system. Similarly, evangelical preoccupation with defining the boundaries of its community and its continual efforts at preserving its group boundaries from possible encroachment make sense when one considers such behavior in terms of how group boundaries order social experience and define an individual's place in a larger social-cultural system.

The work of anthropologist Anthony Cohen on the "symbolic construction of community" outlined an approach to the study of social life that defined community not according to its structural forms but in terms of its symbolic meaning, that is, "as a system of values, norms, and moral codes which provides a sense of identity within a bounded whole to its members" (Cohen 1985:9).[33] Cohen's primary concern was with the ways in which individuals and groups create their sense of community and "the resourcefulness with which they use symbols in this regard to re-assert community and its boundaries when the processes and consequences of change threaten its integrity" (1985:28). As had Barth, Cohen argued that boundaries, which mark a group's beginning and end, exist because social interaction often threatens the integrity of individual and group identity. Cohen stressed, however, that group boundaries are neither always nor necessarily apparent. Rather, they are imbued with symbolic meaning and should therefore be thought of as existing in the minds of those who observe and respect them. But meanings vary. As Cohen pointed out, "the boundary may be perceived in rather different terms, not only by people on opposite sides of it, but also by people on the same side" (1985:12).

While the boundary marks the "geosocial" extent of the group, the boundary is not merely the difference between one group and another. As Cohen put it, "the community boundary is not drawn at the point where differentiation occurs. Rather, it incorporates and encloses difference . . ." (1985:74). It is, in effect, a symbolic representation of difference. If the boundaries were merely the observable differences between groups, then identifying and defining those differences would be a matter of classifying and then ascertaining the "meaning" of a particular community's symbolic boundaries. But if the boundary "incorporates and encloses difference," then in order to explain the diversity within a community, it is necessary to examine the processes whereby those differences are symbolically represented.

Cohen identified several characteristics of group boundaries that are instructive to this study on twentieth-century evangelicalism in that they move beyond metaphorical language, classification schemes, and "two-party" typologies. First, community boundaries are symbolic by nature and are therefore interpreted and even symbolized differently by groups that oppose one another and even by members of the same community. A second characteristic is that because boundaries are oppositional in character, they are relative and arbitrary rather than fixed (1985:58 and 115). Third, boundaries do not merely signal group differences but embody those differences, making their existence of vital importance to a group's identity. The importance of the boundary for defining group identity and difference cannot be overestimated.

As with Barth, a final insight we might draw from Cohen that will aid our explication of postwar evangelical diversity is that the intensity with which boundaries are defended is equal to the intensity of the boundary threat members perceive. Likewise, the threat to the group boundary changes as social relations between one group and another changes. In this way, change can reduce tension between groups as well as increase it. But the relaxing of tensions without can produce unexpected tensions within. In the case of evangelicalism, its changing relations to liberalism gradually brought an easing of tensions with modern culture. Internally, however, its move toward social acceptance was greeted by resistance and eventual alienation from elements not welcome to such changes.

Thus, the dynamic nature of group boundaries, outlined in the above model, will help explain not only the emergence of the new evangelical coalition in the early 1940s, but also its oppositional relationship to fundamentalism, its growing definitional quandaries with respect to liberalism in the 1950s and 1960s, the disintegration of its coalition in the 1970s, and its expanding diversity of expression in the 1980s and 1990s.

CHAPTER THREE

The Liberal and Conservative Divide in American Protestantism, 1880-1930

WHEN MARTIN E. MARTY set out to map the changing religious landscape of modern America over two decades ago, he noticed among other things a sharp line between what he called "public" and "private" emphases within Protestantism's "Righteous Empire." This two-party system that Marty wrote about was barely discernible at the onset of the twentieth century. Before then, most chroniclers of American religious history had generally discussed Protestantism according to its denominational types. But in the period from about 1880 to 1900, denominational distinctions began to blur, and American Protestants squared off into theologically liberal and conservative corners. By the 1920s, when the fundamentalist-modernist controversy drove a sharp wedge between these groups, two distinct camps emerged—one concerned primarily with private or individual salvation, the other with the public or social consequences of the Christian Gospel (Marty 1970).[1]

The "private" party, Marty went on to explain,

> seized that name "evangelical" which had characterized all Protestants early in the nineteenth century. It accented individual salvation out of the world, personal moral life congruent with the ideals of the

saved, and fulfillment or its absence in the rewards or punishments
in another world in a life to come (1970:179).

Abandoning the modern world as irretrievably secularized, this
"private" type of Protestantism (known later as "fundamentalism"
because of its tenacious insistence upon a literalistic interpretation of
the Bible) had as its main goal the conversion of individuals instead of
the transformation of society. The oft-quoted statement by the nineteenth-century evangelist Dwight L. Moody came to characterize the
outlook of the private party within Protestantism: "I look upon this
world as a wrecked vessel. God has given me a lifeboat and said to me,
'Moody, save all you can'" (quoted in Noll et al. 1983: 294).

Conversely, said Marty, the "public" or social sphere of Protestantism "was public insofar as it was more exposed to the social order and
the social destinies of men." As a result, the public party "pursued a
Social Christianity, the Social Gospel, Social Service, Social Realism,
and the like." Moreover, while "private" Protestantism pursued more
expressly a revivalistic agenda for the conversion of individuals and
thereby the revitalization of the churches, "public" Protestantism
gradually abandoned revivalistic techniques and relied instead on
modern social theories to help them transform a fallen world
(1970:179; cf. May 1949 and Szasz 1982). In time, these two opposing
emphases effected an irreparable breach within American Protestantism, a breach that continues to this day.

Complicating Marty's typology, however, was the emergence of the
"new evangelicalism" out of the soil of fundamentalism during World
War II, a coalition of conservative and moderate evangelicals who
sought to regain intellectual respectability for orthodox Protestantism
and to reassert a conservative religious and social agenda for postwar
America. Unlike the many typologies discussed in the previous
chapter, Marty's typology does leave room, at least implicitly, for a
mediating "third party." Indeed, in a later essay, Marty pointed to the
evangelicals as one orthodoxy among several competing Protestant
orthodoxies. As Marty explained, "most of the energies expended
recently by evangelicals have been directed chiefly to the cause of
demarcating or delineating boundaries between themselves and American Protestant liberals on the one hand or fundamentalists on the
other" (1977:190). In this case, then, the rise of this coalition of

evangelicals might be interpreted as an attempt to reconcile these "public" and "private" Protestant parties.

The aim of this chapter will be to review the history from which a distinct liberal and conservative ("public" and "private") Protestantism took shape, and, in doing so, to situate the rise of the new evangelical coalition within its historical context. This brief historical survey will identify two ideological shifts within Protestantism. First, following the observations of Martin Marty and Ferenc Szasz, it will trace the increasing tendency among Protestants after 1880 to define themselves less in terms of denominational affiliation and more along conservative/liberal lines, polarizing Protestants into rival conservative and liberal factions. The second shift in Protestantism this chapter will trace is the consequent movement of the conservative faction, in light of its "defeat," away from America's religious mainstream—a move that took it from center to periphery. As it will become clear, conservative "marginalization" came about as a result of its increasing alienation from a culture it once seemed to dominate and believed it could "Christianize" (Handy 1984) but now saw as both secularized and secularizing—an influence it must now seek to escape.

Indeed, the twentieth century seemed to be an era the orthodox Protestants were ill prepared to enter, an age when religion and society were both becoming increasingly more secular. Whereas in the nineteenth century religion and American culture seemed to commingle without the slightest ripple of protest from either, in the twentieth century conservative Protestantism's social and moral prescriptions appeared to many as carry-overs from an unsophisticated time. With the advent of industrialization and its resulting urbanization, American society had changed almost overnight (May 1949). Fundamentalism's biblical dictates appeared anachronistic to people who now turned to the miracles of science for enlightened solutions to society's problems. As Marsden observed, "Fundamentalism emerged from an era in which American evangelicalism was so influential that it was virtually a religious establishment; eventually, however, fundamentalism took on the role of a beleaguered minority with strong sectarian or separatist tendencies" (1980:6-7). For fundamentalists, who as a rule were deeply imbued with dispensationalist views of the world, the social order appeared to be "lost" and therefore beyond redemption. This shift in fundamentalist thinking about American culture—from viewing it as the "New Israel" (Cherry 1971) to viewing it as a "fallen nation"—likewise effected social structural changes within conservative Protestantism itself. These two dynamics played a significant role in defining the conflicts that took place between liberal and conservative Protestants.

Thus, the following discussion will chart the turn-of-the-century liberal/conservative realignment within evangelical Protestantism and fundamentalism's exile from the center to the periphery of American cultural and religious life. This historical sketch will highlight several of the decisive and divisive events that took place roughly from 1880 to 1930, focusing primarily on fundamentalist reactions. Although such a condensed treatment of these issues belies their theological, social, and historical complexities, it serves, in any case, to acquaint the reader with the character of the fundamentalist-modernist controversy and to set the stage for the more detailed discussion of the emergence and expansion of the new evangelicalism in the chapters to follow.

THE INCHOATE LIBERAL/CONSERVATIVE THEOLOGICAL DIVIDE

The "roots" of fundamentalism extend to the controversies that during the early decades of this century rent Protestantism asunder and set into motion two competing religious agendas. As with liberalism, Protestant fundamentalism constituted various streams of theological and philosophical thought that coalesced sometime before 1920 (Marsden 1980). For a time, this rightward movement was known simply as conservatism. The term "fundamentalist," coined by Baptist editor Curtis Lee Laws in 1920 to describe the growing party of vocal conservatives within the Baptist churches (Marsden 1980:107), was later adopted by conservative Protestants as a rallying point for those loyal to the "Fundamentals of the Faith" who were bent on combatting Darwinism in the public schools and liberalism in the churches. The major differences that developed between liberals and conservatives centered primarily on their beliefs regarding God's relation to the phenomenal world, the human condition, and the authority of biblical revelation.

In very general terms, liberals came to view God as immanent and his self-evident nature as unfolding through time and within the framework of human cultural history. Liberals also emphasized the redemption of society from human ignorance—and not human depravity—as the chief goal of preaching the Gospel. In addition, while liberals did consider the Bible to be a source of knowledge about God and Jesus Christ, they relied more heavily on the depth of personal religious experience or "feeling" (Schleiermacher) for religion's confirmation. They also came to value modern historical and linguistic means of interpreting and understanding the Bible, readily adopting the methods of so-called higher criticism that were anathematized by conservative Protestants in the latter decades of the nineteenth century.[2]

As a rule, conservative evangelicals believed that God transcended this evil fallen world. The line between Holy God and sinful Earth was sharply and immutably fixed. In stark contrast to the Divine nature, human nature was inherently evil. Humankind had descended from Adam and Eve, who, through their disobedience to God, had caused the fall of all humanity and subsequently had infused the whole human race with a sinful nature. As a result, this evil nature had alienated all of humanity from God.[3] Conservatives understood God's revelation of himself and his saving grace as it was contained in the Bible, a divinely-inspired revelation that affirmed both the transcendence of God and the utter helplessness of humankind. The sharp break between the pure heavenly world and the carnal earthly realm implied the need for individual believers to make a radical break from their sinful natures and to seek salvation through a change of heart and lifestyle. Sinful society was doomed, the conservatives taught, but through a conversion experience individuals could escape its damning influences (cf., Ahlstrom 1975:224-87).

The debate between conservative and liberal evangelicals, however, came down to the inspiration and authority of the Christian scriptures. Conservatives held tenaciously to the verbal inspiration of the Bible. Their writings, especially those of Charles Hodge, B. B. Warfield, and, later, J. Gresham Machen, set out to prove the authenticity of the Christian religion by proving the unerring reliability of the Bible. The most famous formula for divine inspiration was the Princeton Theology.[4] Liberals, on the other hand, refused to be shackled by outmoded and uninspiring theories of the Bible's origins and salvific claims. In turn, they did not feel compelled to "prove" the authority of the Bible as did the conservatives, but accepted it, instead, on the basis of the relevance of its message to the modern age. As William Newton Clarke wrote in 1898, "the authority of the Scriptures is the authority of the truth that they convey." It is not necessary for Christians to prove the inspiration of the Bible, for "if God is in a book," Clarke argued, "he will be found: we do not have to justify our sense of his presence there by building up a theory to show how he got there. God shines by his own light" (quoted in Hutchison, 1976:120,119).

In the face of Darwinism, biblical criticism, the comparative study of religion, and the new social sciences, liberals felt compelled to respond rationally, not dogmatically. They were honestly attempting to salvage what they could of biblical truth. As Winthrop Hudson pointed out, one of the advantages of liberalism's New Theology "was that it enabled its proponents both to maintain what to them was the heart of their inherited faith and at the same time to come to terms with the whole intellectual temper of the modern world" (1981:276). For example, in 1872, Henry Ward Beecher, one of the great pulpiteers of the nineteenth century, extolled the virtues of modern thought to Yale seminarians when he said, "the providence of God is rolling forward in a spirit of investigation that Christian ministers must meet and join." Beecher warned that they would become simply "apostles of the dead past" if they allowed "the development of truth [to] run ahead of them" (quoted in Hudson, 1981: 269). The conservatives, however, did not see it quite the same way. They interpreted the changes that the liberals were instigating as nothing less than an insidious attack on the "faith once delivered." Accordingly, conservatives would brook no hint of the liberals' compromise with either biblical criticism, modern science, or secular culture.

Fundamentalists, as they shortly came to be called, saw in the New Theology a threatening challenge to their claim that the Bible is the only true and objective revelation of God's salvation for the human race. Rather than stand idly by and allow liberals to harmonize the Bible with the claims of science and with the spirit of the age, fundamentalists challenged liberalism's authority to speak on behalf of God and the Christian religion—or even to speak as Christians. Poised for the attack, the fundamentalists vowed to fight until every vestige of modernist "unbelief" had been purged from the churches.

THE "MILLENNIAL" DIVIDE

One of the ways by which the early fundamentalists became an organized movement and developed a cohesive sense of identity was through a series of Bible and Prophecy conferences held almost annually from 1868 until 1901 and then intermittently until 1918 (Sandeen 1970 and Dayton 1988a).[5] In a curious way, the Prophecy conference movement became one of the ways in which fundamentalists fought modernism. Pressing their case for an error-free Bible, fundamentalists believed that history had been outlined in the pages of the Scriptures. Because all of history pointed to the Second Advent of Christ, they confidently pointed to historical events in the late nineteenth and early twentieth centuries as "signs" that clearly confirmed the truth of the Bible.

The centerpiece doctrine of these conferences was the belief in the literal and visible return of Jesus physically to earth to reign over it as king. Prior to his return, however, the Church would fall into apostasy and the world would grow ever more godless and wicked. Coming in judgment and glory, Christ would destroy evil and establish his kingdom of righteousness in Jerusalem for a millennium, a thousand years. Because Christ's return would occur *before* the millennium, this view of the endtime period came to be known as *pre*millennialism. In contrast, *post*millennialists believed that Christ would return only after the world had, through the redeeming work of the Church, established a millennial period of peace.[6]

These conferences exerted an enormous influence on a significant number of conservative church leaders and, by extension, their parishioners. In addition, the Bible and Prophecy conferences, as well as the periodicals that grew out of them, helped popularize premillennial-dispensationalist doctrines of the second coming of Jesus. Indeed, some scholars argue that without the peculiar historiography that resulted from the blending and refinement of millennial expectation and dispensational thought through this series of conferences, the fundamentalist movement might have been merely a footnote in

American religious history.[7] Because of the importance of premillennial-dispensationalism to an understanding of the development of early twentieth-century fundamentalism, the essence of the theologies of William Miller and John Nelson Darby and the impact of premillennial-dispensationalist doctrines will be discussed briefly below.

Through detailed study of the prophetic passages of the Bible, William Miller (1782-1849), a Baptist lay minister, concluded that all signs pointed to 1843 as the year of Jesus' Second Coming to earth to establish his long-awaited kingdom of peace. Though Miller had made his calculations between 1816 and 1818, it was not until 1835 that he published his predictions, and not until 1839 that his message was broadcast to any effect. It was at that time that Miller was greatly assisted by the keen organizational and promotional prowess of the Reverend Joshua V. Himes, a man whose enthusiasm for crowds and knack for publicity gave Miller the boost he needed to get his message out (Sandeen 1970 and Hudson 1981).

By the end of the 1830s, Miller had gathered around him a fairly large following of some 50,000 adherents from the churches in upper New York State and New England. By early 1843, expectations among these Adventists began to run high. But as Miller's original date passed, the mood began to change from excitement to disappointment. Refiguring his prophetic calculations, Miller announced that he had erred; the date of Christ's Second Advent would be October 22, 1844. When that date likewise passed with not even the least sign of a heavenly visitation, the movement collapsed. While the "Great Disappointment," as it was called, had certainly dashed the hopes of tens of thousands of Adventists, American millennialists did not give up their hope that Christ would return someday soon. Indeed, many would take up where Miller had left off, with the exception that they were usually careful not to set specific dates for Christ's return.[8]

The dispensational theology of John Nelson Darby (1800-1882), a one-time member of the Church of Ireland and a leader of the Plymouth Brethren, provided American premillennial evangelicals with a simple historical framework within which to organize and interpret their prophetic findings.[9] In America, millennial expectation had been prevalent within the Protestant churches since before the Revolution. In this climate, Darby's message seemed almost destined to thrive.

To put it briefly, Darby taught that God had divided human history into seven historical periods, or dispensations. Each dispensation was governed by a different divine principle by which God dealt with and ultimately judged humankind (Scofield 1896).[10] Basing his dispensational notion upon a cyclical theory of historical development, Darby taught that each dispensation begins in Edenic innocence and peace—peace between God and humanity and peace among humans in harmony with themselves and the created order. But this quickly changes. The new dispensation—as the old one before it—slowly degenerates into sin and disobedience, culminating in social upheaval, divine judgment, and the inauguration of the next era. With each new dispensation, however, creation is brought closer and closer to the final golden age of peace—the seventh dispensation. Darby held that humankind was currently passing through the sixth and final period before Christ would return to bring the age of millennial peace. Darby also believed that the various social and political crises of his time indicated that the consummation of the sixth age was imminent (Sandeen 1970).[11]

What is more, Darby taught the "any-moment" return of Christ—what came to be called the "secret rapture." Before the cataclysmic end of the sixth and present dispensation, Jesus would remove his faithful remnant of Bible believers from the earth to wait with him in heaven until God the Father had destroyed the old heavens and earth and created them anew. After that, Christ and his faithful remnant would descend to the newly restored earth to reign with him for one thousand years, the seventh and final dispensation, the millennium (Sandeen 1970:62). Because this secret rapture of the faithful could happen at any moment, Christian dispensationalists were admonished to be prepared morally and spiritually at all times for their "rapture" to heaven.

In addition to his emphasis on the secret rapture, Darby also taught that the Christian churches and the "true church" were not coextensive. The true church, Darby maintained, was spiritual, not institutional. All religious institutions and denominations were, in fact, fallen; they had apostatized. In order to avoid possible contamination and even condemnation by association, Darby, who travelled extensively throughout North America between 1862 and 1877, encouraged his followers to separate themselves from their churches.

Despite his admonition, most American dispensationalists, while accepting Darby's theology, were somewhat reluctant to embrace his ecclesiology. They remained in their churches, teaching a more modified version of Darbyite dispensationalism (Sandeen 1970:136 and Stone 1993:33-34).

Interestingly, these two points—apostasy of the churches and the necessary separation of the believer from them—reappeared in the thinking of later dispensational fundamentalists during the early days of the fundamentalist-modernist controversy. For instance, at the Prophetic Bible Conference held in Chicago in 1914, Arno Gaebelein, a popular conference speaker, Bible commentator, and longtime editor of the Jewish Christian publication *Our Hope,* scolded his fellow premillennialists for their failure to obey God's call to separate from apostates. "Brethren," he said, "God calls you to separate yourselves from all that denies His Word, His Name, His Son, and His Gospel. Listen! God always has called to that in every proceeding crisis. He expects his people to have no fellowship with the works of darkness." With even greater emphasis, Gaebelein questioned, "How dare you support men and institutions who deny your Lord? How dare you keep fellowship with the enemies of the cross of Christ?" (1914:154). Thus, dispensationalism brought to the emerging fundamentalist movement two of its signature characteristics: its endtime historiography and its separatist impulse (see Stone 1993).

PROPHECY POPULARIZED AND POLEMICIZED

The blending of millennial expectation and Darby's dispensational historiography came about as a result of the long process of writing and revising by prophecy conference speakers and by the editors of and contributors to the dozen or so millennialist periodicals of the day. This process culminated in the publication in 1909 of C. I. Scofield's detailed reference notes in the *Scofield Bible.* In it, the millenarian interest in the signs of the times and dispensational historiography were expertly blended by Scofield in a useful and appealing format. The *Scofield Reference Bible* soon became the most popular reference work among American fundamentalists. Indeed, the *Scofield Bible,* Sandeen argued, has been "subtly but powerfully influential in spreading premillennial dispensationalist views among hundreds of thousands who have regularly read that Bible and who often have been unaware of the distinction between the ancient text and the Scofield interpretation" (1970:222).

Premillennial dispensationalist notions of historical development came to color fundamentalists' understanding of world events. The Bible, millenarians believed, had foretold the very conflicts that the world was presently experiencing. World War I, for example, had been predicted in the Bible. Aerial combat had been foreseen by the prophets (see Evans 1986). The return of the Jews to Palestine had also been predicted in the Bible.[12] In addition, there would be drought, famine, disease, and economic disaster. The churches would likewise apostatize; the Bible had foretold it. This view, that ancient Bible prophecy was being fulfilled in the modern age, assumed an inerrant Bible whose reliability depended upon the necessary literal fulfillment of its prophecies. What is more, because this literal interpretive scheme placed historical events within the context of the prophetic predictions revealed by God in the Bible, it allowed millenarians personal insight into the meaning of world events. It seems, then, that long before the Swiss theologian Karl Barth urged Protestant ministers to preach to the contemporary situation with the Bible in one hand and the newspaper in the other, premillennial dispensationalists were reading the Bible as if it *were* the daily paper. As Samuel Kellogg, an early dispensationalist leader, averred, "Prophecy is simply history written in advance" (1893:90).

As expected, liberal Protestants scoffed at the "end-time" speculations of their millenarian brethren. The reason for this disdain was quite obvious. While dispensational theories were heavily dependent upon a literal interpretation of the Bible, the historical-critical methodologies of the liberals did not allow for such literal and idiosyncratic interpretations of the Bible. To a new breed of highly educated liberal churchmen, the fundamentalists' hermeneutical methodology appeared simplistic and naive.

In this way, the conflict between conservative and liberal Protestants at the turn of the century came to represent two mutually exclusive interpretations not only of the Bible, but of human history and cultural development as well. Conservatives, in the main, read history according to the dispensational patterns set forth in the premillennial dispensationalist interpretation of the Bible. By contrast, liberal Protestants, looking to scientific models of natural development and evolutionary progression, did not impose a strictly biblical grid on history. As George Marsden observed, "these totally opposed views of history lay at the heart of the conflict and misunderstanding between theological liberals and their fundamentalist opponents." The sharp disagreement between transcendent and immanent views of God and his relation to the natural world profoundly informed conservative and liberal views of the historical process. "The liberal party," Marsden continued, "came increasingly to view history in the sense of natural development as the key to understanding all reality, including Scripture." The fundamentalists, however, "insisted more and more that the supernatural account of things in Scripture was the key to understanding anything about natural reality, including history" (1980:63). Therefore, by the early decades of the twentieth century, signs of an irreparable breach within the Protestant establishment were beginning to reveal themselves, especially in interpretative differences over the Bible. Conservative Protestantism was beginning to move institutionally as well as symbolically from center to periphery. This seismic shift is no better evident than in Protestantism's debate over science and fundamentalism's subsequent crusade against evolution.

FUNDAMENTALISM'S FAILED CRUSADES: FROM CENTER TO PERIPHERY

The story of fundamentalism's crusade against science and secularism is well documented and need not be recounted here in historical detail.[13] The bitter road from the Charles Briggs heresy trial (1891-1893) to the John T. Scopes "monkey" trial (1925) was paved with one conservative defeat after another. In less than fifty years, conservative evangelical Protestantism found itself removed from the center of American cultural and religious life, having been displaced by scientific modernism and religious liberalism (Marsden 1977). But the fundamentalists would not go down without a fight. As a result, Protestantism was wracked by disagreement and riven by dissent.

America's entry into the European war in April 1917 turned Protestants' attention, if only briefly, away from their increasingly bitter ecclesiastical conflicts against each other to a greater enemy abroad. Winthrop Hudson suggested that one possible reason for this truce might have been the ideological stake that both liberals and fundamentalists had in the outcome of the "war to end all wars." Liberals mobilized themselves in order to save Western culture and humanity— "to make the world safe for democracy." The fundamentalists, on the other hand, were fighting German intellectual and cultural unbelief, which they believed was responsible for the liberal-modernist scourge that "plagued" the Protestant churches (Hudson 1981:368-369; cf., Longfield 1991). Even though World War I provided a hiatus from denominational infighting, conservatives and liberals continued their rivalry, periodically sniping at each other in the public arena.

For instance, Shirley Jackson Case charged that, in propagating their pessimistic "end-of-the-world" views, the premillennialists were, in addition to spurning "all serious effort to secure the betterment of the world by means of popular education, social reforms, remedial legislation" (1918:241), diverting attention and funds from the war effort (see Noll, *et al.* 1983:373). This charge implied that the fundamentalists were indirectly aiding the Germans. In addition, there came other attacks accusing fundamentalists of receiving money from German sources. The editors of the Biola Institute's dispensationalist monthly magazine, *King's Business,* responded promptly and in kind to such allegations. Said the editors, "While the charge that the money for premillennial propaganda 'emanates from German sources' is ridiculous, that the destructive criticism that rules in Chicago University 'emanates from German sources' is undeniable" (quoted in Noll, *et al.* 1983:373).[14] Thus it was that both liberals and fundamentalists, though for different reasons, exhibited a great amount of patriotism in the war effort. When the war ended, however, the controversy in the churches was resumed, this time with even more vigor and acrimony.

The fundamentalist-modernist controversy of the 1920s was simultaneously fought—and lost—by fundamentalists along two major fronts. Briefly, the first line of defense was against the teaching of evolution in the public schools and the propagation of antibiblical scientific theories in the universities. The second battle line was drawn by fundamentalists in an effort to stem the rising tide of liberal theology (or modernism) in the mainstream Protestant churches. The fight against evolution, which took place during the first half of the decade, left fundamentalist ideology discredited in the eyes of the American public. The conflict in the churches, which continued for sometime longer, left liberals and fundamentalists embittered toward each other, leaving the churches sorely and almost hopelessly divided (Ahlstrom 1975b:396-403).[15]

THE MENACE OF EVOLUTION

The campaign against the teaching of scientific theory in place of biblical religion in the public schools—culminating in the Scopes Trial—captured the attention and absorbed the energies of fundamentalists from roughly 1919 to 1927 (see Furniss 1954 and Szasz 1982). In typical revivalistic style, fundamentalists campaigned across the country, alerting fellow conservative churchgoers to the dangers that Darwinism posed to American society and to the Christian faith. As Norman Furniss put it in his landmark study on fundamentalism of this period, "in their conviction that the theory of evolution would destroy acceptance of the Bible as an authoritative guide in religion and conduct, they had sought to make instruction in the biological sciences conform with the narratives found in Genesis" (1954:3).

Fundamentalists believed that the evolutionary theory of human origins, if left unchecked, would lead to a breakdown of the moral and social order. Indeed, conservative Protestant fears of evolutionary theory had changed little since S. A. Hodgman warned in 1867 that the spread of Darwinism would touch off "a wave of 'defalcations and robberies, and murders, and infanticides, and adulteries, and drunkenness, and every form and degree of social dishonor'" (quoted in Furniss 1954:11). But evolutionary theory, which during the nineteenth century had almost exclusively been the preoccupation of elites, did not attract the attention of laypersons until the early 1920s, when William Jennings Bryan made evolution a major cause célèbre around which fundamentalists could rally in force (see Szasz 1982, Roberts 1988, and Longfield 1991). As it was, before Bryan had taken the field in the war against modernism and unbelief, other conservative Protestant spokespersons such as William Bell Riley and George McCready Price had loosely organized their followers to fight Darwin's "satanic" influences through legislative means.[16]

William Jennings Bryan gave fundamentalists a needed boost when he joined the fight in 1923, quickly becoming biblical orthodoxy's most impassioned spokesperson (Furniss 1954:3, 76-100 and Russell 1976:162-189).[17] For some years before, Bryan had been travelling throughout the country warning Americans of the social and religious evils of evolution. But with greater urgency, he now lobbied state lawmakers on behalf of laws preventing the dissemination of evolutionary theories through the public schools. His efforts led to the passage of the Butler Act in Tennessee in the spring of 1925—the strongest anti-evolution statute in the country. But Bryan's finest triumph for fundamentalism's crusade against evolution would soon prove to be a cause of its own eventual undoing.

By the summer of 1925, the struggle against evolutionary theory came to a dramatic climax when Tennessee's new anti-evolution statute received its first and fiercest challenge from a high school science teacher in the sleepy little borough of Dayton. Prompted by the American Civil Liberties Union's advertised offer to provide free legal services, John T. Scopes was persuaded by some local businessmen in Dayton to test the legality of Tennessee's ban on teaching evolution. Not long after giving his students a lesson in biological evolution, Scopes was arrested and charged by local officials with defying the Butler Act. When the ACLU learned of Scopes's arrest, it responded quickly, providing Scopes with the finest lawyers in the country. Among them was the renowned criminal lawyer Clarence Darrow, who was appointed counsel for the defense. The fundamentalists were also quick to act. Seeing this court case as an opportunity to crush the anti-Christian proponents of evolutionary theory and modern science, William Jennings Bryan, sponsored by William Riley's World's Christian Fundamentals Association, which had been founded in 1919 to fight evolution and modernism, took upon himself the mantle of defender of the faith. The two giants met on a battlefield some have represented as the symbolic clash between the nineteenth- and twentieth-century worlds—between traditional and modern cultures. While the modern view did not prevail that hot July week in Tennessee, Dayton would prove a Pyrrhic victory for anti-evolutionary forces. Bryan would win the day, but he did so to the discredit of fundamentalism and its proponents generally.

Some days before the trial began, reporters and curiosity-seekers converged on Dayton. A circuslike atmosphere pervaded the region. Hotdog and lemonade stands appeared along Dayton's main street and a peculiar array of enterprising rag dealers and medicine men likewise came to peddle their notions. But the trial itself was over almost as quickly as it had begun. Although Scopes was the defendant, it was fundamentalism—as the press portrayed it—that actually stood trial. Bryan, who accepted Darrow's call to the stand as biblical orthodoxy's expert witness, could not parry Darrow's rigorous and penetrating cross-examination, which aimed at discrediting literal interpretations of the Bible. Bryan's answers appeared foolish, providing Darrow with the decisive victory over biblical obscurantism he had sought. Bryan, who had sought to scourge Darwinism, was himself pilloried; fundamentalism was a laughingstock. As Bradley Longfield related, "Bryan's performance [on the stand] confirmed all the worst stereotypes of fundamentalists as uneducated, unthinking, and reactionary" (1991:155).[18] Though the Tennessee statute banning the teaching of evolution was upheld, the fundamentalist cause was severely discredited. As satirist H. L. Mencken, with characteristic sardonic wit, observed, "if any man stands up in public and solemnly swears that he is a Christian, all his auditors will laugh" (quoted in Marsden 1980:3). Bryan would not live long enough to repair the damage he had done to the cause of fundamentalism. Ironically, before he arrived in Dayton in July 1925 to do battle with the forces of modern science, Bryan had declared, "The contest between evolution and Christianity is a duel to the death." By week's end, Bryan himself was dead, presumably from exhaustion (Gatewood 1969:330; Szasz 1982:122). Despite fundamentalism's best efforts, during the first decades of the new century conservative Protestants steadily lost what influence they had had on American society. The Scopes Trial merely served to accelerate their alienation from mainstream American culture.

FIGHTING MODERNISM IN THE CHURCHES

Almost immediately after the Scopes Trial, the major battleground of the modernist controversy moved away from the public courts and back to the various denominational conventions, theological seminaries, and missionary societies. Without missing a beat, fundamentalists returned to the controversy over the infiltration of liberalism and modernism into the churches that had been suspended in 1917 by the U.S. entry into World War I.

After the Great War, fundamentalists discovered, much to their horror, that they were losing control over their respective denominations; they found themselves exerting less and less influence over denominational programs and agencies. In addition, fundamentalists increasingly discovered that they had more in common with conservatives in other denominations than with liberals within their own churches. Groups like the World's Christian Fundamentals Association (1919), the Fundamentalist Fellowship (1921), and The Baptist Bible Union (1923), for instance, were early examples of efforts by fundamentalists to exert greater influence on the churches and contemporary society through cooperative action outside established denominational associations.[19]

Then, in an effort to wrest control of their denominations and purge them of modernist heresy, fundamentalists precipitated further controversy within the Protestant churches. Fundamentalists such as J. Gresham Machen, William Bell Riley, J. C. Massee, John Roach Straton, and even the affable hayseed revivalist Billy Sunday were vicious and relentless in their strong condemnation of liberalism and modernism. The denominational battles were especially fierce in the Northern Baptist and Northern Presbyterian churches, causing irreparable rifts and resulting in many new denominations, such as the Orthodox Presbyterian, Bible Presbyterian, Conservative Baptist, and the General Association of Regular Baptists, all fundamentalist in cast. With each defeat for orthodoxy, however, it became clear to the fundamentalists that their respective denominations had compromised the Gospel by tolerating modernism within their ranks (Massee 1954). Many fundamentalists came to believe that their churches had fallen precipitously away from God, an event that many fundamentalists referred to as the "Great Apostasy" of the churches, the apostasy they believed was predicted in the Last Days (See Russell 1976, Marsden 1980, and Longfield 1991).

Fundamentalists' attitudes toward liberal Christianity were poignantly expressed in J. Gresham Machen's classic denunciation of modernism, *Christianity and Liberalism* (1923; cf., Machen 1922).

Liberalism, Machen argued, was not only theologically wrong, but "un-Christian," an altogether different religion from Christianity. "What the liberal theologian has retained after abandoning to the enemy one Christian doctrine after another," declared Machen, "is not Christianity at all, but a religion which is so entirely different from Christianity as to belong in a different category" (1923:6-7). Let no one be deceived, Machen warned, "despite the liberal use of traditional phraseology modern liberalism not only is a different religion from Christianity but belongs in a totally different class of religions" (1923:7). As Machen saw it, the solution was simple: liberals should either discard their atheistic heresies or leave the church. As he put it, "A separation between the two parties in the Church is the crying need of the hour" (1923:160). Ironically, it was Machen who eventually left the mainstream, founding the Orthodox Presbyterian Church in 1936, which itself split after Machen's untimely death in 1937 (see Russell 1976, Longfield 1991, and Hart 1994).[20]

Machen was not the only fundamentalist to denounce liberal Christianity. But his rebuke, while clear and uncompromising, was refined and quite restrained in tone. By contrast, the majority of fundamentalists who voiced opposition to modernism were not as polite as Machen. For example, Billy Sunday, in his typical down-home style, declared during the war that "when the word of God says one thing and scholarship says another, scholarship can go to hell!" (quoted in McLoughlin 1955:132). After the war, Sunday gave even greater heat to his verbal attacks on liberals and modernists. Similarly, Judson E. Conant, in an antimodernist diatribe published by the Moody Bible Institute in 1922, denounced liberals for their "unbiblical" view of the virgin birth of Jesus. "The Modernist," impugned Conant, "juggles the Scripture statements of His deity and denies His virgin birth, making Him a Jewish bastard, born out of wedlock, and stained forever with the shame of His mother's immorality" (quoted in Furniss 1954:22).

The fundamentalists were not the only faction to raise the temperature of the debate. Liberals likewise joined the verbal fracas, voicing their dislike and distrust of the growing fundamentalist movement within their churches. Among the most ardent and eloquent defenders of the modernist cause was the Baptist clergyman Harry Emerson Fosdick. Fosdick, perhaps the most popular liberal

Protestant minister of the era, saw Protestantism dividing, if not already divided, into two sharply defined camps. Fosdick addressed this division in his famous sermon of 1922, "Shall the Fundamentalists Win?," which he preached while pastoring New York City's First Presbyterian Church.[21] Fosdick pointed to the emerging boundary between conservatives and liberals. As Fosdick observed:

> Here in the Christian Church today are these two groups, and the question which the Fundamentalists have raised is this, Shall one of them drive the other out? Do we think the cause of Jesus Christ will be furthered by that? If He should walk through the ranks of this congregation this morning, can we imagine Him claiming as His own those who hold one idea of inspiration and sending from Him into the outer darkness those who hold another? You cannot fit the Lord Jesus into the Fundamentalist mold. The Church would better judge His judgment (reprinted in Hutchison 1985:177).

Though Fosdick did acknowledge certain irreconcilable differences between fundamentalists and liberals, he still held out the possibility for a peaceful coexistence between the two factions. Nonetheless, Fosdick was noticeably discomfited by the fundamentalist push to exclude liberals and modernists from the churches. Fosdick's candor and equanimity earned him the respect of both liberal and moderate Protestants—and the opprobrium of the fundamentalists. Though Fosdick was eventually forced to resign his pulpit in 1925, he was later installed as minister of Rockefeller's interdenominational Riverside Church of New York City in 1931, a position he held until his retirement in 1946 (Ahlstrom 1975:399).

By contrast, C. C. Morrison, editor of the liberal journal *The Christian Century*, responded to fundamentalist diatribes much more forcefully. His editorial "Fundamentalism and Modernism: Two Religions" (1924) characterized the fight between liberals and fundamentalists the same way that Machen had: as a conflict comparable to the clash of two distinct religions. Morrison wrote about their developing distinctions thusly:

> The God of the fundamentalist is one God; the God of the modernist is another. The Christ of the fundamentalist is one Christ; the Christ

of the modernist is another. The Bible of the fundamentalist is one
Bible; the Bible of the modernist is another. The church, the kingdom,
the salvation, the consummation of all things—these are all one thing
to fundamentalists and another thing to the modernists. . . . Which
God is the Christian God, which Christ is the Christian Christ, which
Bible is the Christian Bible, which church, which kingdom, which
salvation, which consummation are the Christian church, the Christian kingdom, the Christian salvation, the Christian consummation?
The future will tell (1924:6).

Responding more directly to Machen's barbed attacks, William P.
Merrill, minister of the Brick Presbyterian Church in New York City,
published *Liberal Christianity* (1925). In it, Merrill attempted to
answer Machen's indictment of Protestant liberalism point by point.
Annoyed by Machen's misrepresentation of liberalism as "a type of
faith and practice that is anti-Christian to the core" (Machen
1923:160), Merrill offered an apologetic that aimed both to clarify the
liberal position and to defend "with deep assurance and joy" his
argument "that liberal Christianity is a legitimate and important part
or phase of the development of Christian doctrine and practice, . . .
worthy of confidence and respect" (1925:14-15). What is more, liberal
Christianity is not at all un-Christian, but, Merrill contended, is
"essentially in harmony with the New Testament" (1925:15). Contrary
to Machen's charge, then, liberalism is not "the greatest menace to the
Christian Church" (Machen 1923:160). Far from it, argued Merrill,
"liberal Christianity is the religious hope of the world" (1925:15).[22]
    Distrust on both sides of the aisle grew to the point that separation
of the two parties seemed almost inevitable. "The inherent incompat-
ibility of the two worlds," as Morrison phrased it, "has passed the stage
of mutual tolerance" (1924:6). It was not long before fundamentalists
within the mainstream Protestant churches found themselves increasingly "out of step" and in disagreement with the progressive programs
of their respective denominations. With the exception of Charles
Erdman, whose moderate position helped still the tempest at least
temporarily, most conservatives found themselves without influence
in their own denominations (Longfield 1991). Although Bryan,
Machen, and other fundamentalists sought to purge the churches of

liberals and modernists, in the end, it was the fundamentalists who would leave the Protestant mainstream.

THE RETREAT OF FUNDAMENTALISM

Thus, in response to their embarrassing defeats, many of the most ardent fundamentalists eventually withdrew from the mainstream churches and formed their own denominations and established their own missionary and educational enterprises. In their minds, these separatists became, as it were, "voices crying in the wilderness." David F. Wells and John D. Woodbridge referred to the 1930s as a "wilderness experience" for fundamentalism (1977:13), while George Marsden likened post–Scopes Trial fundamentalism to the American immigrant experience (1977:150). This particular metaphor that Marsden offered vividly describes the self-understanding that fundamentalists themselves articulated: the sense of being strangers in a strange land, of being on the periphery of American religious and cultural life. The worldview of the fundamentalists before World War II might therefore be thought of as in some ways similar to the "ghettoization" mentality of many immigrant groups that came to the shores of America during the late nineteenth and early twentieth centuries and were consigned to living in isolated enclaves. Fundamentalists became religious and cultural outsiders, a phrase that implies a developing tribal mentality within the fundamentalist movement.

Thus, what this brief historical survey of the battles that erupted between fundamentalists and modernists early in this century has shown is that the division these events created within the churches produced a clear separation that sharply divided American Protestantism into two adversarial camps. It is against this backdrop that the new evangelicalism of the 1940s and 1950s emerged.

CHAPTER FOUR

The Emergence of a "New" Evangelicalism, 1940-1960

BY THE END OF THE FUNDAMENTALIST-MODERNIST CONTROVERSIES of the 1920s, American Protestantism found itself sharply divided into two major opposing alliances: liberalism and fundamentalism. The liberal contingent had won the day, retaining control over the mainline denominations. The fundamentalist contingent, however, had rejected the mainstream religious and cultural establishment and had removed itself to the "margins" of religious and cultural life. The literature on this period presents two popularized views of this dark time of defeat for American fundamentalism. Some interpreters have tended to see the experience as not unlike the Israelite diaspora, a "faithful remnant" (Marsden 1980) crying out for divine consolation as well as judgment against an evil world. Other interpreters have painted an even bleaker picture of this period, likening it to the Hebrew wanderings in the desert (Wells and Woodbridge 1977). Indeed, the image most scholars invoke is of a demoralized movement in irreversible decline. As Wells and Woodbridge wrote, "Truncated by splits, understandably beset by a defensive mentality, suffering from a loss of confidence, it [fundamentalism] was but a shadow of its earlier strength." Moreover, they continued, "The period from the 1930s to the 1960s . . . was in many ways one of lonely consolation. Wounds were licked, losses were counted, defenses were shored up" (1977:13). Thus, according to some scholarly assessment, it seemed that the prospects for a revival of fundamentalism during this period were indeed bleak.

But, as Joel Carpenter has more recently and more persuasively documented to the contrary, although the "failed crusades and eroded intellectual credibility [of the 1920s] were staggering setbacks," nevertheless "the movement survived its defeats and in fact, it thrived in the following years" (1984c:15-16). The main reason for fundamentalism's survival can be linked directly to its penchant for establishing parachurch organizations and extra-ecclesial agencies. As Carpenter reported, even before fundamentalists retreated from their denominations, they had already put in place cooperative agencies and organizations to facilitate the spread of the Gospel and to preserve orthodox Christianity. These cooperative efforts among fundamentalists during the 1920s and 1930s spawned a vast religious empire, replete with educational institutions, evangelistic associations, radio ministries, publishing houses, summer conferences, and the like (Carpenter 1980).[1] This elaborate infrastructure enabled fundamentalism to expand its base of operation virtually unnoticed and unchecked by the liberal mainstream Protestant denominations. As a result of its independent organizations, however, fundamentalism, though thriving, remained an isolated and relatively ineffective enclave.

Though it had developed a fairly cohesive substratum in the 1930s, fundamentalism began to separate slowly into two opposing camps.[2] Organizationally, the first visible signal that such a breach was developing within fundamentalism came when these two emerging factions chartered two competing ecclesiastical associations within the space of one year. The first of these, the American Council of Christian Churches, organized in 1941, had a membership that consisted primarily of independent and nondenominational churches. The second organization, the National Association of Evangelicals (NAE), the larger and more doctrinally diverse of the two, was founded in 1942 and was made up of clergy and laymembers from within many of the established churches; it became the basis of the new evangelical coalition.[3] But while the goals of these associations were similar, and while the membership of these groups differed little from each other doctrinally, their methods and strategies for obtaining their objectives differed markedly.[4]

What is more, though both organizations sought to stir religious revival in the United States, the issue that eventually drove a wedge between them was their conflicting positions on ecclesiastical separation from secular society. The American Council, which called on the faithful to separate themselves from a sinful world, believed revival would come as the churches in America cleansed themselves of their modernist taint. The NAE, however, taught that a united Christian coalition could effect revival only by leaving its cloister, engaging the world directly, and showing the relevance of the Gospel to modern life. They maintained that their separatist fundamentalist colleagues held too rigidly to methods that worked against revival, primarily because such separatist methods alienated the believer from mainstream American society. It would therefore be necessary, they believed, for fundamentalists to moderate the ecclesiastical and doctrinal excesses that alienated and separated them from the religious and cultural mainstream, to revive, reform, and perhaps even reconstruct Protestant orthodoxy.

The trick, as the leaders of the NAE understood it, was to bring together Protestants of all stripes into one greater evangelical coalition without falling into the same trap as the well-intentioned liberals of an earlier generation. The liberals, fundamentalists charged, had sacrificed the divine message of the Gospel and compromised the Christian faith on the altars of intellectual respectability, cultural relativity, and evangelistic expedience. While NAE leaders also believed that the liberal churches were indeed apostate, they did not make separation an essential test of doctrinal purity. Unlike the American Council, membership in the NAE was not contingent upon one's complete separation from the liberal mainline denominations. As a result of this and other positional differences, a boundary between fundamentalists and new evangelicals slowly began to divide conservative evangelicals; two Protestant orthodoxies emerged where before there had been only one.

In this chapter, then, the goal will be to trace this developing boundary between evangelicals and fundamentalists as it came to be articulated by new evangelical leaders during the 1940s, 1950s, and early 1960s, and to examine specifically the process by which the new evangelicals differentiated themselves from historic fundamentalism.[5] The boundary developed as a result of a shift in the self-definition of the new evangelicals from "fundamentalist" to "not fundamentalist," a shift that took place in several phases and was articulated by a number of spokespersons. At first, the evangelicals attempted to revive fundamentalism and its impact on American culture. When it became apparent that its doctrinal and cultural positions worked against "mainstreaming," the evangelicals then sought to reform fundamentalism. The third shift came when spokespersons for the evangelical coalition, frustrated by attempts to reform historic fundamentalism, rejected fundamentalism and their ties to it. While the original intention was "united evangelical action" among conservative Protestants, the unintended consequence of the evangelical coalition was the creation of an evangelical identity distinct from fundamentalism. Indeed, by the early 1960s these two aspects of conservative Protestantism "would be so irreconcilably divided that for all practical purposes they would cease to be parts of the same movement" (Carpenter 1984c:228; cf., Marty 1977:192-196). This growing separation of Protestant orthodoxy into two camps, then, frames the argument of this chapter.

UNITED EVANGELICAL ACTION

The rise of moderate, cooperative fundamentalism in the 1940s was a direct consequence of the desire by fundamentalists and other conservative evangelicals represented in the National Association of Evangelicals for United Action to bring about a religious revival throughout the United States.[6] If orthodox Protestants were to make any measurable Christian impact on American society, these "new" evangelicals reasoned, then both unity of purpose and cooperation of effort were of the utmost importance. "The moderate fundamentalists' quest for a new alliance," Carpenter confirmed, "stemmed from their desire for a national awakening. Their country's future looked grim, but revival, they thought, would renew the nation's moral integrity and prosperity." But, Carpenter continued, "A sweeping revival would require evangelical cooperation" (1984c:187, 188; see Carpenter 1989:110-116).[7]

But as evangelicals considered the divided state of American Protestantism, the possibility for revival seemed hopelessly remote. What was needed was a revival of fellowship among orthodox Protestants that would lead the way to cooperative evangelical endeavor. As Carpenter thus reported, "Revival would come, many of them thought, [but] only as evangelicals put aside their quarrels and formed a great united front to accomplish the task" (Carpenter 1984a:12).[8] The major stress of the NAE lay in its cooperative approach, which encouraged evangelicals to reach out to previously excluded conservative Protestants, such as the Pentecostal and Holiness groups, in order to broaden their constituency beyond the narrower orbit of separatist fundamentalism (see Ockenga 1947c).[9]

The prospects for including the more extreme separatist fundamentalists in this cooperative enterprise, however, seemed nearly impossible. The moderates recognized that the denominational battles of the 1920s and 1930s had made fundamentalism "insular and defensive," and made cooperation seem synonymous with liberal/ modernist compromise. As Carpenter noted, "Their leaders drew sharp doctrinal boundaries to separate themselves from the 'apostasy' of modernism and formed exclusive alliances, whether or not they actually left their old denominations." What is more, because fundamentalists were somewhat skittish and excitably suspicious, "They often lashed out at other evangelicals whose beliefs did not meet their standards" (1984c:18). The popular Brethren minister and longtime secretary of the Foreign Mission Society, Louis S. Bauman, for example, unapologetically denounced pentecostalism as a "demonic imitation" of the apostolic gifts (quoted in Carpenter 1984c:188).

By the late 1930s, many of the moderates, tired of the divisive internecine battles within the denominations and among independent fundamentalists, began to call for and work toward a national coalition of orthodox believers who would pledge themselves to put aside party splits. The most notable of these was J. Elwin Wright of New England (Lindsell 1951:112-113 and Evans 1991:115-119). But by the time Wright launched a national association made up of would-be "new evangelicals," there was already in place the separatist fundamentalist American Council of Christian Churches, founded with the expressed two-pronged purpose of opposing the Federal Council of Churches and exposing the apostasy of the denominations. To Wright and his younger Bostonian colleague, Harold John Ockenga, the oppositional disposition of the American Council appeared counterproductive to the goals of reviving orthodoxy in the churches and exciting religious revival in America.

The American Council, founded in September 1941, urged fundamentalists of all stripes to separate from both churches and denominations associated with the Federal Council of Churches. Separation was imperative, they argued, because "co-existence between liberals and fundamentalists in one church was not only impossible but also scripturally wrong" (Gasper 1981:25). Under the direction of Carl McIntire, the younger and more tenaciously fundamentalist protegé of the late J. Gresham Machen, the American Council became notorious for its second objective: to expose the evils of apostasy within the denominational structures.[10]

For most fundamentalists, the clearest symbol of this apostasy *was* the Federal Council, which, they believed, had drafted an unscriptural charter, "one which included unbelief and promoted the inclusivist church" (McIntire 1944:21). As McIntire charged, "The exposures that the American Council has made of the Federal Council's position have been mainly along the line of [the FCC's] loyalty to the faith and its denials of the great doctrines of the Christian Church" (1944:67). These denials, he argued, have allowed unbelievers to remain comfortably within the churches, thus defiling the churches and, worse, weakening the power of the Gospel message. To quote McIntire once more, "It is the presence of pagan forces inside the Federal Council's testimony that has nullified it and made it weak and helpless in dealing with paganism. There is no hope for victory in such a body" (1944:22). For these reasons, at every turn the American Council challenged the right of the Federal Council to speak on behalf of the Christian church (see Roy 1953).

The official tactic of the NAE concerning the Federal Council was not to attack it but to challenge it by being a positive witness for an orthodox evangelical faith. Though fundamentalists such as the editors of the *Sunday School Times* warned that those who refused to attack the Federal Council would eventually be engulfed by its paganizing influence (*SST* 1942:494), moderates thought otherwise. As Harold John Ockenga, first president of the NAE, optimistically pointed out, "Our positive doctrine and deeds will be enough to differentiate us from all kinds of apostasy in all places" (1942a:2).

The NAE leaders thus sought to overcome the bitter animosity that fundamentalist and liberal Protestants exhibited toward each other, not wanting, as Ockenga put it, "to waste our time and energy in such fruitless controversy" (1942a:2). These leaders believed that Protestant Christianity had already spent too much precious time battling against itself, battles which the American Council seemed almost too eager to revive. As Ockenga asserted, the founders of the NAE "believe too much energy, money and time have been lost in this kind of mistaken strategy already." By contrast, these moderates, Ockenga announced, "desire a positive, aggressive, dynamic, unified program of action by those who are evangelical, a program of evangelism, of missions, of Christian education, of Gospel broadcasting, and of unity in every realm touching our Christian faith" (1942a:2).[11]

In addition to its less oppositional stance toward the Federal Council, the NAE was much more tolerant of evangelical diversity than the American Council. The reason for this is that moderate fundamentalists were seeking to build the broadest possible base of support from which to launch its revival, a base built upon evangelical "affirmation" rather than fundamentalist "negation." As Ockenga phrased it, evangelicals "are praying for and awaiting a national revival. They do not want to be diverted to participate in some back-alley scrap while religion other than evangelical seizes American loyalties, as is being done now" (1942a:2). James DeForest Murch, recalling this formative period of the NAE's history, elaborated on this positive cooperative objective. As he put it, evangelicals "were determined to break with apostasy but they wanted no dog-in-the-manger, reactionary, negative, or destructive type of organization. They were determined to shun all forms of bigotry, intolerance, misrepresentation, hate, jealousy, false judgment, and hypocrisy" (Murch 1956:51). Spokespersons for the NAE seemed convinced that the doorway to revival could be opened by the keys of unity and cooperation among evangelicals and sought to revive fundamental Protestantism accordingly.

J. Elwin Wright and the other leaders who founded the National Association of Evangelicals, while they did not initially desire to break with their fellow fundamentalists or with the American Council, seriously endeavored to tread a more moderate and inclusivist path. As Carpenter observed, these moderate fundamentalists "believed the new association should welcome all evangelicals and aim primarily at a positive program, rather than mounting a crusade against the Federal Council" (1984c:191-192). Even so, an unintended consequence of the formation of the NAE was the departure of a "new" evangelical contingent from the fundamentalist movement (Carpenter 1984c: 228). Indeed, the attempts by moderates in the early 1940s to revive fundamentalism would soon give way to calls for reform within fundamentalism. In the end, by the mid-1950s, efforts by most new evangelical leaders and spokespersons toward reform would eventually give way to outright rejection of Protestant fundamentalism. This threefold dynamic has functioned as a subtext of their attempts to revive the spirit of nineteenth-century evangelicalism by fostering cooperation among orthodox believers, engaging in responsible social initiative, and offering relevant theological reflection on issues of deepest concern to the thinking public.

THE "VOICE" OF EVANGELICAL PROTESTANTISM

The addresses given at the first national conference of the newly formed National Association of Evangelicals for United Action at the Coronado Hotel in St. Louis in April 1942 set a course that not only differed from both the fundamentalist and liberal agendas but consciously separated American Protestantism into evangelical, fundamentalist, and liberal-modernist camps.[12] The foreword to this published series of speeches clearly indicated that those assembled for united evangelical action were determined to transcend the bitter animosity that came to characterize the fundamentalist position. But, in founding the NAE, these evangelical leaders felt it necessary to justify the existence of yet another "alignment of Christian forces . . . in a world already overburdened with a multiplicity of organizations" (*Evangelical Action!* 1942:v).

Reviewing the religious scene in the wake of over twenty long years of fundamentalist defeats, the NAE founders saw the Protestant church in a "fragmentized condition," drawn up into two sharply defined and staunchly opposing camps, neither of which had "succeeded in winning the confidence and support of the vast section of Protestantism still loyal to the historic doctrinal positions of the Church" (1942:v). There seemed to be little hope for a religious revival. The founders of the NAE, however, believed that they could stir the "great body of evangelicals" who were not as yet unified into any cohesive or comprehensive religious association. They believed that both the Federal Council and the American Council had failed to balance adequately the Church's evangelistic mission with its social message, making a new association of united evangelicals necessary (cf., *Evangelical Action!* 1942:vi-vii, and *United . . . We Stand* 1943). These moderates, who purposely adopted the title "evangelical," understood that they were bringing together a movement of Protestants who eschewed the extremes of both the liberal and fundamentalist positions. While they agreed with the fundamentalists that the Federal Council was apostate, they were not convinced that the separatist path was the truly "biblical" solution.

To some degree, each of the addresses presented at this first plenary meeting of the NAE expressed the desire to advance an "evangelical option" so as to rekindle the evangelistic spirit lost during the fundamentalist/modernist debacle of the previous generation. This is especially evident in the keynote speeches by Harold J. Ockenga and Stephen W. Paine.

In his address, Harold John Ockenga, pastor of Boston's Park Street Church and first president of the NAE, insisted that if there was to be a true revival of Protestant Christianity in America, then unity among evangelicals and coordinated effort by conservatives were imperative. Ockenga saw himself as one of the many millions of American evangelicals who supported neither the Federal Council nor the American Council—those persons he called "The Unvoiced Multitudes." But Ockenga lamented that such "believers" were so independent in spirit as to be almost incapable of cooperation. They were "lone wolves," who, while "in a measure have been greatly blessed by God in their own particular fields of endeavor," were gravely endangered because of "ominous clouds of battle [on the horizon] which spell[ed] annihilation unless [they were] willing to run in a pack" (1942:20). The time had come, he entreated his fellow moderates, "this millstone of rugged independency which has held back innumerable movements before . . . must be utterly repudiated by every one of us" (1942:32).

Though, as one would expect, Ockenga spoke disapprovingly of the Federal Council, interestingly, he reserved his harshest criticism for his fundamentalist brethren who, he argued, were more interested in division than in united action. Leveling a charge at the more extreme fundamentalists—but a challenge to moderates—he said, "a terrible indictment may be laid against fundamentalism because of its failures, divisions, and controversies. This must be admitted by those of us who believe in the fundamentals and who seek a new outlook" (1942:32).

Ockenga maintained that the two organizations that claimed to speak on behalf of historic Protestant Christianity had severely discredited its message and, as a result, had greatly undercut the Christian church's mission to the world. On the one hand, because of its extreme dogmatism of spirit, fundamentalism could no longer gain a wide hearing for its views in an increasingly pluralistic society. On the other hand, the liberal denominations had so compromised the Gospel that its inspired message—now relativized—had lost its distinctive edge. In the hands of the liberals, Ockenga argued, the Gospel became merely one more social philosophy among others. The message that the major liberal denominations preached sounded so similar to the philosophies devised by "human" inspiration as to be almost indistinguishable from them. As Ockenga observed, "the denominations are no longer the boundary line between the world and the church but rather help to increase the confusion" (Ockenga 1942:32-33). Interestingly, Ockenga's challenge, by which he sought to reassert the distinctive relevance of conservative Christianity to modern life, was quite reminiscent of the sharp boundary language in Machen's *Christianity and Liberalism* (1923). "The division is no longer between denominations," insisted Ockenga; "the division is between those who believe in Christ and the Bible, and those who reject Christ—the Christ of the cross and the Bible. Now is the time to forget all these differences and join together as one with the Crucified One" (1942:33). Clearly, because the worldliness of the denominations had obscured, if not altogether erased, the boundary between believers and unbelievers, the liberal path of the Federal Council was not to be the new evangelical path. But, he might have added, neither would the extreme separatist path of the American Council be theirs.

Stephen W. Paine, then president of Houghton College in New York, considered what he called "The Possibility of United Action," admitting that coordination of effort would be an enormously difficult task for conservatives used to defending orthodoxy with uncompromising vigor. "The task of uniting orthodox Christians," Paine remarked candidly, "has always been fraught with extreme difficulty. . . . Men who have strong convictions . . . are often unable to tolerate any deviation from these convictions, or to have fellow-ship with those who do not agree with them" (1942:50).

Paine differentiated three groups within American Protestantism according to how strictly each defined orthodoxy. By referring to these groups as "orthodox," "super-orthodox," and "unorthodox," Paine gave little doubt that he believed that this new evangelicalism more closely approximated orthodox Protestantism than either "super-orthodox" fundamentalism or "unorthodox" liberalism. In Paine's typology, orthodoxy, super-orthodoxy, and unorthodoxy are distin-guished from one another by their willingness or unwillingness to cooperate with other Christians and by their willingness or unwilling-ness to compromise the faith in order to do so. As Paine argued, super-orthodoxy is unwilling to cooperate with others or to compromise the faith while unorthodoxy is willing both to cooperate and to compro-mise the fundamentals of the faith. In either case, Paine maintained, Satan is pleased. "[Satan] is glad for unorthodoxy if he can get it," Paine explained, "and failing in that he is glad for super-orthodoxy, because that will prevent any effective cooperation among Christian people" (1942:50). Orthodoxy differed in that it held up common cause and reaffirmed doctrinal integrity as mutually beneficial aims of Protestant religion. Indeed, the NAE's desire to achieve balance between these two opposing emphases is appropriately captured in the NAE's clever but paradoxically worded motto, "Cooperation Without Compromise" (Paine 1949 and Murch 1956).

It is important to note, however, that Paine did not distinguish orthodoxy, unorthodoxy, and super-orthodoxy according to such *theological* disagreements as how to interpret the Bible. He based his typology on how broadly or strictly each set its membership bound-aries. Unorthodoxy, Paine pointed out, lacked definiteness. "As a result," he charged, "membership has become broad enough to include everybody and anybody. There has been a lapse into modern-ism" (1942:53). By contrast, super-orthodoxy, which strictly monitors the beliefs of its members, draws boundaries that are highly exclusive. "This has sometimes happened," Paine observed, "with the result that many Bible-believing Christians are excluded, and the movement loses its uniting force" (1942:54). At best, unity within super-orthodoxy remains precarious. As Paine reminded his colleagues, "Hatred of a common foe will often unite factions which otherwise could never work together. But remember also that these negative motives for united action contain within themselves the very seeds of disintegration" (Paine 1942:55). In light of these two extremes, Paine portrayed orthodoxy as a broad coalition of "Bible-believing Christians" that placed its emphasis on positive objectives and shunned "a spirit of controversy and opposition" (1942:50, 59).

The problem of inclusion and exclusion was voiced earlier in the collection of conference addresses in the introductory essay by J. Elwin Wright, in which he presented a history of events leading to the 1942 NAE St. Louis convention. In his attempts to invite as many groups to the conference as possible, he related, he had aimed at inclusiveness. Still, he remarked, out of necessity a line had to be drawn. As he went on to explain, "if we build something worth while, it must be upon a definite doctrinal basis sufficiently broad to include all groups which have remained faithful to the great doctrines of the Church, our common heritage through the centuries. It must, at the same time," he stressed, "be narrow enough to exclude those who have rejected the authority of God's Holy Word" (1942:14). Moreover, he continued at length,

> We must speak out with courage against apostasy and apostate movements, but we must, at the same time, be wise and gracious enough to recognize that there are differences of doctrine among Bible-believing members of the Church of Jesus Christ upon which there is little hope that we will see eye to eye until the day when we no longer "see through a glass darkly," but face to face with our Lord. We must not allow our fellowship with each other to founder upon the rocks of profitless controversy over issues which are relatively unimportant, except as a matter of our own conviction (1942:14-15).

Wright then offered a seven-point statement of faith to which he hoped all participants would give assent and asked that all "adopt a declaration of our essential solidarity as evangelicals" so as to "heal the wounds caused by these many generations of multiplied dissensions among the Children of God" (1942:15) and thereby present a united front to an unbelieving world.

The need to draw boundaries that were neither too inclusive nor too exclusive was also a concern that some prominent evangelical leaders expressed in their comments, published along with the NAE convention addresses. For instance, C. Gordon Brownville, pastor of the Tremont Temple Baptist Church in Boston, voiced support for the cooperative platform of the NAE and wrote that "the new organization in its doctrinal stand is broad enough to include those who believe in the great essential facts of our most Holy Faith, and narrow enough to exclude those whose mind and heart are not in agreement with these truths" (*Evangelical Action!* 1942:143).

The specific question that concerned these new evangelicals therefore—one that would continue to resurface throughout the 1940s and 1950s—was how inclusive was too inclusive. For the NAE, the Federal Council (later the National Council of Churches, or NCC) was an example of indiscriminate inclusion and therefore an unacceptable model to follow. Evangelicals knew they were not *that* inclusive. On the other hand, the American Council was, for them, an example of harshly discriminating exclusion—sometimes over somewhat trifling nonessentials—and thus equally unacceptable. Evangelicals knew also that they were not *that* exclusive.

Still, although the National Association of Evangelicals became the most visible symbol of this new force in conservative Protestantism, a clear distinction between separatist and this more moderate and less exclusivist contingent was not, as yet, completely discernible.[13] The intention was to unite Protestants, not to divide them further. Their intention is borne out by the inclusion of reputed "fundamentalists"— and even some "liberals"—among the new evangelical fold.[14] Indeed, some fundamentalists were even vocal proponents of the NAE's agenda for united action. "Almost no one seems to have regarded the formation of the NAE as a sign that 'evangelicals' were now breaking from 'fundamentalists' over the principle of separatism (or exclusivism)," wrote Marsden. At this point, "there was not a practical distinction between fundamentalist and evangelical: the words were interchangeable. All involved in the NAE were frankly fundamentalists, and among fundamentalism only a minority would make separation a test of fellowship" (1987:48).[15] But while some fundamentalists sought to revive fundamental Protestantism through a positive, cooperative program, at the same time, others within the NAE orbit were calling for a recovery of an evangelical social conscience, one that had defined evangelical Protestantism's relation to American society in the decades before the fundamentalist-modernist disruption. A move to reform fundamentalism was clearly on the horizon.

FUNDAMENTALISM AND SOCIAL CONCERN

Troubled by fundamentalism's failure to apply effectively "the great Biblical verities" to the problems facing postwar American society, Carl F. H. Henry, professor at the Conservative Baptist Seminary and later a founding faculty member of Fuller Theological Seminary, attempted to prick the social consciences of fundamentalists who, for the most part, had abandoned this-worldly concerns and left them to liberals and modernists. Henry's little book, *The Uneasy Conscience of Modern Fundamentalism* (1947), is significant not simply because in it Henry called fundamentalists to a renewed social vision, but, and more importantly, because in it Henry attempted to reclaim the social imperative of the nineteenth-century evangelical heritage from which fundamentalists had consciously cut themselves loose. Concern for society and social welfare was not on the agenda of early twentieth-century fundamentalism, which put a higher premium on individual conversion. As a movement, however, nineteenth-century evangelicalism had effected great social changes during that century (see Smith 1957 and Dayton 1978). Henry pressed this specific point again and again.

Henry chastised fundamentalists for their entrenched attitudes and called on fundamentalists to leave aside their party strife and seek instead to rediscover Christianity's social message, preached by the church since apostolic times. For, as Henry warned, "unless we experience a rebirth of apostolic passion, Fundamentalism in two generations will be reduced either to a tolerated cult status or . . . become once again a despised and oppressed sect" (1947:preface). Henry feared that the socially relevant message of historic fundamentalism would be completely obscured by separatist fundamentalism's unyielding doctrinal sectarianism and by its overly pessimistic view of modern secular culture. "I voice my concern," he wrote, "because we have not applied the genius of our position constructively to those problems which press most for solution in a social way. Unless we do this, I am unsure that we shall get another world hearing for the Gospel" (1947:preface).

Henry was direct: "The hour is ripe, if we seize it rightly, for a rediscovery of the Scriptures and the meaning of the Incarnation for the human race" (1947:preface). He urged conservatives to apply the fundamentals of biblical orthodoxy in a practical manner, not to revise or revolt against the faith as fundamentalists believed the liberals and modernists had done a generation earlier. Henry's quarrel, then, was not with the fundamentalists' faith but with the callous self-righteous attitudes that had developed within fundamentalism, what Henry, citing William Ward Ayer, referred to as "pharisaical fundamentalism" (1947:63). Henry believed that self-righteous fundamentalists, like the Pharisees of Jesus' day, had limited the social effectiveness of the biblical message. Additionally, thought Henry, "the world crisis serves to embarrass Fundamentalism," because its methods were out of step with modern problems. What is more, most fundamentalists were, in Henry's view, not even the least bit concerned with modern problems, content instead to let the world waste away from its own moral and social depravity. Thus, because of its "lack of social passion," fundamentalists, not wanting to be sullied by sin, were not unlike "the modern priest and Levite, by-passing suffering humanity" (1947:15).

Henry used several interesting metaphors to describe fundamentalism. Though somewhat uncomplimentary, these metaphors appear to represent symbolically the unintentional shift in Henry's thinking from the existence of one historic fundamentalism to a fundamentalism dividing between separatists and moderates. For instance, in a chapter entitled "The Fundamentalist Thief on the Cross," Henry used the image of Jesus hanging between the two thieves at the Crucifixion to illustrate how both fundamentalism and modernism had robbed the Gospel message of its transformative and redemptive power through misapplication of its dual emphasis on this life as well as the life to come. As Henry argued,

> The two thieves between whom Jesus was crucified might, without too wild an imagination, bear the labels of humanism and Fundamentalism. The one on the left felt that Jesus had no momentous contribution to suffering humanity, while the one on the right was convinced of His saviourhood but wanted to be remembered in the indefinite future, when Jesus would come into His kingdom (1947:60).

The implication of this metaphor is that neither the liberal-modernist nor the fundamentalist, like the thieves crucified with Jesus, fully understood the social impact of Jesus' life and death. "Contemporary Fundamentalism," said Henry, "needs to meditate long hours on the Saviour's reply: 'Today shalt thou be with me in paradise.' The message for decadent modern civilization must ring with the present tense. We must confront the world now with an ethics to make it tremble, and with a dynamic to give it hope" (1947:60).

Fundamentalists took notice. To some, Henry's little book was frighteningly reminiscent of the message of the Social Gospellers of an earlier generation who, these fundamentalists insisted, had brought the present calamity down on American Protestantism through their romancing of humanism and socialism. Not surprisingly, even with Henry's cautious approach to this subject, because of its controversial dimensions, fundamentalists still misread Henry's intentions. Here was the modernist tare sprouting anew among the wheat of orthodoxy, some fundamentalists thought. It must be rooted out before it is allowed to spread.

In June 1947, the editors of *United Evangelical Action* printed excerpts from Henry's book and asked their readers if they agreed or disagreed with Henry's view. In July the editors printed side-by-side a pro-Henry and a con-Henry letter. The con-Henry letter was written by Bernard Ramm, a professor of apologetics at Biola Institute in Los Angeles.[16] The pro-Henry letter was authored by Paul L. Arnold, pastor of Northwest Presbyterian Church of Detroit.

Ramm disagreed with Henry's view that Christian ethics must be applied at the macro-social as well as the micro-social level: that Christian ethics has both personal and social implications. As Ramm contended, "the one who affirms [that Christian ethics touches on political, social and economic aspects of modern life] would have a difficult case to prove from the pages of the New Testament." For Ramm, "Christian ethics in the New Testament is the quality of life that arises from the redemptive experience of the gospel. It is a life characterized by Christ-likeness, by the fruits of the Spirit, and not a matter of meat and potatoes, governments and economics" (1947:5,16).

Sandwiched between Ramm's discussion of personal vs. social ethics are two statements that reveal in his thinking not merely the typical fundamentalist disjuncture between church and society, but the major dilemma that the new evangelicals came to face, namely, how to engage the world without being implicated in or corrupted by it. The problem for Ramm, and, by extension, for most fundamentalists, was how to balance one biblical imperative against another. The Bible, as the fundamentalists interpreted it, called for Christian service to the destitute and disheartened yet also extolled the necessity of separation from sinful society. Individuals were urged, as St. Peter on Pentecost had preached to the crowd, to "be saved from this perverse generation" (Acts 2:40). As Ramm cautioned, participating in social amelioration meant that "the Christian would find himself shoulder to shoulder with the unbeliever"—doubtless a terrifying prospect for Ramm and his fellow fundamentalists (Ramm 1947:5). Believers would find themselves working for the benefit of the very perverse society from which they were to be separated. Though evangelism was desirable, cooperation with unbelievers was unthinkable, hence the dilemma. Ramm continued: "If the church actually started to implement its social ethics, it would soon find itself working with liberals and non-Christians which would certainly not be desirable in view of the *confusion* it would create" (1947:5 emphasis added).

One is tempted to pause and ask what Ramm meant by "confusion." In this context, the word "confusion" is especially interesting, because it appears to denote a confounding of the distinction between believer and unbeliever—between fundamentalists, who are "Bible-believers," and the liberals and modernists in the churches, who are not. Ramm's phrase seems to reveal a concern to preserve a sharp boundary around orthodoxy. Although Ramm acknowledged the dilemma of modern fundamentalism, in the end he seemed more inclined to reassert the fundamentalist position: "I too am uneasy about the mess we are in. But I find no injunction in Scripture for me to follow but (1) evangelize, and (2) keep my spiritual life at the right level" (1947:16).

In his pro-Henry letter, Paul Arnold centered his comments on the influence that dispensational eschatology had exerted on the fundamentalist agenda to the detriment of active involvement in social betterment. Arnold encouraged fundamentalists not to focus on the imminent end of the world to the exclusion of other biblical doctrines that were just as fundamental to the faith. As Arnold explained, a balanced emphasis "could help modern Fundamentalism to adhere closely to the Biblical view of the consummation of history in the personal imminent return of Christ to introduce supernaturally His Kingdom, and at the same time to be vitally and practically interested in attacking world evils from both the individual and social viewpoints" (1947:5). The Fundamentalist, continued Arnold, "should find it Biblically desirable to support the general welfare, while he awaits the imminent return of Christ to establish His Kingdom" (1947:16). Thus, the believer could, in good conscience, balance salvation from the sinful world with participation in social uplift.

Arnold focused his thoughts on another point from Henry's *Uneasy Conscience* in which Henry criticized fundamentalists for preaching an incomplete Gospel theology. It was this incomplete witness, Henry claimed, that was responsible for its lack of social concern. "The problem of Fundamentalism then," to quote Henry, "is basically not one of finding a valid message, but rather of giving the redemptive word a proper temporal focus" (1947:65). In short, "The redemptive message has implications for all of life; a truncated life results from a truncated message" (1947:68). Henry believed that fundamentalists must rediscover the social aspects of the Gospel in order to present to the world what Henry often called the "full-orbed" message of redemption. Fundamentalists, in his view, presented only part of that message, not the "full counsel of God." Thus, for Henry, and for Arnold as well, modern fundamentalism, in its unbalanced emphases—particularly its preoccupation with eschatology— "appears to be only *partially* fundamental. It needs to be *completely* fundamental" (Arnold 1947:15, emphasis added). For Arnold, as for Henry, this complete fundamentalism included participation in the amelioration of urban decay and social injustices. "A Biblical Fundamentalist," entreated Arnold, "should not fear the support of movements intent upon general welfare, even with the taint of sin present in them—for Fundamentalism itself cannot escape a taint of sin in its every action" (Arnold 1947:15-16).

What is implied in both Henry and Arnold, although not fully developed, is the notion that Protestant fundamentalism as a movement had lost sight of its goal to revive apostolic Christianity, becoming instead a bastion of sectarian extremism. Fundamentalism had strayed into nonessentials, making adherence to certain nonessential beliefs and behaviors a test of fellowship.[17] Somewhere along the way, fundamentalism had withdrawn into its own comfortable cloister and had consequently become an isolated community that, according to Henry, had lost sight of the Gospel's message for the modern predicament. "If Fundamentalism ceases to 'work'," Henry charged, it is because "we have imported into it elements which violate the innermost essence of Christianity." What Henry desired instead was "for the whole evangelical movement [to rekindle] a new life and vigor on the destitute world front" (1947:61). "The time has come now for Fundamentalism to speak with an ecumenical outlook and voice." If it does, Henry continued more optimistically, "if it speaks in terms of the historic Biblical tradition, rather than in the name of secondary accretions or of eschatological biases on which evangelicals divide, it can refashion the modern mind" (1947:63).

In contradistinction, therefore, to fundamentalism, the message that the new evangelicals announced was billed as a recovery of orthodoxy with both a personal and social message of redemption. The new evangelicalism would be, as it were, fundamentalism with a heart. By 1947, it seemed that moderate fundamentalists were beginning to move away from their avowed attempt to revive fundamentalism through cooperation and a renewed social conscience toward a platform that called for a reform of fundamentalism itself.

EVANGELICALISM: "SOMETHING MORE THAN FUNDAMENTALISM"

At about the same time that Carl Henry was uncovering the uneasy conscience of fundamentalism, Harold John Ockenga, soon to be named founding president of evangelist Charles Fuller's newly formed seminary in Pasadena, was reassessing the influence of fundamentalism on postwar American society. Ockenga would conclude that even more substantial changes needed to take place in order for fundamentalism to be an effective force in the modern world. In a published speech, Ockenga (1947a) asked the blunt and penetrating question: "Can Fundamentalism Win America?" His answer was a categorical No! "Fundamentalism as presently constituted," Ockenga boldly announced, "is impotent." It watches helplessly as the cancers of modernism, secularism, and Catholicism spread throughout American culture, destroying it. "As for a diagnosis and a possible antidote [to the world's ills], fundamentalism," Ockenga said sharply, using apocalyptic imagery from the prophetic Book of Daniel, "has been weighed in the balances and found wanting" (1947a:13).

Ockenga accused fundamentalists of divisiveness and negativity, which he found much more odious than holding slight doctrinal variations on minor creedal points. "Fundamentalism is divisive," Ockenga charged. "Fragmentation, segregation, separation, criticism, censoriousness, suspicion, solecism, is the order of the day for fundamentalism. Utter incapacity for cooperative action is evident" (1947a:13). This divisive spirit, which Ockenga believed had prevented unity and harmony among fundamentalists, strongly militated against its hopes for winning America.

Ockenga listed several ways in which he believed division is fostered among fundamentalists. First, there is "division in the ranks over a minor point of eschatology" (1947a:14). In addition, there is division because of "the attitude of many fundamentalists that when error or evil appears in a denominational organization they must separate themselves from it [the organization]" (1947a:14). It is not enough that these fundamentalists call for separation, but, Ockenga inveighed, they are themselves schismatics, attempting to divide from those who choose to remain within their "apostate" churches as a positive witness for orthodoxy or the fundamentals. Although in a follow-up response to this article Ockenga mentioned that he was not pointing an accusing finger at any one fundamentalist group (1947b:53), the American Council did seem to be implied when he disapprovingly declared that it is the position "of some so-called cooperative groups of fundamentalists to smear and besmirch their brethren with such names as disloyal, compromiser, coward, for not renouncing all previous Christian connections and placing themselves under a new hierarchy of intolerant bigots" (1947a:14).

The negativity so pervasive in the fundamentalist movement, Ockenga argued further, prevented fundamentalism's unique biblical testimony and its solution for a lost world from being heard, with the result that "fundamentalism stands isolated and aloof, while all other religious groups are rolling up their sleeves to tackle the threat to their very existence" (1947a:14). Both divisiveness and negativity of spirit were therefore counter-productive and prevented fundamentalism from bringing the Gospel message to bear on the social, political, and economic difficulties facing a war-torn world still suffering the consequences of World War II's human and material destruction. In sum, and alluding to Henry (1947), "the fundamentalist Christian has an uneasy conscience about abandoning education to the secularist or to the modernist, about the fatalistic view of human events, about his divorce of the Jesus of pity, service, healing and human interest from the Jesus of fundamentalism. He knows there is a need for a progressive fundamentalism with an ethical message" (1947a:14).

Keeping in mind that Ockenga still thought of himself as a fundamentalist, we might note that his criticism of fundamentalism is all the more revealing. If "no particular group was in mind as the object of attack," as he claimed, then Ockenga was unwittingly drawing a distinction between these two representative bodies of conservative Protestantism. This point can be underscored even more when one considers his assertion that though "fundamentalism" cannot win America, "united evangelical action" can and will. As he put it, "A ray of hope has broken through the clouds in the organization of the National Association of Evangelicals. Here has been displayed the spirit of cooperation, of mutual faith, of progressive action, and of ethical responsibility, so conspicuously lacking elsewhere" (1947a:15). But, so there will be no doubt about the theological position of this new organization, Ockenga added prudently that the "NAE unites on a common statement of evangelical faith which is fundamentalist" (1947a:15).

As with Henry's manifesto, Ockenga's article seems to have been quite pivotal. A negative assessment by one of fundamentalism's own would doubtless have been unthinkable ten or twenty years earlier. That Ockenga's article caused quite a stir among fundamentalists can be discerned from the unusually voluminous response that came from those who read it. If the many letters received by *Christian Life* are an accurate gauge, then one might see in them the subtle emergence of a new evangelical consciousness, one that would later reject the fundamentalist movement in favor of a coalition of moderate evangelicals.

The editors of *Christian Life* received 127 letters (*CL* October 1947:49)—of which they printed only a representative sample of 26—some praising Ockenga's timely and honest assessment, but others voicing concern over his "liberal" leanings. According to the editors of *Christian Life,* "the unprecedented volume of correspondence pro-voked by this article indicates an undercurrent of dissatisfaction with Fundamentalism as presently constituted" (*CL* September 1947:35). But the editors cautioned their readers by reminding them that the purpose for presenting this open forum was "not as a springboard for further controversy, but as a possible panacea for the weaknesses it reveals" (*CL* September 1947:35). The editors appeared to be unaware that the conflict between new evangelicals and fundamentalists was slowly moving out of the limited arena of the NAE and American Council rivalry to the wider fundamentalist movement, a transition that would become quite evident by 1956.

The 26 letters printed in the September and October 1947 issues of *Christian Life*—a fundamentalist version of the flashier *Life* maga-zine—provide an interesting sample of fundamentalist opinions. Responses to Ockenga's article ranged from pronounced disapproval to enthusiastic support. As expected, most of the readers who dis-agreed with Ockenga's prognosis took exception to his exhortation to fundamentalists that they should involve themselves in social projects, as the modernists and liberals did. The focus of fundamentalism, they argued, should be not on social welfare but on the salvation of souls.

Among the responses by staunch fundamentalists was a lengthy reply from the aged and ailing William Bell Riley, a towering figure in the Northern Baptist Convention and a tireless champion of various fundamentalist causes during the modernist controversies (cf., Russell 1976). In his letter, Riley, who identified himself "as one who has given his life to the defense and propagation of fundamentalism," expressed deep sadness over the infighting among his younger colleagues (1947:33). Much like a great prophet giving a last testament before his passing, Riley called on fundamentalists to reunite themselves as brothers and redirect their criticisms elsewhere. As he put it, "Every member of the family knows that the household is not perfect; but the best members of families do not go about calling attention to family faults. . . . [S]ince our enemies—modernists—are constantly blasting at our weaknesses, why should our brothers be handing stones to them?" (1947:84).

But far more interesting and important are the comments of those who concurred with Ockenga's assessment and came to his defense

Many called for reform but left open the possibility for the rejection of fundamentalism. For example, S. R. Kamm of Wheaton, Illinois, encouraged "orthodox, evangelical Christians" to "face frankly the issues which [Ockenga] presents." Kamm then went on to confess,

> I have never found any great spiritual power in "fundamentalism" as such. Although many people within the movement have been characterized by an earnest desire to preserve a sound Biblical, Christian message for our generation they have often dissipated their energies in fruitless controversy with fellow believers. As a result, the entire movement is seriously weakened by an internal strife which is strongly condemned by the New Testament. I see no future usefulness for such a movement in the Christian community until there is a deep and sincere repentance before our Lord for the sins of backbiting, slander and religious pride which has [sic] characterized the life of many of the movement's adherents (CL October 1947:50).

Another reader, who requested to remain anonymous, believed that because fundamentalism had brought dishonor to historic orthodoxy, it was discredited and therefore had no future. As that reader explained,

> Fundamentalism must inevitably fail. It has brought historic Christianity into an unmerited disrepute and made it difficult, if not impossible, to reach the educated groups in this country. . . . Its failure is not only inevitable; its collapse is imminent. Separation will not survive in the next twenty years of American history. It cannot. . . . I draw a sharp distinction between fundamentalism and historic orthodoxy (CL October 1947:107-108).

Still another letter, this one from Frank Nelson of Pasadena, California, presented a more critical analysis of fundamentalism in which he offered an explanation for its defensive posture. "While I am far from being a liberal," Nelson admitted, "yet I cannot help feeling that the main impulse for the defense of fundamentalism stems from a deep-seated fear for its tenability. Personally, I am a *convinced* evangelical (John 3:3)[18] and I have no fear for the validity of historic Christianity" (CL October 1947:108.) In saying this, Nelson, much like the anonymous reader cited above, appeared to be placing fundamentalism outside the symbolic boundaries of historic ortho- doxy, which, the above respondents seemed to be saying, were best expressed in evangelicalism. Unlike the "fundamentalist," they inti- mated, the "evangelical" is convinced of the truth of historic Protes- tant Christianity and thus does not have to defend it tenaciously. Nelson seemed to imply that since the fundamentalist, uncertain of the legitimacy of his position, felt compelled to defend it, then fundamen- talism must be something other than historic Christianity.

Cornelius Jaarsma of Wheaton College also placed fundamental- ism outside the boundaries of Protestant orthodoxy. He agreed with both Ockenga and Henry that "the real weakness of the current fundamentalist movement" is that in overreacting "to the socialization of the Christian message, fundamentalism ignores the social implica- tion of the Christian faith. . . . This neglect and one-sidedness has led to all kinds of aberrations and distortions of Christian truth among evangelicals. I thank God for the awakening among some of us to *a better way*" (*CL* September 1947:38, emphasis added).

This "better way" is identified by some respondents as the cooperative platform of the NAE. As Leslie R. Marston, Bishop of the Free Methodist Church in Greenville, Illinois, and a contributing editor to the *UEA,* explained, "Some of us have viewed the National Association of Evangelicals from its founding as the vehicle of the 'something more than fundamentalism' which can win America" (*CL* September 1947:36).

In October 1947, Ockenga wrote a stinging reply to the negative responses his article had elicited (*CL* October 1947:52-55). In his remarks, Ockenga identified fundamentalism as an ideology that was counterproductive to the redemptive goals of the Christian churches. Ockenga's incisive rejoinder, in which he reiterated his charge that "fundamentalism is impotent," invites lengthy citation here.

> The emphasis of these fundamentalists is that of winning individuals
> to Christ and of leaving the social conscience to the awakened and
> regenerate individual. This belief that Christian doctrine carries over
> from a religious experience to ethics is what I call "a pious hope."
> English fundamentalism has not made "teetotalers" of the English
> clergy. German fundamentalism has not made pacifists out of the

German clergy. American fundamentalism has not made humanitarians out of the American clergy, much less to say brothers in spirit. The social conscience of fundamentalism must be awakened on liquor, race, labor, war, etc. It would be simple to name northern fundamentalists who drink hard liquor, southern fundamentalists who are Nazi on race questions, eastern fundamentalists who are blind on labor rights, and western fundamentalists who glory in war. Religious doctrine and experience must be supplemented by ethical teaching. Too many fundamentalists are on the wrong side of the ethical questions (Ockenga 1947b:52).

It becomes clearer with each exchange between evangelicals and fundamentalists that the goals of ecclesiastical and social reform that the evangelicals had originally set for themselves—especially as articulated by Henry and Ockenga—could not be achieved within the fundamentalist movement as it was presently constituted. A change in agenda, or rather, a shift in emphasis, necessitated movement away from the separatist ecclesiological and dispensationalist eschatological tenor of fundamentalism. The formation of the National Association of Evangelicals was a large step in this new direction. Indeed, as reported above, the NAE was a first step toward an eventual rejection of fundamentalism.

What followed in subsequent years was a near avalanche of articles and editorials by these new evangelicals (and, of course, responses by their fundamentalist detractors). A war of words soon ensued. In each of these works, the evangelicals, in attempting to outline their positions more clearly and carefully, distanced themselves further from fundamentalism and what the spokespersons for the new evangelicalism regarded as fundamentalism's doctrinal and ecclesiastical excesses. The works cited in the next section illustrate an interesting aspect of this emerging boundary differentiation: evangelicalism became defined in opposition to fundamentalism. New evangelicals claimed to be fundamentally orthodox, but not fundamentalists.

This definitional process was couched primarily in theological terms, of course, but more than a theological debate was taking place. While doctrinal issues certainly became salient points of distinction between evangelicals and fundamentalists, what is of greater fascination is the way social structural boundaries were forged by the evangelicals. That is, while their language was clearly theological, and while they thought they were debating theological questions, the new evangelicals were unwittingly drawing a boundary between themselves and fundamentalists by defining normative orthodox Christianity in terms of the new evangelical coalition. Clearer definition of the evangelical coalition did not come until the mid-1950s, when a pair of articles on the nature and organizational purposes of the new evangelicalism were published in *Eternity* magazine and *Christian Life,* and when evangelicals launched a journal of their own, *Christianity Today.*

THE NATURE OF EVANGELICALISM

In an article published in *Eternity* magazine in February 1956, entitled "The Nature of Evangelicalism," Vernon G. Grounds, then president of the Conservative Baptist Seminary in Denver, asked provocatively, "What is the nature of Protestant orthodoxy, that embodiment of historic Christianity which sometimes bears the label evangelicalism, sometimes the libel fundamentalism?" (1956:12). Although Grounds began his discussion on the nature of evangelicalism with what some might call a backhanded slap at fundamentalism, his actual intention was not to divide conservative Protestants so much as to call them back to their historic roots. The division, he believed, had already been brought about by separatist fundamentalists who had, in effect, separated themselves from historic orthodoxy. But Protestant orthodoxy, Grounds asserted, in its new evangelical form, was "a twentieth century continuation of the historic faith which springs from a bloody cross and an empty tomb," a claim no other religion, not even liberal Protestantism or neo-orthodoxy, could support (1956:43).

Indeed, Grounds denied for all types of Christian movements other than the new evangelicalism any legitimate tie to historic orthodoxy. Comparing first Eastern religions and then Western religions and then other forms of Christianity to evangelicalism, Grounds identified those elements that each of these religions shared with Protestant orthodoxy. Then, with great candor, Grounds pointed out that evangelicalism "parts company with" each of the world's religions in significant ways. In addition, Grounds argued that evangelicalism "parts company with liberalism," "parts company with neo-orthodoxy," and "parts company with Roman Catholicism" (1956:12-13).

But, while one could have expected this distancing from liberalism, neo-orthodoxy, and Catholicism, Grounds's subsequent treatment of fundamentalism—which comprised the main section of his article—displayed an abrupt parting of company with fundamentalism that had not yet been as clearly enunciated in earlier evangelical writings (cf. Butler 1976:116). For instance, Grounds admitted that "undeniably evangelicalism is fundamentalism," but only "if by fundamentalism is meant a tenacious insistence upon the essential and central dogmas of historic Christianity" (1956:13). Otherwise, Grounds stated, evangelicalism more than parts company with fundamentalism. "Evangelicalism," he asserted, "is *not* fundamentalism as fundamentalism is ordinarily construed" (1956:13, emphasis added).

Why the change in pattern and emphasis in his article? Given Grounds's concern to distinguish historic orthodoxy from its pretenders, one might suppose Grounds assumed that while people do not tend to confuse Protestant orthodoxy with Buddhism or Catholicism, some might easily and unconsciously confuse evangelicalism with fundamentalism. The tendency among non-evangelicals to equate evangelicalism and fundamentalism may explain Grounds's careful concern to distinguish the two, to draw a clear line between evangelicals and fundamentalists. Indeed, in this paragraph, Grounds can almost be heard to say, "Make no mistake about it, evangelicalism and fundamentalism are different!" Throughout the remainder of his article, Grounds outlined the differences.

How, then, does fundamentalism as "ordinarily construed" differ from evangelicalism? Grounds, in what was perhaps one of the most forceful denunciations of fundamentalism by an evangelical so far in the debate, dissociated evangelicalism from the excesses of fundamentalism. To quote Grounds's characterization of fundamentalism at length:

A thoroughgoing evangelical recognizes with a wry smile the truth in the liberal jibe: "Fundamentalism is too much fun, too much damn, and too little mental"! A thoroughgoing evangelical realizes that with unfortunate frequency Protestant orthodoxy has degenerated into a rabid sectarianism which furnished many recruits for the lunatic fringe of religion. But if America is not adequately represented by the conduct of some irresponsible tourists, neither is evangelicalism adequately represented by every snake handler, every holy roller, every bigoted fanatic. No, evangelicalism ought to be judged by its truly representative creeds and spokesmen. . . . [T]here is no good reason why, after two thousand years of glorious history, mainstream Christianity should suddenly degenerate into an *ism* and become fundamentalism. Actually, instead of being an *ism* of recent vintage, evangelicalism is main-stream Christianity in modern form (Grounds 1956:13).

Grounds's denunciation of fundamentalism's theological obscurantism and sectarian spirit was indeed quite strong. But Grounds's criticism should not be interpreted as a repudiation of orthodoxy but of fundamentalism itself. Evangelicals were doctrinally fundamental but not organizationally fundamentalists. As Grounds cautioned, "With this distinction in mind, then, one may speak of evangelicalism as fundamentalism, if he chooses, but he may not do so in all fairness if he equates the two terms uncritically" (Grounds 1956:13). Grounds seemed to be arguing his case against fundamentalism by stating how fundamentalism fell short of historic orthodoxy. In this way, Grounds said little that one might characterize as positive affirmations of evangelical faith. His aim was not to compare the two in order to reconcile them. Instead, Grounds placed emphasis on the aspects of new evangelicalism that were *not* fundamentalistic or similar to fundamentalism—a contrast he felt needed to be drawn.

CHANGING EVANGELICALISM

The profound significance that the March 1956 *Christian Life* article "Is Evangelical Theology Changing?" had on the future of American evangelicalism cannot be overstated. The divided response it elicited from conservative Protestants marked the end of the old fundamentalist coalition. As Farley Butler affirmed, "The fundamentalist reaction to the *Christian Life* article left little doubt that here was the beginning of two movements, where before one had stood" (Butler 1976:138). Taken by itself, this article said little that learned fundamentalists would dispute theologically. But when viewed against the backdrop of previous books and articles that attacked, among other things, fundamentalism's separatist ecclesiology, intellectual and theological stagnation, and its lack of social concern, this article provided the watershed moment for the new evangelical coalition's repudiation of old fundamentalism. As one moderate after another abandoned the fundamentalist movement, reform of fundamentalism no longer seemed to be a central component of the new evangelical agenda.

While for over a decade much of the literature coming out of the new evangelical camp obliquely attacked a number of fundamentalist positions, most of these paper assaults had gone virtually unnoticed by fundamentalists. But, as Butler stressed, by 1956 "fundamentalist leaders knew that the controversy which had been confined to the classrooms of evangelical seminaries and colleges and pulpits of individual churches would now be fought in the pages of the evangelical press" (1976:138). A clearer separation between evangelicals and fundamentalists would soon become unmistakable.

In rather straightforward fashion, the editors of *Christian Life* laid out the new currents of thought among conservative Protestant theologians. But while, as in Grounds's discussion, the editors' focus was primarily theological, one can discern in the editors' comments a sharp distinction being made between "fundamentalist" and "evangelical" coalitions and a differentiation of conservative Protestant religion into two rival communities.

The editors of *Christian Life* argued somewhat implicitly—as many new evangelicals did more explicitly—that fundamentalism as an ideology and as a movement had diverted and distorted Protestant orthodoxy. What began in the 1920s "as a high-level theological discussion [within the churches and seminaries] degenerated into a cat and dog fight" (1956:16). Fundamentalist anti-intellectual sensationalism brought shame to evangelical orthodoxy in the eyes of American society. "The Virgin Birth," the editors continued, "ran neck and neck with murder on the front pages of the newspapers. Evolution was pitted against the Bible in the Scopes trial of 1925. Fundamentalism began to be a catch-all for the lunatic fringe; Holy Rollers, snake handlers, even Mormon polygamists were calling themselves fundamentalists. That's why to the man on the street *fundamentalism* got to be a joke. As an ignorant, head-in-the-sand, contentious approach to the Christian faith," the editors concluded, "it seemed as out-dated as high button shoes" (1956:16). The trivialization of orthodox beliefs by fundamentalists was an embarrassment to evangelicals because it ignobled and discredited historic orthodoxy.

Scandalously discordant, the editors sadly observed, fundamentalism no longer commanded the respect of American society or spoke for Christianity with an authoritative voice. Evangelicalism, the editors of *Christian Life* intimated, was a movement not to be identified with fundamentalism but a movement that had preserved the central core of biblical Christianity. Fundamentalism had become like a circus sideshow, they told their readers, "But all the while there was a solid core behind the garish shell. Even before World War II that core began to push out. When the war was over, the crust split wide open. Out popped a younger generation. They agreed with their elders. But they thought there was more to Christianity than being on the defensive all the time. They wanted to build on the contributions of older leaders a positive, not a reactionary, movement" (1956:16). In this analysis, fundamentalism is seen as an aberration of traditional Protestantism, an outgrowth of the controversies of an earlier era, a residual by-product of that time to be rejected as deviant and ineffectual.

With the rise of the new evangelicalism, the editors noted, fundamentalism had been transformed: "fundamentalism has become *evangelicalism*" (1956:17). The emphasis had changed from defense of the faith to a "positive witness for God's redemptive love, wisdom and power as revealed in Jesus Christ" (1956:16-17). The shift was from a dogmatic and often intolerant insistence on the "fundamentals" to a positive proclamation of the "evangel" or the good news about Jesus of Nazareth.

According to the editors of *Christian Life,* "new currents" were "churning evangelical waters"—a fresh spirit of theological and ecclesiastical openness had shifted the emphasis of theological debate from defensiveness and suspicion to positive affirmation and dialogue.

The changing emphasis of evangelical thought, however, revealed stark differences between fundamentalists and evangelicals in their attitudes and approaches to modern society and biblical scholarship. The editors mentioned eight new directions that characterized this new evangelicalism:

1. A friendly attitude toward science
2. A willingness to re-examine beliefs concerning the work of the Holy Spirit
3. A more tolerant attitude toward varying views of eschatology
4. A shift away from so-called extreme dispensationalism
5. An increased emphasis on scholarship
6. A more definite recognition of social responsibility
7. A re-opening of the subject of biblical inspiration
8. A growing willingness of evangelical theologians to converse with liberal theologians (1956:17-19).

These eight shifts in evangelical theology—especially with regard to its attitudes toward science, biblical scholarship, and social responsibility—were understood by evangelicals not as a movement away from orthodox Protestantism but as the restoration of an orthodoxy either abandoned or neglected by fundamentalists.

In many ways, this lengthy editorial served as an evangelical declaration of independence from fundamentalism. Moreover, the 1956 *Christian Life* editorial seemed to articulate more concretely the growing separation within old fundamentalism that was only faintly evident a decade and a half earlier when the NAE was founded. By the mid-1950s, however, the separation was almost complete.

Reactions to the *Christian Life* editorial by fundamentalists were predictably critical, falling into at least three categories. Some fundamentalist critiques were simply negative and dismissive. For instance, John R. Rice, editor of the *Sword of the Lord,* dismissed the evangelicals featured in the *Christian Life* article as "young, rather unknown and cocky men" who, "because they have a moderate job in a Bible institute or seminary, are not accepted by the mass of Christian people as authorities on what are the fundamentals of the faith" (*CL* May 1956:3).

Another kind of reaction, illustrated by John H. Stoll of Cedarville College of Ohio, did not acknowledge a growing distinction within conservative Protestantism. "I believe the distinction you make between an evangelical and a fundamentalist is unwarranted," he remarked (*CL* May 1956:3).

Still a third kind of response, expressed in comments made by noted fundamentalists published in the January 1957 issue of Biola

Institute's *King's Business* magazine, acknowledged the differences between themselves and the evangelicals and expressed some irritation at the smugness and insolence of the leaders of this upstart movement.[19] For instance, S. H. Sutherland observed that "throughout the article there is an attempt to differentiate between fundamentalists and evangelicals. . . . [T]hough supposedly discussing the changes in evangelical theology, yet [it] spends its time pointing out the failing of fundamentalism" (*KB* January 1957:23). Similarly, Alva McClain, president of Grace Theological Seminary, was at first angered and then saddened by evangelical betrayal. "It is both curious and disturbing today," he told the editors of *King's Business,* "to find 'evangelicals' who, while bewailing the belligerence of historic fundamentalism and advocating a closer rapprochement with the liberals, are at the same time belaboring and fighting against their own side" (*KB* January 1957:27).

Theologically, fundamentalists believed that the new evangelicals threatened orthodoxy because they appeared to compromise on key doctrines, and this compromise fundamentalists found distressing. But the third kind of response makes it clear that fundamentalists were reacting additionally to the perception of newly drawn lines of demarcation. Evangelical adjustments of the boundary defining the differences between evangelicalism and old fundamentalism were decried by fundamentalists as "compromise."

Evangelicals, for their part, understood their program differently. They were not tinkering with historic orthodoxy, as the fundamentalists charged, but saw their actions as a recovery of orthodox Christianity which had gotten bogged down by fundamentalists accretions—bigotry, narrowness, censoriousness, intolerance, and the like. Even so, during this period evangelicals sought merely to distance themselves from the odium of fundamentalism and, from that point, to work toward reform of historic fundamentalism. It was only later that many of the new evangelicals would come to reject fundamentalism outright.

NEW EVANGELICALISM'S "CLEAR VOICE"

In the midst of the heated debates between fundamentalists and evangelicals over the nature of evangelical theology and the extent of its influence, a new conservative Protestant journal, which claimed to be "a clear voice" for evangelical Christianity in America, was launched (*CT* October 15, 1956:20). Sponsored by Billy Graham and patterned after the theologically liberal journal *The Christian Century,* *Christianity Today* was founded with the expressed purpose of showcasing the theological and intellectual contributions of serious-minded evangelical leaders and scholars.

Graham's interest in a new periodical stemmed from his desire to expand his evangelistic ministry by broadening its support to include the mainline denominations as well as moderate fundamentalists. This broader vision for religious revival through mass evangelism, or "ecumenical evangelism," as it was called, led Graham to "jettison the disastrous fundamentalist images of separation, anti-intellectualism, and contentiousness"—a direction in which the new evangelicals had been similarly moving (Marsden 1987:159). Edited by Carl Henry, *Christianity Today* became a symbol, along with the NAE, Fuller Seminary, and even Graham himself, of the new course evangelicals like Ockenga, Henry, Grounds, and others were charting for Christian orthodoxy. As Butler observed, *Christianity Today* "fully reflected the emphases of the new evangelicalism and was one of its authoritative spokesmen. The outlines of the movement can be seen in its pages" (1976:172).

Graham sought to unite in one journal the many discrete voices in the emerging new evangelical coalition, which had as its common goal the desire to build an orthodoxy that adopted the biblical elements within both fundamentalism and liberalism, while at the same time distancing itself from the unsavory extremes of both. The new periodical, as Graham envisioned it, would "plant the evangelical flag in the middle of the road, taking a conservative theological position but a definite liberal approach to social problems. It would combine the best in liberalism and the best in fundamentalism without compromising theologically" (quoted in Marsden 1987:158).

The articles and editorials published in *Christianity Today's* early period reflect the attempt by evangelicals to gain some measure of intellectual and theological respectability. They tried to accomplish this goal, however, by distancing themselves not merely from the obscurantism of modern fundamentalism (see Ramm 1957) but, more interestingly, by drawing a boundary that placed fundamentalism outside of orthodox Christianity (see Carnell 1958). That is to say, the new evangelicals came to characterize fundamentalism as a movement that could not legitimately trace its roots back through the Reformation to the Apostolic Church. The implications of this position would, of necessity, lead to a complete rejection of old fundamentalism by the new evangelicals—a rejection, they would add, not of fundamental doctrines but of fundamentalist organizations and attitudes.

For example, in one of the first major editorial pieces in *Christianity Today*, Carl Henry outlined the positions of the new evangelical coalition, not only distinguishing a clear line between fundamentalist, liberal, and evangelical, but subtly shifting the way evangelical leaders began to classify fundamentalism as well. His two-part editorial identified the "perils" inherent to both fundamentalism—which he called "Independency"—and liberal ecumenism—which he termed "Organic Church Unionism" (1956:20). Henry, however, did not define these "diametrically opposed" positions with reference solely to their theological stances. Henry also classified these "contradictory forces" according to their organizing principles. To Henry, their most evident features were not theological but organizational. "The two clashing movements of which we speak," argued Henry, "are Independency and Organic Church Unionism embodied in agencies familiar to all [i.e., the American Council and the National Council of Churches]" (1956:20). Henry then examined their contrasting "tensions and perils," viewing neither movement with much favor. Wrote Henry,

> Independency tends to be intolerant, Church Unionism tolerant. The former moves in the direction of exclusivism, the latter toward inclusivism. Independency remains highly creedal in minute detail, while Church Unionism becomes vague and ill-defined in theological basis. One can easily become Pharisaic [i.e., highly literalistic in beliefs and legalistic in actions], the other Sadducean [i.e., more open] (1956:20).

In the second part of his editorial, Henry once more pointed out the inclusive/exclusive boundary dynamic, a dynamic evangelicals tended to associate with fundamentalism and liberalism (cf., Paine 1942 and Henry 1947). As Henry maintained, "Whereas Independency errs on the side of exclusivism, tending to spell out its position so minutely that it separates itself readily from true believers as well as from unbelievers, the ecumenical adherents tend to be so inclusive that they regard outsiders as members of the body. One group excludes some persons who really ought to be included; the other includes some whose lack of adequate credentials ought to exclude them from an apostolic fellowship" (1956b:21). "Ecumenicity," Henry argued further, "tends to be just as intolerant as Independency, although this intolerance is expressed in a somewhat different fashion. Whereas Independency draws narrow lines, defining beliefs in such a detailed and technical fashion that it rules out many, ecumenicity also draws lines which are narrow and intolerant" (1956b:22). To Henry, ecumenicity, though proclaiming theological openness, was narrow because it did not tolerate conservatives. Henry thought it blatantly hypocritical that the acceptance of conservative Protestants by liberal ecumenists depended upon conservative willingness to abandon orthodoxy.

In Henry's scheme, as in earlier evangelical writings, evangelicalism occupied the middle position between these two extremes. He noted that "Between Independency and Church Unionism stand the middle parties. Many of them have found a mutual ground in the National Association of Evangelicals." One feature held in common by "the middle parties," Henry pointed out, is their mutual opposition to both the American Council and the National Council. "But its position is not so easily defined," Henry admitted, "since the lines are not so sharply drawn. It subscribes to some concepts of each of the extremist groups, but opposes others, finding its rationale in a mediating view, or perhaps better described as a perspective above the extremes" (1956b:21). In substance, Henry's evaluation of the current divisions within American Protestantism differed little from the assessments made by earlier new evangelical commentators (cf., Paine 1942). Of note, however, is the explicit way in which Henry staked out evangelicalism's location by reference to the two "extremes" from which it differed.

What is more, Henry's editorial pointed to a demonstrative shift in the new evangelical characterization of fundamentalism. Quite apart from placing both fundamentalism and liberalism on extreme opposing ends of the Protestant spectrum, Henry carried this critique of Protestant fundamentalism and liberalism one step further. He moved them off the spectrum almost entirely by intimating that both fundamentalism and liberalism had departed from historic orthodox Christianity. By contrast, the new evangelicals had recovered the true message and mission of the Bible and the Apostles. "Both [fundamentalist and liberal Protestant] attitudes are essentially heretical," Henry provocatively declared. "While they are opposite in polarity, they both rise from a departure from the apostolic base. One narrowly excludes divergence of opinion, so that it becomes difficult for some undoubted Christians to find standing room. The other is so broad and so indefinite that one cannot be sure on what ground he stands. Neither one is truly biblical nor finally acceptable. . . . [T]he one is no less a peril than the other" (1956b:22). Evangelicals who had held firm to the convictions of the Apostles, then, were viewed as reasserting those themes that had been drowned out by the din of controversy between these two deviant expressions of Protestant Christianity. But how do evangelicals know they have the true faith? By comparing themselves with those two deviant extremes and finding them both wanting, Henry might well have answered. One can almost hear in Henry the very words that William Ward Ayer confidently proclaimed at the NAE's first convention in 1942: "We unhesitatingly declare that *evangelicals* have the 'keys of the kingdom'" (*Evangelical Action!* 1942:46, emphasis added). The one difference, however, would be that for Henry, writing in 1956, "evangelical" did not include fundamentalism or liberalism.[20]

Henry returned to this theme the next year in a four-part lecture published in *Christianity Today* as a series that broached the question, "Dare We Renew the Controversy?" (1957). Once again, Henry's portrayal of fundamentalism, though greatly tempered when compared with his previous editorial, depicted a movement that had broken continuity with historic Christianity, indeed, a movement of only recent vintage characterized mainly by what it opposed. "The fundamentalist movement," Henry insisted, "became a distinctly twentieth-century expression of Christianity, characterized increasingly by reaction against liberalism" (Henry 1957a:23). As a movement, however, fundamentalism quickly devolved from a conservative theological position to an intolerant and fragmenting "disposition"—"'a morbid and sickly enthusiasm'" (G. B. Wurth quoted in Henry 1957a:23). As Henry observed, "Its early leadership reflected balance and ballast, and less bombast and battle. Only later did a divisive disposition show itself, plunging the evangelical movement into internal conflict" (1957a:26).

One result of the conflicts within the churches was the emergence of fundamentalism as a mentality. True, theological fundamentalism as a religiously orthodox position was, for a time, obscured. But, Henry continued,

> The recrudescence of fundamentalism during the Second World War involved a diversification within the movement. On one side were those eager to detach the great theological affirmations from a recent negative reactionary spirit and to strengthen constructive theological and ecclesiastical activity; on the other, those who add to the reactionary spirit by multiplying divisions and by disowning brethren in the former category. The first group insists that fundamentalists of the latter definition are severing themselves from the spirit of historic evangelical Christianity; the second group claims that evangelicals of the former category are making a subtle retreat to a compromised fundamentalism (Henry 1957a:26).

In Henry's view, neither modernism nor fundamentalism accurately represented true Christianity; both groups had been discredited: modernism because it was "a perversion of the scriptural theology," and contemporary fundamentalism because it was "a perversion of the biblical spirit" (1957:26). But the continuity with the past was retained by an evangelical remnant, the new evangelicalism, whose theology and ecclesiology, according to Henry, corresponded to that of the Apostles and Protestant reformers.

In another *Christianity Today* editorial, "Evangelicals and Fundamentals," published later that same year, Carl Henry came back to his discussion of evangelicalism vis-á-vis fundamentalism. Henry noted that the term "evangelical" had caused considerable confusion among Protestants—both liberals and fundamentalists—especially with regard to the ministry of Billy Graham, which had itself received a flood of criticism from both corners. As Henry saw it, "Further confusion has been caused by criticism of the 'fundamentalism' of Billy Graham by liberal and neo-orthodox leaders and the censure of the 'modernism' of Mr. Graham by some fundamentalists. All this semantic confusion calls for clarification" (Henry 1957b:20). As a descriptive title, "evangelical,"

Henry confessed, has become an ambiguous term. To clarify its significance, Henry sought to sharpen its referential meaning.

While fundamentalists such as John F. Walvoord, president of Dallas Theological Seminary, defended the label "fundamentalist" as honorable and respectable (Walvoord 1957),[21] Henry and others preferred the term "evangelical" for two reasons. For one thing, Henry explained, "the word is scriptural and has a well-defined historical content," and, for another, "the alternative, *fundamentalism,* has a narrower content and has acquired unbiblical accretions" (Henry 1957b:20). By contrast, Henry argued, the term "fundamentalism does not possess biblical background nor has it gained a rich and well-defined content that history has endowed on evangelicalism" (1957b:20). However, in the process of untangling the "semantic confusion" about the word "evangelical," Henry went a step further: "Because fundamentalism cannot be biblically defined, it cannot authoritatively define what is fundamental and what is not fundamental to Christianity" (1957b:20).

Henry looked to *Webster's New International Dictionary* for an historic definition of "evangelical." He reported that "evangelical" designates "that party or school among the Protestants which holds that the essence of the Gospel consists mainly in its doctrines of man's sinful condition and the need of salvation, the revelation of God's grace in Christ, the necessity of spiritual renovation and participation in the experience of redemption through faith" (quoted in Henry 1957b:20). This definition, insisted Henry, placed the new evangelicals in the direct succession of "evangelical" Christians from Augustine through the Reformers to Moody and Machen. "These men, for the most part, not only proclaimed the great doctrines which concerned salvation, but made the evangel apply to the whole of life" (1957b:20). In the final analysis, "Evangelicals are turning away from the term fundamentalism not because of any inclination to disavow traditional fundamentals of the Christian faith," as some fundamentalists charged, "but are prompted by its inadequate scriptural content and its current earned and unearned disrepute" (1957b:21).

What Henry seemed to be implying in this discussion is that the "new" evangelicalism was, in fact, the true historic orthodoxy. Moreover, for Henry, "evangelical" described that which is continuous with the message and mission of the Gospel as set forth by the Apostles and reclaimed by the reformers. As a movement, however, contemporary fundamentalism had emerged from historic evangelicalism and perverted its meaning.[22] "We," the new evangelicals seemed to be saying, "are *not* part of that perversion." Because fundamentalism, as the evangelicals defined it, had no connection to historic orthodoxy, new evangelicals could not and should not identify themselves with the fundamentalist movement. The next logical step, then, would be for evangelicals to reject fundamentalism. Indeed, after the mid-1950s, we find some of the harshest criticism of fundamentalism by new evangelical spokespersons. It seemed that evangelicals no longer strove either to revive or reform fundamentalism. To the contrary, at nearly every turn, many now began to repudiate it.

"NEGATING" MODERN FUNDAMENTALISM

By the late 1950s, several spokespersons for the new evangelicalism were taking their case against fundamentalism to a wider audience, most notably to the "liberal" readership of *The Christian Century*. What makes this move especially interesting is that evangelicals were also beginning to entertain rapprochement with their mainline Protestant brethren, however measured and stipulatory such ecumenical dialogue might become. One of the first articles to appear in *The Christian Century* by a "fundamentalist"—albeit a disaffected one—since J. Gresham Machen was a piece entitled "Fundamentalists and Ecumenicity" by Sherman Roddy, son of Fuller Theological Seminary professor Clarence Roddy (Marsden 1987) and himself formerly a professor at Conservative Baptist Seminary in Denver. Aside from the fact that Roddy attacked fundamentalists as religious, social, psychological, and economic "have-nots," "unable to come to terms with modern life" and, at heart, "victim[s] of fear," he labeled the fundamentalist movement as perhaps the main hindrance to Protestant reconciliation. "No one can seriously deny," Roddy remarked, "that any single group poses more difficult problems for the ecumenical goal than the fundamentalists" (1958:1109). And while "the easiest way to deal with them is to ignore them," he reminded his more liberal readers that "the nature of the ecumenical responsibility does not allow this" (1958:1109).

What one finds intriguing about Roddy's article is not that Roddy's criticisms of fundamentalism were harsh—this became a commonplace among evangelical writings of the time—but that in attacking fundamentalism, Roddy identified himself with the mainline's concern for open channels of dialogue between liberals and conservatives. Although Roddy himself had left the fundamentalist orbit, the primary purpose of his article was not to denounce fundamentalism so much as it was to make "new evangelicalism" accessible to the liberal religious mainstream. He wanted to open lines of communication through mutual understanding and Christian charity. By confirming the negative stereotypes liberals held of fundamentalists, Roddy consciously sought to distance evangelicals from old fundamentalism. At the same time, however, Roddy tried to introduce the liberal religious establishment to a "new breed" of fundamentalist—"a group of younger men who are impatient with fundamentalism as they find it" who "call themselves the new evangelicals" (1958:1110). These new evangelicals, Roddy explained, "are often well trained scholars who in consequence of their learning have shed much of the fear implicit in fundamentalism. Hence they constitute a bridgehead to which contacts may be made" (1958:1110). Roddy encouraged liberals to seek to cultivate fruitful dialogue with this new breed of educated fundamentalist, in effect, holding up the new evangelicalism as the sole representative of orthodox Protestantism.

But, Roddy cautioned, reconciliation between liberals and moderate conservatives would not be easy because of some of the serious issues faced by the new evangelicals, who were still linked at some points to fundamentalism. As Roddy explained, the new evangelicals "must wear the old garments of fundamentalism while changing the man within. For economic and political reasons they are reluctant to appear as friends of the enemy, even though privately they recognize the enemy as part of the Christian community. They live with a double standard" (1958:1110). Roddy appealed to the "enlightened leaders of the main stream" not only to accept new evangelical appeals for understanding and respect, but, more importantly, to "do much to provide these pilgrims a new home" (1958:1110).

Though it could be argued that Roddy's "olive branch" to the liberal religious mainline did not represent new evangelical thinking in the main, his comments did at least indicate the beginnings of an evangelicalism seeking to sever its ties to fundamentalism in order to build lines of communication with liberals. Whereas earlier, evangelicals sought to unite conservative and moderate fundamentalists, these later new evangelicals seemed to be broadening their coalition to include some liberal elements. To create a broader coalition, Roddy not only sought to distance the new evangelicals from the extremes of fundamentalism, but he also characterized fundamentalism, by implication, as orthodox Christianity at its most perverse.

The next year, the editors of *The Christian Century* printed another article that attempted to explain the new evangelical position in relation to, but as wholly apart from, fundamentalism. This time, the comments in the provocatively titled article, "Post-Fundamentalist Faith," were those of Edward J. Carnell, then president of Fuller Seminary. "Let me say a word about that anxious breed of younger men," Carnell wrote autobiographically, "who are conservatives in theology but are less than happy when they are called 'fundamentalists.' These men are both the cause and effect of a radical atmospheric change within American orthodoxy" (1959b:971). This "radical atmospheric change" within orthodoxy had produced what Carnell referred to as a "post-fundamentalist faith," the revivification of the conservative tradition in Christian theology and not, as some might contend, a revival of old fundamentalism.

Carnell then recounted a brief and selective history of twentieth-century fundamentalism, taking care to note its various departures from orthodox Christianity. As he pointed out, during this period, which saw "a series of subtle internal changes, fundamentalism shifted from an affirmation to a negation. The result was a cunning pharisaism that confused possession of truth with possession of virtue. Fundamentalism stood in the temple of God, thankful that it was not like modernism" (1959b:971). According to Carnell, fundamentalism defined its "status by negation," denying the truth of any other system or community other than itself. To fundamentalism, wrote Carnell, "All other elements in the Christian community were apostate" (1959b:971). But in contrast to fundamentalism, Carnell seemed to suggest, evangelicalism derived its status by affirming its orthodox biblical heritage.

This "new breed" fundamentalism, Carnell maintained, is therefore not fundamentalism at all, and should, moreover, not be mistaken for its deviant or "cultic orthodoxy." "Since a goodly company of younger conservatives are trying to restore the classical lines of orthodoxy," Carnell was quick to assert, "philosophy of religion ought to reserve the term 'fundamentalist' for the person who confuses possession of truth with possession of virtue or who defends a separatist view of the church." Orthodoxy, he stressed, "does not affect a monopoly on truth. It rejects the cultic quest for negative status"— and here he sounded a soft but hopeful ecumenical note—"it is ready to entertain friendly conversation with the church universal" (1959b:971).

Carnell was troubled by the many labels that it seemed were indiscriminately applied by both modernists and fundamentalists on those with whom they disagreed. Though Carnell was disturbed by the use of labels, however, he recognized the utility of labels in combatting the tendency for theological boundaries to become blurred and for the honorable aspects of orthodoxy to become obscured by the cultic disposition of fundamentalists and, he would add, modernists. As he put it, "It is too bad, in a way, that we have to use labels at all. In Antioch they were content to be called Christians. But all is not lost. By using carefully selected labels, we at least clarify our position in the theological spectrum" (1959b:971).

The following year, Edward Carnell wrote a second article on the new evangelicalism for *The Christian Century* that was published under the title "Orthodoxy: Cultic vs. Classic" (1960). This essay, published as part of the "How My Mind Has Changed" series, was a summary of the argument he had made against fundamentalism as "orthodoxy gone cultic" (1959a:113) in his monograph, *The Case for Orthodox Theology.* This slender book, published in 1959 by Westminster Press, was the third in a series of three books on contemporary theology by prominent liberal, conservative, and neo-orthodox theologians.

Orthodoxy, Carnell believed, could be divided into two distinct manifestations, one classic, the other cultic. Carnell defined orthodoxy as "that branch of Christendom which limits the ground of religious authority to the Bible" (1959a:113). According to Carnell, "classic" orthodoxy is that expression of Christianity that remains faithful to the authority of the Bible and that defines itself by these sacred scriptures. In contrast to "classic" orthodoxy is "cultic" orthodoxy. In Carnell's opinion, "cultic" orthodoxy perverts true orthodoxy either by including or by excluding principles or practices that are not derived ultimately from the authoritative voice of the Christian scriptures. Defining fundamentalism as a perversion of orthodoxy, Carnell then took fundamentalism to task on each of its signature doctrines—separation, dispensationalism, biblical literalism—and argued forcefully that each of its peculiar beliefs, from which it obtained its identity, were derived from its "cultic mentality" and not from biblical authority.

In Carnell's view, the reason why modern fundamentalism went "cultic" was because of its transformation shortly after World War I from a movement that "preserved the faith once for all delivered to the saints," to a mentality that, having become "an army without a cause," perpetuated its war against a discredited modernism (1959a:113-114). Negating all other Christian groups became fundamentalism's new *raison d'être*. "Status by negation," Carnell charged, "is the first order of business. When there are no modernists from which to withdraw, fundamentalists compensate by withdrawing from one another" (1959a:117). "Ever occupied with the work of negative status," Carnell contended later in his *Christian Century* piece, "the Fundamentalist must blame others for evil [the evil he refuses to see in himself]; he must find a scapegoat" (1960:378). Fundamentalism, then, rather than becoming a synonym for "classic" orthodoxy, became instead an aberration, a mutant subspecies of Protestant Christianity—one that should be rejected.

Though apparently tempted in his conclusion to dismiss fundamentalism as "cultic" and hence "heretical," Carnell, whose expressed interests were ecumenical, tried instead to be empathetic. "Although fundamentalism is orthodoxy gone cultic," Carnell remarked demurely, "the perversion is fathered by misguided zeal, not malice" (1959a:124). In his later *Christian Century* article, however, Carnell adjusted his earlier assessment. With feigned optimism—what some might take as thinly veiled contempt (Marsden 1987)—Carnell "hoped" that "perhaps the day will come when the fundamentalist will temper his separation by the wisdom of the ages. Perhaps not. But in the meantime let us not be too disturbed by his vanity" (1960:379). Concluding his remarks in a somewhat patronizing tone, Carnell saw little hope for a reform of "cultic" orthodoxy: "The fundamentalist means well. He wants status in the church, but he errs in the way he goes about getting it. Having missed the way, he needs our pity, not our scorn" (1960:379).

The boundaries that Carnell drew between fundamentalists and the new evangelicals, groups represented respectively by the terms "cultic" and "classic" orthodoxy, were extreme when compared to the boundary distinctions that earlier new evangelical spokespersons such as Ockenga, Henry, and Grounds had alluded to in their writings. Nevertheless, Carnell's precise articulation of the differences between evangelicals and fundamentalists provided clearer lines between the two groups that many later evangelicals came to adopt. Indeed, by 1960, the rejection of the fundamentalist movement by the new evangelicalism was all but complete.

The Evangelical Boundary Dilemma: Checking the Drift toward Liberalism, 1940-1965

THE EMERGENCE OF A NEW EVANGELICALISM in the 1940s and 1950s signaled the end of the old fundamentalist coalition, effectively dividing conservative Protestantism into two rival orthodoxies. While fundamentalists reinforced their separation from secular culture, evangelicalism, the more moderate of the two, put forth a program that envisioned the great multitude of unrepresented and unaligned Protestants united together into a greater evangelical coalition that would regain for orthodox Protestant religion the respected place in American society it had once enjoyed.

By the end of the 1950s, evangelicals such as Carl Henry and Harold Ockenga could look back on two decades of success that the new evangelical coalition had experienced. Gone were the embarrassing days of fundamentalist defeats. As Henry related in a lengthy editorial in *Christianity Today*, "The day is gone when religious couriers bear tidings only of loss after loss for the evangelical movement; of conservative scholars dwindling until at last Machen and Warfield seem almost to stand alone; of revealed religion demeaned as fundamentalist cultism and fundamentalism disparaged in turn as sheer anti-intellectualism." Indeed, Henry continued, "The day is gone. One fact stands sure: evangelical claims are being reasserted today with a vigor and wideness surprising to most interpreters of contemporary religious life" (1959c:3).

In his article on "Resurgent Evangelical Leadership," printed the following year in *Christianity Today,* Ockenga echoed much of Henry's glowing tribute to a revitalized evangelical religion, pointing out its specific aims and various initiatives:

> The evangelical has general objectives he wishes to see achieved. One of them is a revival of Christianity in the midst of a secular world. . . . The evangelical wishes to retrieve Christianity from a mere eddy of the main stream into the full current of modern life. He desires to win a new respect for orthodoxy in the academic circles by producing scholars who can defend the faith on intellectual ground. He hopes to recapture denominational leadership from within the denominations rather than abandoning those denominations to modernism. He intends to restate his position carefully and cogently so that it must be considered in the theological dialogue. He intends that Christianity will be the mainspring in the many reforms of the societal order (1960:14)

But the forging of a new evangelical coalition, predicated as it was on a return to the religious mainstream and on fuller participation in modern cultural life, did not come without complications. Not only were these new evangelicals compelled to rethink the relation of orthodoxy to American culture and its relevance to the modern age, but they were also forced to reconsider their identification with historic fundamentalism. In so doing, the new evangelicals came increasingly to see themselves as not simply another type of fundamentalism but as a coalition of conservatives who had moved beyond the insulated world of fundamentalism. This boundary became more and more evident as evangelicals marked out their differences with the fundamentalists in ecclesiastical, social, and theological issues. What is more, in the course of identifying themselves as *not* fundamentalists, the new evangelicals found themselves suddenly faced with the social structural dilemma of defining how they were also *not* liberals or modernists. That is, in the process of differentiating themselves from fundamentalists, evangelicals soon became aware of their own increasingly "leftward" drift toward liberalism, giving rise to the uneasy question of how far "left" evangelicals could drift and still remain orthodox.[1] Thus, at the same time that evangelicals were delimiting the boundaries that separated them from fundamentalists, they were also devoting considerable attention to preserving the boundaries between themselves and liberalism.[2] As a result, the new evangelicals focused a large amount of their energy on defining what it meant to be orthodox, while simultaneously directing as much, if not more, of their energy to defining how they were not liberals.

To illustrate the new evangelicalism's concern over its boundary with liberalism, this chapter will examine three topical episodes in which this boundary was consciously maintained, retracing much of the same ground covered in the discussion above. First, though evangelicals sought cooperation among themselves, they were on guard not to define this common ground for unity as ecumenical. Second, while the new evangelicals pressed for greater social awareness and social involvement, at the same time they were careful not to confuse their renewed social interest with the Social Gospel. Third, though evangelicals anxiously sought intellectual respectability for orthodox theology, they nonetheless drew a sharp line of distinction between evangelical orthodoxy and Barthian neo-orthodoxy, the most prominent liberal theological movement at that time. Additionally, each of these themes, though relating to conservative Protestantism's symbolic boundary with liberalism, reveals evangelical ambivalence toward identifying with and participating fully in modern secular society.

EVANGELICAL UNITY CONTRA LIBERAL ECUMENISM

The evangelical leaders who organized the National Association of Evangelicals for United Action (NAE) in 1942 did so with the specific intention of bringing together evangelical Protestants who did not already have a voice in or sympathize with the policies of the Federal Council of Churches (FCC), but who at the same time could not support the separatist position of the fundamentalist American

Council of Christian Churches. NAE supporters were convinced that neither the FCC nor the American Council could unite the majority of Protestants, who, they maintained, were as yet unaligned with or unrepresented by either association (*Evangelical Action!* 1942). As the members of the NAE executive committee explained,

> Between these poles of thought along the lines of coordinated effort is found the great body of evangelicals, still a majority in number in the Church, still without commitment to any correlating organization, already convinced in many instances that the solution has not been found in previous attempts at coordination but ready and anxious to give sober consideration to another effort in that direction (*Evangelical Action!* 1942:vi-vii).

Nearly two hundred delegates, representing about forty denominations, gathered for the NAE meeting in St. Louis in 1942 to attest to their desire for unity among conservative Protestants (Wright 1942:3). They believed that while Protestantism was fragmented, the situation was not entirely hopeless. If the various churches and individual believers who made up the "great body of evangelicals" could be united on a common doctrinal base, a revived Protestant evangelicalism could become a major force for orthodoxy in America. All that was needed, they argued, was the necessary "glue" to hold such a movement of evangelicals together. "The force is in waiting," the NAE committee reported, "but it must become cohesive" (*Evangelical Action!* 1942:v-vi).

The speeches presented at this first conference of the NAE set the terms for an evangelical ecumenism, but one that would come to distinguish itself from the broader ecumenical movement. For example, in his historical overview of this uniting of evangelicals, J. Elwin Wright, whose tireless efforts toward unity among conservatives in New England during the 1930s helped bring about the creation of the NAE (Evans 1991), expressed uncommon candor in his desire for unity among evangelicals. "It is obvious to all of us," Wright averred, "that the Church in this generation is sadly in need of a return to the unity of purpose which characterized it in apostolic days" (1942:3). Although Wright acknowledged the many barriers to unity among evangelicals, he encouraged his colleagues "to cultivate a spirit of love and consideration toward those with whom we differ on less essential matters" (1942:16). The remaining speeches followed closely Wright's heartfelt desire for unity among evangelicals.

In his comments on the need for an association of evangelicals, Harold J. Ockenga spoke in a rather ecumenical vein, calling conservatives to recognize that unity could not be achieved by defending denominational differences but by transcending them. "If the cross of Christ Himself, cannot unite true Christians," Ockenga told his fellow delegates, "there is no other possibility for their unification." Indeed, he continued, "Different church governments and many other differences are insignificant and almost foolish if Christ is put in the highest place, where He belongs" (1942:32). Denominationalism compounded the problem of disunity because those who defended denominationalism believed that they were defending the Gospel of Christ. But they were often mistaken, Ockenga intimated, since "denominations are only monuments of old arguments of our forefathers; the reasons for most of these have long since passed out of existence and only the separation created by the arguments continues to live on" (1942:33). Although the differences that divided Christians were often insignificant, the disunity such differences caused was great, so much so that "between many of us in our denominations," Ockenga noted, "there is less fellowship than there would be in a good Rotary club, for the simple reason that we do not have any sense of unity. Satan's greatest stronghold is the division of Christians into denominations as they are today" (1942:33). Even so, Ockenga seemed hopeful "that from a body of men such as this a very forward step in the unity and the progress of evangelical forces will be taken" (1942:19).

In his brief keynote address, William Ward Ayer, pastor of Calvary Baptist Church in New York City, urged evangelicals to seek common ground upon which to unite for action. The basis of Protestant unity, he told his audience, could only be found in "a common meeting place for common purposes" (1942:42). As he explained, "there must be a hub in which the spokes of our several organizations can meet in order to make for firmness of purpose and service, and for solidarity in testimony" (1942:42) Such unity, he noted, was not to be found in either the Federal Council or the American Council (1942:43-45).

In his remarks before the delegates, Stephen Paine echoed much of Ayer's speech, adding that in order for evangelicals to secure unity, they must eschew questions over sectarian doctrines that might merely provoke further controversy. To this end, Paine argued that in order for orthodoxy to be more inclusive, it should be defined "in the simplest possible terms" (1942:59). "Simplicity of creed will be a great asset," he said (1942:59). As Paine elaborated further and in a more tolerant spirit, "we should always place our emphasis upon positive objectives and shun a spirit of controversy and opposition to existing organizations, even when we question their orthodoxy" (1942:59-60).[3]

Not long after the first conference of the NAE, representatives of the NAE travelled throughout the country calling for united action among evangelicals and establishing NAE chapters wherever there was sufficient interest. At one such NAE regional gathering in early 1950, the usually staid Carl Henry spoke to his Los Angeles–area audience with the enthusiasm of a tent revivalist: "What could occupy us more appropriately than reflection upon evangelical unity, evangelical purpose, and evangelical activity? *United for action*! Like the beat of drums, or a call to hoist the colors, it quickens the spirit, as if someone had shouted from the heavenlies: 'To your tents O Israel!'" (1950:6).

Chief among their aims was to counter the influences of the Federal Council of Churches in education, radio broadcasting, social services, evangelism and missions, and to provide evangelicals with a voice in the affairs of church and state. Their efforts met with success in that by the second convention of the NAE held in Chicago in May 1943, the number of delegates had grown to almost 1,000, representing some 50 denominations with an estimated constituency of perhaps 15 million (Gasper 1981:27; cf., Shelley 1967:69-72). Even so, though they sought to make the NAE the voice of a united evangelical Protestantism, evangelical spokespersons were continually faced with the problem of defining unity in terms different from the liberal ecumenism they challenged. In short, they did not want their efforts confused with those of the liberal mainstream.

One reason for this problem was the inherent distrust by conservative Protestants of "human" organizations and hierarchical structures, especially those which might stifle individualism and independence. As William Ayer had proclaimed to the delegates of the first NAE convention, "The boast of evangelical Christianity is its liberty of thought, freedom of expression, and the right to differ, especially on non-essentials" (1942:31-32). But Ayer left room for the possibility of united action among conservative evangelicals, going on to say that "if there cannot be unanimity, there must be unity, even in division" (1942:32). Fundamentalists displayed little sympathy toward the agenda of the Federal Council or the broader ecumenical movement and were readily suspicious of any church or person that supported ecumenism, however casually.

What supporters of the NAE and the American Council had in common, at least early on, was their belief that the ecumenical movement blurred, if not altogether erased, the line between the church and the world, between sacred and profane, between the saved and the damned. To them, ecumenism not only represented the acquiescence of Christianity to the erosive forces of modernism, but it also gave evidence that the fallen sinful world had penetrated into the church itself. Indeed, many fundamentalists interpreted the emergence of the ecumenical movement as a sign that the future "anti-Christ" envisioned in St. John's revelation of the end times would soon appear on the world scene to forge a one-world church.[4] The NAE's attempts to unify a fragmented evangelical Protestantism made them all the more aware of its boundary with liberalism; strengthening this boundary occupied much of the efforts of evangelical spokespersons. Thus, when evangelicals connected with the NAE sought unity, they did so conscious of their separation from the liberal mainstream, and they expressed their separation in terms that distinguished evangelical "unity" from ecumenical "union."

Postwar evangelicals were not sparing in their denunciation of the ecumenical movement. Ockenga, along with the other speakers at the first NAE meeting, appears to have set the terms for the new evangelical critique of ecumenism when he declaimed that "Along side of Roman Catholicism is that terrible octopus of liberalism, which spreads itself throughout our Protestant Church, dominating innumerable organizations, pulpits, and publications, as well as seminaries and other schools. Because of our divided condition, the Federal Council of Churches bids fair to control all government relationships for Protestantism" (1942:26-27; cf., Gordon 1948). This situation, he believed, was one that evangelicals must fight to reverse.

The threatening results became all the more apparent to the evangelicals as both the Federal (after 1950, "National") and the

World Council of Churches (WCC) became more and more identified in the minds of the American people with the Protestant ecumenical ideal. Comments such as those cited below from an 1950 article by *UEA* editor James DeForest Murch on the founding of the National Council of Churches are typical. Murch, who penned numerous articles and editorials deriding the ecumenical vision of the liberal mainstream, wrote,

> Thousands of evangelicals look upon the proposed NCCCUSA [i.e., National Council] as a serious threat to all they hold dear. They see it as a potential Protestant monopoly in America—a super-church which can regiment and eventually rob both its constituent members and all non-member bodies of their individual freedom of thought and action (Murch 1950:4).

The goal of liberal ecumenism, as embodied in the Federal/ National Council and World Council, was completely unacceptable to the evangelicals. One reason for this stems from their strongly held belief that if unity were obtainable, it had to be founded upon unwavering trust in the Bible and not in human ingenuity or goodwill. Murch saw no evangelical alternative but to seek unity outside the orbit of a "compromised" liberalism. As Murch explained, defending evangelical resistance to liberal ecumenism,

> From such a grandiose project evangelicals instinctively turn away. They see an apostate Roman Catholic hierarchy on the one hand and an apostate Protestant ecclesiasticism on the other and are being persuaded that the only hope lies in building a new structure of Christian co-operation, such as the National Association of Evangelicals, which will hold fast the cardinal doctrines of the historic Christian faith and perpetuate the freedoms of historic Protestantism (1950:6).[5]

Although evangelicals decried the monopolistic or, as they liked to call it, communistic tendencies of ecumenism as well as its alleged unity through compromise, evangelical suspicions of liberal ecumenism were still in large part a matter of authority. In short, Who would speak for Protestantism? Indeed, one of the original resolutions at the initial conference of the NAE voiced opposition to any body that claimed to represent Protestant Christianity that did not pledge loyalty first to the Gospel of Christ (*Evangelical Action!* 1942:8-16; see *United . . . We Stand* 1943 and Shelley 1967:80-82).

One example of this challenge to Federal/National Council authority can be seen in Carl Henry's critique of liberal ecumenism. Henry, speaking at the 1950 NAE rally in the Church of the Open Door in downtown Los Angeles, took exception to the National Council's ecumenical program, saying: "Who gave these men, who run to and from Amsterdam and other conclaves as delegates and representatives of the churches, the right to speak for the body of Christ?" (1950:7). Only those who speak with Christ's authority, he declared, may speak for the church of Christ. A similar sentiment was expressed a number of years later by J. Marcellus Kik, then associate editor of *Christianity Today*. In one editorial, Kik confidently proclaimed that "no choicer group exists to bring the true ecumenical goal than those who yield to the authority of the Word, acknowledge the true deity of the Lord, believe in the vicarious atonement, and wait for the coming of the Lord" (1958:141). In essence, both Henry and Kik appeared to assert that because liberals did not truly *believe* the Bible, as the evangelicals did, they could not rightfully speak on behalf of the Protestant churches. Indeed, Kik added emphatically, liberal ecumenism could never "in a thousand and one years unite Christians until it first accepted the Bible as its only basis of authority" (1958:136-137).

It might seem puzzling that the topic of unity appeared in issue after issue of the NAE's newsmagazine *United Evangelical Action,* as well as *Christianity Today* and other evangelical publications, as if the questions concerning unity were still unsettled. In actuality, the articles differed little one from another. One could make the case that rather than refining their position or pressing their case for an evangelical basis for unity, conservative spokespersons spent most of their energies reinforcing the differences between evangelical and liberal ecumenism.[6] In general, evangelicals distinguished their version of Christian unity from liberal ecumenism in at least three ways: (1) by calling for a recognition of the primacy of "spiritual" unity over "organizational" union; (2) by emphasizing that evangelical unity encouraged cooperation among Christians but did not compromise the orthodox doctrines of Protestantism; and (3) by stressing that, unlike liberal ecumenism, which collectivized Protestantism, their program for united evangelical action (or "evangelical ecumenicity") preserved denominational diversity. As the most visible expression of evangelical unity, the NAE became the focal point for the new evangelical ecumenism, an ecumenism that itself became a symbolic boundary between evangelicals and liberals that new evangelical spokespersons would seek to strengthen and defend.

THE "SPIRITUAL" UNITY OF THE EVANGELICALS

The new evangelicals distinguished their version of ecumenism from the liberals' version by appealing to evangelicals to maintain "spiritual" unity rather than the "organizational" unity that they claimed their liberal rivals promoted. To new evangelical spokespersons, unity was not some tangible structural goal that one should work toward, as liberal ecumenists did, but a spiritual reality that already existed—though only in the mind of God. This point is amply illustrated by conservative evangelicals who claimed that the NAE represented a greater evangelical coalition built on spiritual unity, not organizational union.

For instance, in a speech presented in 1943 to a gathering of NAE members and supporters, reprinted in 1956, Harold J. Ockenga spoke of the inherent unity of believers, a unity not synonymous with ecumenicity or ecclesiastical union. "This body [the NAE] must never be identified with any one organizational church. All true believers are in no one church organization. Even a union of all Catholic and Protestant churches would not be the body of Christ. Only a unity of the Spirit or a spiritual unity fits the description. The existence of such a spiritual body ought to be recognized in the presence of dangers threatening Christianity through organizational union" (Ockenga 1956:3). In this speech, Ockenga made reference to St. Paul's teaching on the unity of the church: "One Lord, one faith, one baptism, one hope of your calling." From this statement Ockenga concluded that "the unity which now exists in the church and which can never be invalidated no matter how much it is repudiated by schisms, by errors or by aberrations of character and practice . . . is the foundation of our spiritual unity" (Ockenga 1956:4).

Eight years later, in 1951, the editors of the *UEA* surveyed their readership in order to determine what evangelicals thought about Christian unity. As the editors explained, "Much is being said these days about Christian unity. . . . [W]e thought evangelicals should make known their views on the subject" (*UEA* Feb 1, 1952:7). Willard Crunkilton's response to the survey was typical of many. Crunkilton pointed out that although the idea of a universal church "is delightful, and designed to interest the most disinterested, . . . there are some flies in the ointment, however" (1952:7). Christians should not commit themselves to the idea of unity until they considered what such a program entailed. Crunkilton warned implicitly that liberal ecumenism was not God's program for the modern church. In fact, he drew a sharp contrast between "worldly" ecumenism and the "spiritual" nature of the church. Sadly, he lamented, the evangelical witness to the church's true nature and mission is continually frustrated by the authoritarianism of liberal leaders. "The world has introduced its program into the church," Crunkilton charged, "and if men speak with holy boldness against this fleshly work they are shunted to obscure corners where they will not be heard" (1952:7).

Crunkilton then took the opportunity to remind conservative Protestants of the spiritual unity inherent in the church of Christ. "If there ever was a day when we needed to be reminded that there is already 'One Church,'" Crunkilton remarked, "that is today. Men are bustling about to form something that is *already formed*. As it takes more than dust to form a body, so it takes more than organization to form a church. . . . God has a better way" (1952:7, emphasis added). Crunkilton's attack on ecumenism illustrates the attempt by evangelicals to draw a sharp distinction between the evangelical vision of Christian unity, which is of the "spirit," and the "man-made" unity of liberal ecumenism, which is of the "flesh" (1952:8). Thus, according to Crunkilton, though they were separated by denominational groupings, evangelicals needed simply to rely upon the spirit of unity implicit in the spiritual nature of the Christian church for unity to occur.

The final point Crunkilton made in his reply was biting in its criticism of ecumenism. "While liberals search for the pot of fool's gold at the end of an ecclesiastical rainbow," he charged, "there is a church more eternal than gold, right at hand" (1952:8). We might think of Crunkilton's response as indicative of the subtle shift in evangelical thinking about Christian unity. While evangelicals had called for unity among evangelicals—fundamentalists, moderates, and even some liberals—at the same time, evangelicals were not at all willing to identify their version of unity, which was ecumenical in spirit, with the conciliar movement among mainstream Protestants. Their version differed, evangelicals argued, in that it was based on the organic unity of the "spirit" rather than the synthetic and mechanical unity of the "flesh." As Paul Rees remarked a few years later while laying out the terms for an evangelical ecumenism, "evangelicals did not *seek* unity, they *had* unity" (cf., Rees 1955:9).

Rees authored a series of articles on "spiritual" unity that were published in *UEA* under the title "The Nature of the Unity We Seek." Rees, minister of the First Covenant Church of Minneapolis and a well-known evangelical writer, stressed that this "spiritual" unity was inherent in the church. As Rees explained, "Any ecumenical stirring and encirclement that you and I may wish to name—whether in the small orbit of the National Association of Evangelicals or the larger orbit of the World Council—will succeed only in so far as it becomes . . . a dynamic expression of an already existing unity in Christ. The unity is never synthetic. It is organic. It is vital. It is of the essence" (1955:9). Liberal ecumenists had misperceived the nature of unity, Rees believed. Evangelicals, however, were working toward an ideal unity that already existed, though on a spiritual plane.

Carl Henry, writing on the nature of the unity evangelicals sought, likewise held that Christian unity is spiritual, not organizational, and could thus neither be achieved nor enhanced by ecclesiastical union. "The body, and its unity, already exists, and does not need to be now produced." Even so, continued Henry, "This unity may be empirically disturbed by dissension, or empirically promoted by cooperation, but the ultimate unity of the church is neither destroyed by separation nor established by organizational union" (Henry 1956:3). In Henry's view, then, the unity proposed by ecclesiastical bodies is of no benefit unless it is grounded in a unity of the spirit. Echoing those before him, Henry remarked that "The model and pattern of the oneness of believers are therefore spiritual, not organizational" (1956:3).

A problem arose, however, when evangelicals surveyed the religious scene and realized that the church, organizationally, was still sorely divided. Henry addressed this discrepancy, as did other evangelicals, by arguing that the "true" church must never be confused with its many humanly constructed denominations. The Christian church, Henry maintained, is a spiritual reality that transcends its many physical expressions. Unity is therefore possible only as Christians come to recognize their common connectedness to this spiritual, ideal "body"—what Calvin had called an "indivisible connection" (Henry 1961b:28). Evangelicals, therefore, who perceived an inherent spiritual unity in a divided "body" could argue that they were closer than liberal ecumenists to the ideal of unity that Jesus had prayed for in St. John 17. Evangelicals could hold in tension the divided state of the Christian church—even their own highly denominated coalition—with the ideal of Christian "brotherhood." For one thing, they believed that organizational division was not necessarily divisive; for another thing, they believed that the unity Jesus urged his followers to seek should lead to spiritual union and not to some man-made superstructure.

Harold Ockenga similarly reminded evangelicals that "true Christian unity, rather than being an ecclesiastical organizational unity, is a unity of which the Holy Spirit is the author" (1956:4). This unity, in fact, had existed from the first century to the present. "In the apostolic day," he reminded evangelicals, "each church was autonomous, but spiritually all the churches were a unit. Their life was one. They had no organizational unity" (Ockenga 1956:4). For all their physical activity, Ockenga charged, liberal ecumenists failed to recognize this simple spiritual fact (cf., Henry 1956:3 and Thurston 1956).

J. Marcellus Kik's view on the spiritual unity inherent in the church, as discussed in his well-received book *Ecumenism and the Evangelical* (1958), concurred with Henry's and Ockenga's. "The ground of unity among believers is their spiritual union with Christ," he held (1958:61). Indeed, Kik wrote in an earlier chapter, in spiritual union there is "true organic unity, a spiritual unity which may disappoint those who feel that visible organizational unity is the high goal of ecumenicity. The New Testament, however, emphasizes the spiritual Headship of Christ and the spiritual unity of believers" (1958:46).[7] To distinguish this spiritual unity among "believing" Christians from liberal ecumenism, Kik called this evangelical form of unity simply "evangelical ecumenicity" (1958:9). To Kik, this was a unity not liberal and not organizational, but orthodox and spiritual. As he explained, "out of this [spiritual union] springs the common consciousness that unites all true Christians in a holy fellowship, however separated by time, space, language, or denomination. . . . [B]elonging to Christ rather than belonging to an organization establishes the bond of unity. The consciousness of being in Christ rather than membership in a world-wide church achieves the sense of unity" (1958:61).

Because evanglicals believed that Christian unity existed on an ideal level but not in the physical realm, efforts by liberals to create unity through organizational means were viewed with suspicion. Liberal reliance on human ingenuity and initiative, they charged, was scandalous because it assumed authority over the Divine program. For this reason, the evangelical program for Christian unity consciously differed from the liberal agenda, which they were determined not to resemble in spirit or substance.

"COOPERATION WITHOUT COMPROMISE"

A second way in which the new evangelicals reinforced the boundary between their program for unity and liberal ecumenism was by speaking of evangelical ecumenism as the one that did not compromise the "truth" of orthodox doctrines for the sake of unity. Interestingly, while "unity" of the church was, for the new evangelicals, a *fait accompli,* they seemed to agonize over unity as much as liberals. One reason for this concern was the emphasis evangelicals placed on fostering a Christian cooperation that would not compromise orthodox faith the way they believed liberal ecumenism had. The NAE slogan, "Cooperation Without Compromise," however paradoxical, became the rallying cry of evangelicals, characterizing, in their minds, the main difference between evangelical cooperation and ecumenical compromise (see Paine 1949).

For instance, Earle E. Cairns of Wheaton College, who expressed excitement over the dawning of "a new era in evangelical cooperation," asked evangelicals to consider carefully the basis for cooperative action and the problems evangelicals might have in attaining it. As he put it, "Organic reunion presents the danger of a compromise on the lowest common doctrinal denominator in order to bring people with differing views together. Essential doctrines may be diluted or given up. Truth as well as love is important in real evangelical cooperation" (Cairns 1955:4).

Similarly, George L. Ford, then associate executive director of the NAE, was himself enthusiastic about the NAE's success in uniting evangelicals for cooperative action. In his article "Why the NAE Is Succeeding," Ford listed several reasons for its success, including the NAE's seven-point statement of faith around which "Bible believing Christians of almost every orthodox denomination have rallied" (1956:5). The most salient reason for its success, he believed, was the NAE's uncompromisingly orthodox basis for cooperation. As Ford observed, "With an emphasis of spiritual unity without organic union, of *cooperation without compromise,* of fellowship of true believers in Christ, and a positive program to facilitate the work of the churches[,] the NAE has succeeded where others have failed" (Ford 1956:29, emphasis added). Indeed, Ford concluded, "The NAE *has* brought evangelicals together and *is* the voice of Bible believing Christians of America" (1956:30; cf., Murch 1956 and Shelley 1967).

In the same way, Marcellus Kik also believed that the hallmark of evangelical ecumenicity, unlike liberal ecumenism, was that it called Christians to cooperative effort on the basis of biblical belief rather than diluted doctrines. In contrast to evangelical cooperation, argued Kik, "The ecumenical movement fights shy of sharply defining Christian faith for fear of its disturbing element. An undefined faith produces a paradise of peace and tranquility (though a heretic's paradise)" (1958:64). Kik was well aware of the liberal charge that, in their reluctance to support mainstream Protestant ecumenism and by establishing their own association of conservatives, the new evangelicals were deepening further the divisions among Protestants that they claimed to be healing. Even so, Kik defended the evangelical call to cooperate without compromising orthodoxy as having biblical precedent. As he observed,

> It is interesting to note that the first contest that disturbed the peace of the early church was with heretics rather than schismatics. . . . The apostles did not labor to broaden the definition of faith so that all shades of belief could live comfortably within the church; they refused to accept peace at the cost of truth and courageously fought

heresy by sharply and fully defining Christian faith (1958:64; cf., Carnell 1958 and Henry 1961b).

But, as the new evangelicals discovered during the 1950s, the line between cooperation and compromise was a difficult one to draw. The various constituents that made up the new evangelical coalition had their own distinguishing practices and signature doctrines, ones that would not be so easily set aside, even for the sake of cooperation and greater evangelical unity. Interestingly, though evangelicals believed that they, unlike the liberal ecumenists, could achieve cooperation without compromise, their coalition remained far from unified, even in spirit. Evangelicals were presented with a quandary: how to achieve unity among evangelicals while preserving the diversity apparent in their ever-expanding conservative coalition.

A UNITY THAT PRESERVES DIVERSITY

While the issue of cooperation without compromise was at the forefront of evangelical boundary concern, a third way in which evangelicals distinguished their form of ecclesiastical cooperation from liberal ecumenism was by claiming that unlike the ecumenical movement, evangelical ecumenicity preserved denominational distinctiveness and Christian liberty. Evangelicals charged that liberal ecumenism forced ecclesiastical regimentation, thus usurping the authority of the local church and dampening individual initiative.[8] At the same time, evangelicals denounced fundamentalists, who, they asserted, sought unity through doctrinal regimentation (Paine 1949). In both instances, unity would be mechanical, not organic. The new evangelical quandary was simply this: how does one maintain Christian unity without forcing either the ecclesiastical regimentation of liberalism or the doctrinal regimentation of fundamentalism?

This quandary might explain why evangelicals like Henry, Ockenga, George Ford, Geoffrey Bromiley, and others, while somewhat discomfited by evangelical disunity, began to lay greater stress on the need to maintain diversity even as they pressed for greater cooperation. "It is part of our dilemma," Paul Rees candidly admitted, "that the very attempt to define our unity must take account of the diversity that is among us" (1955:9). The answer for the evangelicals would once again be found in the vague notion of "spiritual" unity, a unity that transcended boundaries even as it defined them.

In an editorial in which he sought to find "the biblical solution to the organizational [liberal] and the separatist [fundamentalist] views of Christian unity," Carl Henry held the two opposing forces of unity and diversity in tension. On one end of the spectrum there is conformity, he argued; on the other end, there is division and disarray. Pointing to the evangelical ideal as different from liberal ecumenism and fundamentalist divisiveness, Henry explained that "organizational union may exist where spiritual disunion prevails, and spiritual union may prevail in the absence of organizational union. The one indispensable New Testament factor is spiritual unity. Where this exists, other partitions and unities will sooner or later fall under their own weight" (1956c:4).

Henry's greater interest was in the growing influence of liberal ecumenism and its push toward ecclesiastical union. He was concerned that the orthodox message might be obscured by the well-organized machinery of liberal ecumenism that pressed for uniformity of belief as necessary to greater unity among Christians. Henry objected, declaring that "the New Testament does not define the antithesis of 'division' in terms of a single organizational fellowship in which all distinctives blur" (Henry 1956c:4). Henry also believed that the liberal ecumenical emphasis on unity through ecclesiastical union was at variance with the biblical and evangelical pattern for unity. As he expressed it,

> No biblical warrant exists for one visible historical church or orga-
> nization, be it Protestant or Roman Catholic, regarded as the super-
> lative manifestation of the body of Christ. . . . The members of this
> body yearn for the fellowship and spiritual unity of *distinct* churches
> which are true in faith and doctrine. And in so doing, they manifest
> their *continuity* with the Christian community of apostolic times
> (Henry 1956c:15, emphasis added).

The reason for evangelical support for denominational division seemed to arise from their desire *not* to confuse the evangelical program for unity with liberal ecumenism, which in its ideal form called for an end to division and the reunification of Christendom into one ecclesiastical body. Henry's last point is interesting when one recalls that at the first conference of the NAE in 1942, Harold Ockenga called for an end to denominational division. The denominations, Ockenga had declared, "are no longer the boundary line between the world and the church but rather help to increase the confusion; denominations are only monuments of old arguments of our forefathers; the reasons for most of these have long since passed out of existence and only the separation created by the arguments continues to live on" (1942b:32-33).

Ockenga's point seemed to be that the denominations had become "worldly" and no longer embodied true Protestant Christianity. Because of this, Ockenga had called for unity among "believers" irrespective of denominational affiliation or loyalty. "Satan's greatest stronghold is the division of Christians into denominations," he had contended. "The division is no longer between denominations; the division is between those who believe in Christ and the Bible and those who reject Christ." He then concluded, "Now is the time to forget all these [denominational] differences and join together as *one* with the Crucified One" (1942b:33, emphasis added).

Ockenga's 1942 comments stand in interesting contrast to Henry's 1956 editorial on Christian unity. This contrast reveals a change in position, a change indicative of the shifting nature of the evangelical boundary. Evangelicals in the 1940s marked their differences from fundamentalists by calling for ecclesiastical unity under one coalition of evangelicals. But if both liberals and evangelicals sought to unite denominations into one greater Protestantism, how was evangelical unity different from liberal ecumenism? In order to distinguish themselves from the liberal mainline, the new evangelicals had to make adjustments in their original plea for unity. "Cooperation Without Compromise" became one slogan that marked the evangelical boundary with liberalism, "Unity amid Diversity" became another.[9]

CHRISTIAN UNITY THROUGH DENOMINATIONAL DIVISION

One example of new evangelical adjustment is found in the writings of Kik, who believed that denominations had preserved Christianity's witness to the truth. Denominationalism had been brought about not by doctrinal acquiescence, he argued, but by theological conviction. "Denominations have been the target for much criticism that their theological differences have been the great cause of disunion. Nothing is further from the truth," Kik wrote. "Through their theological emphasis the Lutheran, Methodist, Episcopal, Baptist, Presbyterian and other denominations have united large numbers of people. The theological emphasis has been a rallying point and [is] not divisive" (Kik 1958:14).

Another example of this adjustment is found in Ford's article "Why the NAE Is Succeeding," cited earlier, in which he detailed the rationale for united evangelical initiative. By drawing a line that favored denominationalism, Ford reemphasized the sharp line between evangelical and liberal ecumenical agendas for Christian unity. "The urgent need which prompted the organization of the NAE," Ford stressed, "was not the necessity of establishing a 'sameness' or 'organizational oneness,' for God does not work by the assembly line method. He exhibits His *unity in diversity* even down to the individual snowflake." Moreover, Ford continued, "The NAE came into being not to eliminate the denominations, but to protect them; not to force individual churches into a mold of either liberal or racial sameness, but to provide a means of fellowship and cooperative witness, not to do the work of the churches, but to stand for the right of churches to do their work as they feel called of God" (Ford 1956:5, emphasis added). As before, this paradoxical position became possible because of the spiritual nature of unity that evangelicals sought to preserve. What is of interest here is that the original push by evangelicals for unity as a response to fundamentalist divisiveness became tempered over time by the threat of liberal ecumenical unionism. In the paradox of evangelical ecumenism, evangelicals discovered a means for distancing themselves from the "rugged independency" of separatist fundamentalism while at the same time maintaining a measurable difference from ecumenical liberalism (see Henry 1956a and 1956b).

A third example of this adjustment in evangelical thinking on ecumenism is found in E. J. Carnell's *Christianity Today* article "Orthodoxy and Ecumenism." In it, Carnell, reputedly the most candid evangelical intellectual of his generation, attempted to outline the orthodox position on ecclesiastical unity in contrast to liberal ecclesiastical union. While Christian unity is important, he argued, it is a unity not attainable in the present. As Carnell affirmed, stressing his point by using italics, *"The visible unity of Christendom is an ideal which simultaneously inspires and judges the real"* (1958:15). This ideal is merely a guide by which the church measures itself, not a goal it will ever fully realize. As he explained, "Just as we strive for sinless perfection, though we shall never reach it, so we strive for the equally valid, though equally elusive, ideal of visible unity" (1958:15). Carnell's larger point, the one with which he scolded liberals, was that the Christian Scriptures did not allow for the sacrifice of truth for the sake of unity, especially when achieved through a "loose handling of the Word of God" (1958:15). Ecclesiastical division, he claimed, is acceptable in the eyes of God and the Christian Scriptures so long as it be division for the sake of truth; *"for,"* as Carnell asserted, once again setting his comments in italics, *"it is better to be divided by truth than to be united by error."* Indeed, he continued further on, "Sincere and unavoidable divisions should excite a sense of honor, not shame, in us" (1958:17).

While Carnell criticized liberal ecumenists for seeing "the evil in disunity" but not "the evil in untruth" (1958:17), at the same time, he made allowances for evangelical disunity by holding that at least its divisions were due to its uncompromising search for truth rather than liberal ecumenism's unity at all costs. (Carnell's assumption, of course, was that liberals were not really interested in biblical truth.) But not all evangelicals held the same opinions, liberals might have countered, not even on "essentials." If there was "One Lord, one faith, one baptism, one hope of your calling," they might have charged, then even some of the evangelicals were obviously in error. Not every evangelical could logically possess the truth and simultaneously hold contrary positions. How, in good conscience, liberals might further have challenged, could evangelicals criticize liberal ecumenists when they themselves appeared to tolerate vast theological diversity within their own ranks? Thus, in order to defend his position, Carnell seemed to make a number of problematic assertions, some logically difficult to follow. For instance, in the concluding section of his article, Carnell made several curiously disjunctive remarks:

> If the visible unity of Christendom is ever realized, it will be a sad
> day for the Gospel. Just as democratic freedom is preserved by a

prudential balance of social interests, so the freedom of the gospel is preserved by a prudential balance of ecclesiastical interests. . . . Orthodoxy believes that every prudent means should be used to heal the divisions in the Christian church. But before one Protestant denomination joins with another, it must examine its own distinctives in the light of the Word of God. If the exegetical ground of these distinctives is no longer conclusive, overtures of union may be undertaken. But if Scripture affords no such release, separation must remain. Under *no* conditions should truth be subordinated to unity. We are saved by faith in Jesus Christ, not by works of the law—and especially not by the law that the church should be visibly united. Our divisions will continue to scandalize the natural man, but this should not unhinge us. The message of the cross is also a scandal (1958:18).

The most thoughtful and detailed discussion on the unity amid diversity theme during this period was authored by Fuller Seminary professor Geoffrey W. Bromiley. Though Bromiley's argument followed the characteristic evangelical position that the ideal form of the church, that is, the biblical ideal, preserves spiritual unity amid the physical diversity of organizational expression, his vision of church unity took note of the tendency for the church to move away from this proper balance. Bromiley posited two perversions of this ideal: *disunity* and *uniformity,* represented by Bromiley in the fundamentalist and liberal positions respectively. Both have existed throughout church history. Both sprang from an emphasis that saw the incarnation of the church, Christ's body, as either spiritual or physical and not enigmatically joined. Uniformity seeks church unity through purely material or physical means. Disunity disconnects completely the physical aspects of the incarnation from the church's vision of unity. In this second "perversion," unity is only spiritual, never visible.

"Diversity, however, is not disunity," Bromiley affirmed, "and therefore the mere fact of multiplicity is no real answer to the question." The reason for this, Bromiley continued, is that "diversity easily gives rise to disunity, especially when unity itself is confused with uniformity" (Bromiley 1958:20). Bromiley insisted that the tension between the spiritual and physical aspects of the church as the "body" of Christ must be maintained: diversity and unity were complementarities, that is, necessary opposites. Bromiley pointed out that when diversity was emphasized above unity it became *disunity*. Likewise, unity, when stressed over diversity, became *uniformity*. The one tended toward "a fanatical exclusivism" and further disunity, the other tended toward "a liberalizing relativization which seeks compromise" (1958:31). For this reason, Bromiley felt, the complementarity of unity and diversity in this scheme prevented the distortions brought about by liberal ecumenists, who pushed for uniformity, and by separatist fundamentalists, who incited divisions. Evangelical ecumenism not only fostered unity among believers, he might have argued, but it allowed believers the independence that Protestant religion traditionally championed.

EVANGELICAL SOCIAL RESPONSIBILITY

The new evangelicals also sought to clarify their boundary with Protestant liberalism in the realm of social concern. As in the case of evangelical cooperation aimed at Christian unity, the division between conservatives and liberals on the issue of social uplift had been firmly established since the fundamentalist-modernist controversies of the previous generation. But when new evangelicals such as Carl Henry sought to recover nineteenth-century evangelical social concern, they found themselves straddling the fence between two well-established positions: fundamentalist social detachment and the liberal Social Gospel. Though in their writings new evangelicals claimed to be recovering the evangelical social conscience before the "Great Shift" in emphasis a half-century earlier, the main focus in this section will be on the new evangelical use of boundary language, noting the care evangelicals took in drawing differences between their own renewed social conscience, fundamentalism's isolation from social issues, and the secularized Social Gospel of religious liberalism. [10]

THE UNEASY EVANGELICAL SOCIAL CONSCIENCE

Interest in social action by postwar conservative Protestants was by no means consistent. The initial excitement that Carl Henry's *The Uneasy Conscience of Modern Fundamentalism* and the poignant articles of

Harold Ockenga[11] stirred in the late 1940s and early 1950s was not easily sustained.[12] Henry, however, remained a constant voice—at times the lone voice—of evangelical social concern.

In his *Uneasy Conscience,* Henry was "distressed by the frequent failure [of fundamentalism] to apply effectively [the great biblical verities] to crucial problems confronting the modern mind" (1947:preface). He was likewise bothered by fundamentalism's reluctance to address modern social ills, believing that the salvation message that orthodox Protestants preached was better able to meet the needs of modern society than the liberal message; "for there is not a problem of global consequence," he wrote, "but that . . . redemption is a relevant formula." Redemption, Henry argued, "is offered as the only adequate rest for world weariness, whether political, economic, academic, recreational. It stands in judgment upon all non-Christian solutions" (1947:42).

Fundamentalists, to be sure, could point to several relief agencies that they supported, but these did not represent ongoing interest in or an active program for social betterment, only "emergency type" action. As Henry pointed out, "the sin against which Fundamentalism has inveighed, almost exclusively, was individual sin rather than social evil." Indeed, "the Fundamentalist opposition to societal ills has been more vocal than actual" (1947:18,20,17). Social evil was thus a mass epidemic that fundamentalists only treated on a patient-by-patient basis.

This "spotty" approach to social concern was unacceptable to Henry, even inexcusable. "There is no room," Henry stated sharply, "for a gospel that is indifferent to the needs of the total man nor of the global man" (1947:42). Henry lamented the fact that fundamentalists had so divorced themselves from modern secular society that by 1940 their message had lost all relevance to the problems facing humanity. He summarized the sad state of conservative Protestant social action in this way:

> There is a growing awareness in Fundamentalist circles that, despite the orthodox insistence upon revelation and redemption, evangelical Christianity has become increasingly inarticulate about the social reference of the Gospel. The conviction mounts that the relationship of the church to world conditions must be reappraised, even if the

doctrinal limits are regarded as fixed within which solution is likely to be found (1947:26).

What is more, Henry said, persisting in his critique of fundamentalist social isolationism,

> Modern Fundamentalism does not explicitly sketch the social implications of its message for the non-Christian world; its does not challenge the injustices of the totalitarianisms, the secularisms of modern education, the evils of racial hatred, the wrongs of current labor-management relations, the inadequate bases of international dealings. It has ceased to challenge Caesar and Rome, as though in futile resignation and submission to the triumphant Renaissance mood. The apostolic Gospel stands divorced from a passion to right the world. The Christian social imperative is today in the hands of those who understand it in sub-Christian terms (1947:44-45).

But, Henry observed more hopefully, this situation could not continue for long; for "There is a rising tide of reaction in Fundamentalism today—a reaction born of an uneasy conscience and determined no longer to becloud the challenge of the Gospel to modern times" (1947:34).

Henry attributed much of fundamentalism's disinterest in social concern to its marked disapproval of the liberal social agenda, the Social Gospel. Henry strongly chided fundamentalists for their blanket disapproval of all programs for social uplift. Conservatives, Henry maintained, should not be opposed to social action simply because their liberal opponents championed social amelioration. Instead, "because of his opposition to evils [a fundamentalist] ought to lend his endorsement to remedial efforts in any context not specifically anti-redemptive, while at the same time decrying the lack of a redemptive solution" (1947:87).[13]

Though ambivalent about evangelicalism's relationship to liberalism, Henry still thought evangelicals should participate in social action. But even with this more liberal spirit, Henry appeared either unable or unwilling to approach social action from other than the traditional nineteenth-century revivalistic perspective. The salvation of souls, he believed, if properly directed, would readily translate into social revival. In this way, Henry urged that evangelicals should endeavor to keep both individual redemption and social renewal in balance. As Henry phrased it, "The evangelical task primarily is the preaching of the Gospel, in the interest of individual regeneration by the supernatural grace of God, in such a way that divine redemption can be recognized as the best solution of our problems, individual and social" (1947:88). Henry was convinced that if evangelicals could successfully blend individual and social emphases, then a Christian culture would naturally result. Accordingly, Henry's long search for balance between those poles is reflected in his subsequent books and articles, which touched on the need for evangelical social interest and involvement that did not stray from the orthodox Protestant concern for evangelism.

AN EVANGELICAL SOCIAL IMPERATIVE

Evangelicalism's newfound interest in this-worldly concerns was the inspiration for many of Henry's works. Not long after *The Uneasy Conscience,* Henry authored a two-part series for *Christian Life* magazine that touted "The Vigor of the New Evangelicalism" (1948a/b).

In these essays, Henry optimistically laid out his social agenda, a program anchored in nineteenth-century revivalism and its concern for establishing individual salvation as the vital force of social renewal. To some degree, nineteenth-century Protestantism succeeded in blending individual salvation and social amelioration (Smith 1957). This was undone by the turn-of-the-century liberal/fundamentalist split, and the two emphases were thereafter set in opposition. As Henry observed, "Whereas fundamentalism had abandoned this world as lost and under the judgment of God, liberals had lost interest in the world to come, the ultimate goal of redemption" (1948a:31). Henry's social vision reemphasized the preaching of individual salvation and individual social responsibility:

> The prophetic and the social messages find their major key in the regeneration of individual sinners by trust in the redemptive work of Christ. This one message, when once it enlists the total man in the regenerate life, orients him properly both to this world and to the next. Evangelicalism will find a new vitality, in the midnight hour of

the Occidental world, in a message that strikes the proper balance of history and superhistory (1948a:32).

The proper balance, then, was one that acknowledged both this-worldly and otherworldly concerns, a balance both fundamentalists and liberals were unable to achieve because of their differing orientations toward modern culture.

Almost ten years later, Henry, in a series of published lectures given at Northern Baptist Theological Seminary in Chicago, reaffirmed the new evangelical program that stressed the necessary tension between liberal this-worldly and fundamentalist otherworldly positions. Once again, Henry took aim at both positions, criticizing them for their mutual failure to balance their application of the gospel message to sinful individuals and to a fallen social order. As Henry asserted,

> Fundamentalism fails to elaborate principles and programs of Christian social action because it fails to recognize the relevance of the gospel to the social cultural sphere. Modernism defines Christian social imperatives in secular terms and uses the Church to reorganize unregenerate humanity. Its social sensitivity gave modernism no license to neglect the imperative of personal regeneration. Evangelistic and missionary priorities, on the other hand, gave fundamentalism no license to conceal the imperative of Christian social ethics (1957:72).

Even so, what one quickly discovers in Henry is that while he pleaded for balanced social action, he did not give himself over to the task of outlining a detailed plan for evangelicals to follow. In article after article Henry expressed his disappointment in both liberals and fundamentalists but left unfinished the work of constructing a workable agenda. His discussions remained at the level of abstraction and did not progress to implementation. To say this is not necessarily to be critical of Henry, who was, after all, refreshingly honest about evangelical failings. What it does suggest, however, is that Henry devoted much of his time to castigating fundamentalists and liberals, to defining the boundary between evangelical and non-evangelical social concern. As a result, he gave over little space to sketching out the kind of comprehensive programs for social betterment that he thought evangelicals needed to develop.

This search for balance between liberal and fundamentalist extremes is perhaps no better illustrated than in Henry's two-part article on "Perspectives for Social Action" (1959a/b), published while he was editor of *Christianity Today,* a post he held for over a decade. During his twelve-year tenure he vigorously argued for an evangelical social ethic that would not only redeem individuals but would transform society as well. In this particular article, Henry put forth his vision of a "Christian culture."

Henry began his discussion with the usual conservative critique of the liberal social program. Henry's criticisms were not against social interest but its overemphasis by liberal churchmen. Indeed, Henry placed social concern as a centerpiece of the Gospel of Jesus. As he pointed out, "Both Christianity's emphasis on justice and social relevance of redemptive religion throb through the pages of Scripture. Without this balanced approach, Christianity becomes anemic" (1959a:10). Henry was not chastising liberals for their interest in society *per se,* but for their reliance on human solutions to spiritual problems, as well as their overindulgence in social matters at the expense of the church's mission to redeem individual souls. As Henry charged, "The social gospel knowingly surrendered the personal gospel of Jesus Christ's substitutionary death and his supernatural redemption and regeneration of sinful men. Instead, it sought to transform the social order by grafting assertedly Christian ideals upon unregenerate human nature" (1959a:10). Moreover, continued Henry, "The social gospel became an *alternative* to the Gospel of supernatural grace and redemption. . . . Through the social gospel churches were given a task unstipulated by [Christ's] Great Commission. The new preoccupation perhaps came through neglect and at the expense of the Church's divinely appointed mission" (1959a:10).

Henry's critique of the liberal social agenda is similar to G. Brillenburg Wurth's assessment of America's "theological climate." Wurth credited the liberal "attempt to confront with the Gospel of Christ the problems of modern American life" as "itself worthy of respect," but he believed, as did Henry and other evangelicals, that this liberal social gospel had "resulted in great spiritual damage, because of its complete lack of resistance to the dominating spirit of the time"

(1957:11). Like Henry, Wurth was disturbed by liberalism's attempt to define Protestant social concern only in terms of the social gospel, thus discounting evangelical efforts as merely an aberration. As Wurth wrote, "What is characteristic of the social gospel is not so much the application of the gospel to social questions but rather the overwhelming emphasis placed on social problems by this gospel. The entire gospel is seen as a social and ethical totality: everything that does not fit into this framework is discarded "(1957:11).

Evangelicals did not want society at large to confuse liberal socialism for Protestantism's true redemptive mission in the world. Pressing their case with great fervor, evangelicals underscored their belief that the Gospel of Jesus was essentially a message of individual, not social, redemption. According to Henry, classical liberalism had moved Christianity away from its primary task of redemption toward its more secondary concern for the social order. The liberal claim that conservatives had failed to follow the social imperative of Jesus' salvific message was, in Henry's opinion, unfounded. In fact, Henry countered, it was liberalism that had departed from the Gospel of Jesus, the evangel that proclaimed that unless a person be "born again," he or she cannot be part of the kingdom of God.

In Henry's mind, the difference between evangelical and liberal social agendas was therefore patent: "it is clear that the religious experiment dating from Schleiermacher to Fosdick detoured Protestantism into the wilderness of modernity, and that the Great Tradition—the heritage of Moses and the prophets, and of Jesus and his apostles—was not really to be found there" (1959c:3). That is, according to Henry, conservative evangelicals, not liberals, had remained faithful to the "Great Tradition" of the Bible. Evangelicals might have believed that they held the "keys of the kingdom"(Ayer 1942:46), but Ayer's optimism and Henry's goading notwithstanding, they seemed content simply to hold those celestial keys tightly and not use them to unlock the redemptive power of the Gospel for the purpose of social regeneration. One is reminded of the classic statement of Harold Ockenga, who enthusiastically declared at Carnell's presidential inauguration,

> The new evangelicalism embraces the full orthodoxy of fundamentalism, but manifests a social consciousness and responsibility which was strangely absent from fundamentalism. The new evangelicalism

concerns itself not only with personal salvation, doctrinal truth and an eternal point of reference, but also with the problems of race, of war, of class struggle, of liquor control, of juvenile delinquency, of immorality, and of national imperialism. . . . The new evangelicalism believes that orthodox Christians cannot abdicate their responsibility in the social scene (1954c:4; cf., Ockenga 1958).

But all the grandiloquent pronouncements to the contrary, evangelicals were not, in the main, at the forefront of social issues. Indeed, the "uneasy conscience" of which Carl Henry spoke was itself a revealing phrase—a double entendre—indicating no small amount of ambivalence on the part of orthodox Protestants who appeared "uneasy" to enter the modern arena in order to put their social agenda into action. Evangelical ambivalence toward social engagement was perhaps one reason why their uneasy social conscience did not, in fact, translate into a workable social program.[14]

THE BOUNDARY DILEMMA OF NEO-ORTHODOXY

This final section considers the evangelical boundary response to Barthian neo-orthodoxy. The challenges neo-orthodoxy presented to evangelical leaders were similar to those of liberal ecumenism and the liberal social Gospel, namely, how to participate in the modern world without becoming liberals or modernists. More specifically, postwar evangelicals faced the dilemma of how to be both theologically sophisticated and intellectually respectable without surrendering their orthodox position. It would seem only natural that in distancing themselves from fundamentalist obscurantism, new evangelicals would move closer to the liberal camp. Their desire to engage the modern world and return evangelical theological discourse to a place of prestige and prominence within the intellectual and religious centers of American life made it necessary for evangelicals to seek more effective means toward that end.

In this section, as in those above, the primary concern will not be to explicate thoroughly the theological positions of the evangelicals. Rather, the focus will be to illustrate evangelical boundary concerns over the neo-orthodox threat posed by Karl Barth's own "evangelical" theology, by fitting those concerns into the larger portrait of the postwar American theological scene. In so doing, this section will argue two points: first, that evangelicals, who wanted not only to discredit liberalism but to press their case for a credible orthodox theology, showed early interest in neo-orthodoxy as a means through which to reassert their orthodox position and regain theological legitimacy; but, second, that because of its liberal assumptions, especially concerning the inspiration of the Bible, evangelicals could only go "part-way" with Barth's neo-orthodoxy (Bolich 1980 and Patterson 1983). Much to their dismay, evangelicals found in neo-orthodoxy a "hybrid" theology that, while promising theological sophistication and intellectual respectability, threatened evangelicalism's distinct boundary with liberal theology. As a result, the new evangelicals abandoned their original positive support for neo-orthodoxy, becoming as critical of it as they were of liberalism, if not more so.

EVANGELICAL THEOLOGICAL AMBIVALENCE

While the new evangelicals were almost as suspicious of liberals as their fundamentalist brethren were, being quick to denounce the National Council and the World Council and being less than complimentary of the liberal social vision, they were nevertheless interested in liberal scholarship. In fact, though they kept their distance from liberalism in most other endeavors, many evangelicals took it upon themselves to study liberal theological positions. What is more, not a few of the new evangelicals, after attending Wheaton College or some other fundamentalist institute or seminary, sought advanced study at major liberal institutions. Carl Henry, for example, received his Ph.D. from Boston University. George Ladd took a Ph.D. from Harvard University. Not to be outdone by his colleagues, E. J. Carnell earned two doctoral degrees at the same time: a Th.D. from Harvard Divinity School and a Ph.D. from Boston University. Later evangelicals would likewise follow this pattern (see Marsden 1987 and Nelson 1987). Their interest, however was not so much in liberal theology as in the advantages they believed a degree from a prestigious institution offered them. Evangelicals entered the lion's den of liberal learning to wrestle with its vicious beasts, hoping that they might emerge with greater credibility as orthodox scholars. They also hoped that by understanding liberal theology they might be in a better position to defend orthodoxy against modern thought. In neo-orthodoxy, which flourished during the post-war period, evangelicals thought that they had found a defensible position between fundamentalism and liberalism.

Historian Farley Butler underscored this point in his work on the new evangelicalism. Though writing on the influence of Billy Graham in the split between fundamentalists and new evangelicals, Butler summarized the theological objective of the evangelicals as basically the desire to develop a credible apologetic for evangelical orthodoxy. "Most [new evangelicals] looked forward to the restoration of ortho-doxy to a position of respectability inside the major denominations. They spoke confidently of the conservative swing in the churches, and produced analyses which exaggerated the similarity of dialectical theology [i.e., neo-orthodoxy] to evangelical orthodoxy. They felt orthodoxy must be maintained, but a less strident tone should be adopted for theological debate. They spoke of new approaches to theologians of other viewpoints, and strove earnestly to earn the respect of non-evangelical theologians" (Butler 1976:7-8).

This portrayal certainly holds true for Edward Carnell, professor and second president of Fuller Seminary, who, according to Rudolph Nelson, seemed to have spent much of his adult life trying desperately to escape the "stigmata of fundamentalism" (1987:16-27). Carnell believed that in order to gain respect for orthodoxy, evangelicals must first gain the respect of their liberal opponents. In his autobiography, Carl Henry, for example, recalled a September 1953 letter from Carnell in which he confided, "'There is a parochialism in evangelicalism from which I must withdraw. I trust that the fruit of this withdrawal will be a richness and breadth of comprehension that will serve as a new point of rallying for the evangelicals. . . . I want to command the attention of [Paul] Tillich and [John C.] Bennett; then I shall be in a better place to be of service to the evangelicals. We need prestige desperately'" (quoted in Henry 1986a:137). One sees in this letter Carnell's desire to fight for orthodoxy not by blindly repudiating liberalism but by adopting intel-lectually defensible positions that would command liberal attention and liberal respect. This desire seems to have been a central concern of new evangelical churchmen and theologians more generally.[15]

For instance, in his 1960 article in *Christianity Today* on the resurgence of conservative evangelicalism, Harold Ockenga spoke of the desire by evangelicals to be more open to liberals and to engage in greater dialogue. As Ockenga observed, "The younger orthodox scholars are repudiating the separatist position, have repented of the attitude of solipsism, have expressed a willingness to re-examine the problems facing the theological world, have sought a return to the theological dialogue and have recognized the honesty and Christianity of some who hold views different from their own in some particulars" (1960:13).

Twenty years later, Gregory Bolich also noted the growing interest among evangelicals in the late 1950s and early 1960s to engage liberalism. "Rather than separating themselves from the nonevangelical theological world, they welcomed open and honest dialog." Indeed, Bolich wrote, "The new evangelicals were active in bringing their message to the world by every means and in every way open to them" (1980:45).[16] This included, if not a concerted attempt at rapprochement with liberal theology, at least a desire to engage liberal theologians on a more neutral turf—the neo-orthodox playing field.

The development of an "orthodoxy" that garnered the respect of liberal theologians held out promise to many new evangelicals anxious for acceptance and recognition. But evangelicals did not find adopting neo-orthodox theological categories as easy as the above comments might suggest. Evangelicals remained cautious in their limited engagements with liberals and were likewise careful to observe the boundary between themselves and liberalism. As Marsden affirmed, "Attitudes toward neo-orthodoxy [became] an increasingly important issue as the postwar fundamentalist community was struggling to define its boundaries" (1987:111).

Interestingly, so long as liberalism remained "modernistic" in approach, evangelicals had not appeared threatened; the line between these two theological communities remained clear. Evangelicals could court liberals without much fear of confusing the two camps. However, with the introduction of so-called crisis theology, or neo-orthodoxy, into the American religious landscape during the 1930s and 1940s, the plot became more complicated. The twist in the "crisis theology" of Karl Barth and Emil Brunner was its attempt to reintroduce orthodox categories of thought into mainstream liberal circles (see Berkhof 1950 and Mueller 1957).

Indeed, though they came from opposite sides of the theological spectrum—evangelicalism, having begun at the orthodox end, moved "leftward," and neo-orthodoxy, having started from the liberal end, moved toward the orthodox pole—evangelical orthodoxy and neo-orthodoxy had similar goals. Both were attempting to moderate the excesses of their respective theological camps: neo-orthodoxy tempered the naive optimism of liberalism; evangelicals moderated the obscurantism of fundamentalism. There was therefore a natural and obvious attraction. But above all else, neo-orthodoxy, especially "Barthianism," was attractive to evangelical scholars because they believed it "provided a route for those who wished to avoid liberalism and at the same time find a theological position that was intellectually respectable" (Barr 1978:221-222).

The rub for evangelicals came when they slowly began to realize that in neo-orthodoxy they would be sharing too much common ground with liberalism. Though neo-orthodoxy sought to correct the excesses of liberalism by recasting Christian theology in orthodox categories, at the same time, it accepted the judgments of modern science and the canons of the historical-critical method. In short, "While clinging to many orthodox affirmations it refused to release some liberal convictions" (Bolich 1980:59).

What evangelicals had originally welcomed as a new form of orthodox theology soon presented evangelicals with an acute threat to orthodoxy itself. Here, it seemed, was a credible "orthodoxy," but an orthodoxy founded on liberal theological assumptions. Evangelicals discovered that they could not, in good conscience, align themselves with this apparent inconsistency. After only a brief courtship, the evangelicals broke off their developing interest in neo-orthodoxy and denounced it as liberal, modernist, and even treacherous. Neo-orthodoxy was too close to liberalism to be acceptable to most evangelicals, but near enough to orthodoxy that it posed a threat to evangelicalism's boundary with liberalism.

BARTHIAN NEO-ORTHODOXY

It is difficult to summarize so comprehensive a theological system as Barth's in this brief section. But for the purposes of this study, a few key points should suffice to make the evangelical boundary reaction against neo-orthodoxy more explicable.

The Swiss theologian Karl Barth began his long career in 1911 as minister of a small parish in the Swiss village of Safenwil. Though thoroughly schooled in German theology and the optimism of the liberal tradition, Barth was made increasingly uneasy by the destructive turn of world events in 1914. Shocked by the devastation and savage barbarity of World War I, Barth struggled to explain these global problems to his parishioners in his weekly sermons. He soon found that his liberal theological assumptions were ill-suited to speak directly and with certainty to the human situation. "Finding no help in theology," theologian William Hordern explained, "Barth turned to the Bible where he found a 'strange new world' that was more alive than the latest philosophy" (1986:131).

The result of Barth's turn to the Bible was the publication in 1919 of his famous commentary on St. Paul's Letter to the Romans. This monumental work catapulted Barth into the center of theological debate and unquestionably altered the shape of modern theology. Barth modestly compared this turn of events to "a man who was falling in the dark and reached out for support. To his surprise he found that he had caught a bell rope and the ringing of the bell had awakened the whole town" (Hordern 1986:132).

In essence, Barth's theology called on Christians everywhere to return to the foundation of their religion: the revelation of God to humanity in the Word of God, Jesus Christ. This proclamation, of course, sounded quite similar to what fundamentalists and evangelicals had been saying for decades, but evangelicals were no longer being heard by liberal churchmen. Barth, on the other hand, was lauded by many mainstream Protestants for his fresh and persuasive recasting of biblical theology. As James Barr recounted, "The polemic of neo-orthodoxy against liberal theology was infinitely more effective than that of traditional conservatism, because Barth and his associates, unlike conservative apologists, had thoroughly studied liberal theology and knew what it was" (1978:214).

Moreover, while Barth called Christians back to the Bible, he made a distinction between the Word of God *revealed* and the word of God *written:*[17]

> The revelation of God . . . was uniquely witnessed to in the Bible. The
> Bible, however, was not itself the revelation of God, but only a witness
> to that revelation. The Word of God was in the first place Christ
> himself, as witnessed to in the scriptures and preached in the church;
> in the second place the scriptures, in that they witness to Christ and
> are preached in the church; and in the third place the preaching of
> the church, in so far as it witnesses to Christ on the basis of the
> scriptures (Barr 1978:214).

This threefold scheme is an example of Barth's dialectical
approach to Christian revelation. Barth, ever given to paradoxical
language, held that similar to Christ, the Bible has both divine and
human aspects. Barth argued, however, that the admixture of human
and divine aspects does not imply that "parts of the Bible are divine
and parts are human" (Barr 1978:214). On the contrary, "the entire
Bible is human, subject to the strains and weaknesses of any human
product, but at the same time all of it is from God, in that it says
something that does not arise from human culture and is not
immanent within it" (Barr 1978:214-215). It is in this way that
Barth revealed his reliance on the methods of modern historical
criticism.

In his works, Barth seemed to be speaking the language of
orthodoxy. This resemblance to orthodox theology piqued new
evangelical interest. But Barth's paradoxical position—imbuing traditional orthodox concepts with liberal meaning—soon caused
evangelicals to become ambivalent. "At first the fundamentalists
were pleased with the rise of neo-orthodoxy," Louis Gasper related,
"because they believed the latter had exposed 'the utter barrenness
and inadequacies of modernism,' and had proved that the impact of
liberalism on American religious thought to be less than had been
supposed" (Gasper 1981:43). Indeed, as Barr wrote, "Neo-orthodoxy
was bound to be of interest to conservatives because it was, like their
own position, sharply opposed to liberalism" (1978:214). But, at the
same time, Barth was alien to the conservative world of American
evangelicals, especially his views on the inspiration of the Bible. As
Gasper explained, neo-orthodoxy "was not slavishly attached to the
literal details of traditional orthodoxy." What is more, though neo-

orthodoxy undercut modernist theology, it remained faithful to its scientific biblical hermeneutic. From a fundamental theological point of view, "This interpretation appeared to question the divine origin of the Bible." As a result, "The orthodox could not agree and began to denounce the neo-orthodox as a new expression of modernism" (Gasper 1981:43).[18]

Depending on how a person read Barth, he could be seen as either sympathetic to the case of conservative orthodoxy or merely a modified liberal. For instance, as Butler remarked, "New evangelicals stressed the contribution of neo-orthodoxy in dethroning liberalism, while fundamentalists saw in neo-orthodoxy a more dangerous form of liberalism" (1976:8). These conflicting positions help explain the ambivalence with which many new evangelical theologians greeted Barth.

As an example, Harold Ockenga found neo-orthodoxy "helpful to the current liberal-orthodox encounter," even crediting it with having "smashed modernism." As Ockenga related it, "Once a friend of mine was walking with Spiemann and Muller in Nuremberg. They were talking about Barth. Spiemann made the observation, 'The value of Barth is that he has smashed modernism, but he has not yet arrived at orthodoxy. He has done for us orthodox what we could never do for ourselves'" (Ockenga 1946:13).

This early gratitude toward Barth soon presented a problem for many evangelicals (who had originally expressed delight over neo-orthodoxy's relentless attack on the inadequacies of liberalism), for they later came to recognize that their positions would also come under intense fire by Barth. While evangelicals did appreciate Barth's desire to reclaim orthodoxy, they were still apprehensive, primarily because of neo-orthodoxy's tendency to blur the boundary between liberal and evangelical. In an ironic way, Barth was simultaneously too close to orthodoxy and too close to liberalism for evangelical comfort. In fact, many evangelicals argued, it was a more insidious form of liberalism because it pretended to be orthodox and evangelical, personifying the proverbial "wolf in sheep's clothing." Eventually, the evangelicals came to agree with the fundamentalists, but only after a closer encounter with neo-orthodoxy and its chief representative, Karl Barth.[19]

NEW EVANGELICAL
AMBIVALENCE TOWARD NEO-ORTHODOXY

While Harold Ockenga gave credit to neo-orthodoxy for having "smashed modernism," in the same article he strongly argued that neo-orthodoxy should nevertheless be classified with liberalism. "In many ways," he warned, "it may appear nearer to Christianity, but it is a more subtle perversion thereof than liberalism. It cuts from under the Christian certainty of the Word of God and leaves him to legislate for himself" (Ockenga 1946:13).[20] Other evangelical spokespersons followed Ockenga's lead, not only pointing out the liberal foundations of neo-orthodoxy, but also objecting to neo-orthodoxy's claim to having recovered orthodoxy. It galled evangelicals that Barth, like Fosdick, claimed to be "evangelical" yet held to liberal presuppositions about the inspiration of the Bible (see Van Til 1964).

Stephen Paine voiced similar ambivalence toward neo-orthodoxy, praising it for having discredited modernism while at the same time denouncing it for claiming to be orthodox. In his 1950 NAE conference presidential address, Paine referred to neo-orthodoxy as "a respectable and face-saving escape for the thorough-going humanistic religious liberal who is keen enough to discern that modernism is a dead end street." Neo-orthodox theologians such as Barth "have done for religious thinking a great service in exposing the utter barrenness and inadequacy of modernism." But, "In spite of the several important points at which it purports to depart from the position of modernism, neo-orthodoxy still belongs very definitely in the same category with this same religious liberalism" (Paine 1950:12). Edward Carnell, also writing in 1950, was in essential agreement with the assessment of neo-orthodoxy by Paine and many evangelical leaders. Neo-orthodoxy, Carnell flatly charged, "turns out to be but an extension of the fallacy of modernism" (1969:53).

Likewise, G. Brillenburg Wurth, an evangelical scholar at the Kampen Theological Seminary in the Netherlands, warned his fellow evangelicals of the dangers inherent in neo-orthodox theology. As he cautiously observed, "Many hope that neo-orthodoxy will provide the basis of a future ecumenical theology. As a matter of fact, neo-orthodoxy contains something which makes it appropriate for this purpose. It is preeminently a theology of synthesis." But, noting its more specific threat to evangelicalism, Wurth then remarked, "The chasm between orthodoxy and Liberalism appears to be bridged in a genial manner. Basic evangelical sounds are heard and what offends modern man's world view and religious autonomy [are] discarded" (Wurth 1957:13).

Similarly, Carl Henry, whose pen seemed never to run dry, took up the challenge Barthian neo-orthodoxy posed to evangelical ortho-doxy's distinct boundary with liberalism. Though he credited neo-orthodoxy with having "vindicated" the "doctrines that fundamental-ists upheld in the controversy with liberalism" (1957c:55), Henry argued that "it would be an overstatement to imply that in the recovery of these doctrinal emphases Barth and the neo-orthodox theologians return in all essentials to an historic evangelical exposition" (1957c:55).

Henry hesitated to speak of an evangelical "debt" to Barth for having slain the liberal/modernist hydra. In fact, Henry appeared skeptical about Barth's "move" toward orthodoxy. "Doubtless," Henry guardedly remarked, "Barth in a crucial [hour] strategically exposed the inner weaknesses of classic liberalism to its own constituency. Doubtless he raised long-neglected evangelical doctrines to a position of earnest theological importance and study. On the other hand, his present theological position revolts against elements in both Reforma-tion and biblical theology" (Henry 1957c:55). That is, while Henry did not question Barth's important contribution to the restoration of orthodox theology, he was not convinced that Barth had returned to the biblical theology of the Apostles and the Reformation fathers from which Barth believed liberals and modernists had departed.[21]

In an editorial published the next year in *Christianity Today*, Henry continued to press his attack on Barth's seemingly unabashed liberal views. Before the arrival of neo-orthodoxy, wrote Henry, the theologi-cal landscape was distinctly divided between liberal and conservative terrain. The line that separated these groups was the authority of the Bible. "On the modernist side," observed Henry, "it was the rejection of any absolute theology that opened the door to creedal tolerance and theological relativism. On the evangelical side, it was the exaltation of the principle of scriptural revelation that issued in firm defense of a revealed theology" (Henry 1958:20). But, Henry continued, "the *lines of separation* dimmed." There appeared to be some movement between positions. "Some modernists clung to fragments of New Testament teaching . . . with absolute devotion. And some popularizers of fundamentalism . . . encouraged certain views . . . which brought conservative positions into measurable disrepute" (Henry 1958:20, emphasis added). Enter neo-orthodoxy, Henry intimated, whose paradoxical language exemplified this moderating shift within liberalism, threatening the established boundary between orthodox and modernist positions.

Henry's next point appears to be the key to understanding his decided distrust of so-called Barthian evangelicalism. "The historic *dividing line* between evangelical and modernist approaches remained quite unobscured," Henry charged, "until neo-supernaturalism [i.e., neo-orthodoxy] arose to assail the classic liberal view and to profess a return to the theology of the Reformers. This neo-supernaturalism, or dialectical theology, has proved itself to be a midway haven for mobile modernists and discontented evangelicals" (Henry 1958:20, emphasis added).

Henry's conclusion is even more pointed. "Since the infection of religious thought by this medial theology," he asserted, "ambiguity and confusion has resulted from the indiscriminatory practice of divesting the vocabulary of theology of its sacred biblical and historical meanings, and imparting a modern glow to such concepts as original sin, the fall, atonement, second coming, revelation and inspiration." As a result, "Spokesmen today do not even hesitate to misappropriate the labels of 'evangelical,' 'conservative,' and 'fundamentalist.'" Clearly, Henry concluded, "The historic divide, which had once been *fixed,* is now threatened by *fluid* doctrinal definitions" (Henry 1958:20, emphasis added). Henry's concern, then, though eloquently and forcefully couched in theological language, was fundamentally a concern for the maintenance of a clear, unambiguous boundary defining the uniqueness of evangelical orthodoxy as an expression of true biblical Protestantism—an orthodoxy not discredited by fundamentalism, not tainted by modernism.

Similarly, Bernard Ramm, in an article entitled "The Continental Divide in Contemporary Theology," offered some suggestions to evangelicals "for locating the dividing line between biblical theology and modern deviations" (1965:14). Ramm proposed to give evangelicals "criteria . . . for finding this divide in theology" (1965:15). As Henry had done, Ramm likewise divided the theological landscape into two opposing camps, using orthodox beliefs, among other criteria, as his guide and illustrating further the new evangelical boundary concern over neo-orthodoxy and its blurring of the conservative/liberal divide.[22] Ramm's landscape is a familiar one to new evangelicals: "On one side of the continental divide in contemporary theology stand the orthodox; on the other stand the modernists and liberals in their common rejection of supernatural salvation" (Ramm 1965:15). But in his scheme, neo-orthodoxy falls in the middle, or as Ramm cleverly punned, "in the crack." As Ramm put it,

> Barth and Brunner have a theology of cracks! In that Barth stresses revelation as the personal presence of God, God as subject, as encounter and not as knowledge, his view is in the Ritschlian tradition and therefore is modernist. In that he stresses the objectivity of revelation in the Incarnation and the authoritative witness to revelation in Holy Scripture, he assents to revelation as truth. Thus his view of revelation is in the crack *between* modernism and orthodoxy (1965:15, emphasis added).

Thus, to summarize this lengthy discussion, what we find is that while in the decades following World War II, evangelicals were still suspicious of liberal Protestant theology, they were to some degree quite eager to engage liberals in selectively open theological dialogue. In their desire to shed their label as theological obscurantists, new evangelical theologians at first interpreted the rise of neo-orthodoxy as a "godsend," a bridge by which evangelicals hoped to achieve theological acceptability within the religious mainstream. But as evangelicals came into greater contact with neo-orthodoxy, they soon realized that although it claimed to be orthodox, even "evangelical," neo-orthodoxy was still quite liberal by comparison. In the end, evangelicals got cold feet; they could not fully embrace neo-orthodoxy because in mediating liberal and conservative theological positions it threatened to blur one of the major distinctions by which evangelicals had come to define themselves: they were not liberals. "It seems to me," wrote William Fletcher in his 1962 book, *The Moderns,* "that precisely because his thought runs so close to the position of mainstream Christianity, Barth represents the most formidable threat to the Church today" (quoted in Bolich 1980:59-60).

The boundary dilemma of postwar American evangelicalism arose from its efforts to enter modern culture without also becoming modernist or liberal in its approaches to Christian unity through cooperation, social amelioration through direct involvement, and intellectual respectability through theological refinement. These three topical episodes aptly illustrate that the boundary between groups is most in evidence when interaction with members of rival groups threatens to erase or blur the distinctions between the groups. Evangelicalism's announced desire to reenter the modern world after decades of fundamentalist isolation was greatly tempered by ambivalence toward modern culture and efforts to define ecumenical, social, and theological interests as *not* liberal. In the end, rather than put forth a workable program that capitalized on their youthful and energetic vision for an orthodoxy that was socially and theologically vital, evangelicals spent most of their energies reinforcing the distinct boundary between themselves and their "modernist" rivals.

CHAPTER SIX

The End of the New Evangelical Coalition, 1965-1990

BY THE TIME THE NATIONAL ASSOCIATION OF EVANGELICALS celebrated its twentieth anniversary in 1962, the postwar evangelical coalition had succeeded in defining itself as neither fundamentalist nor liberal. Indeed, by 1965, the evangelicals could rightfully speak of three main ideological movements within American Protestant Christianity. After 1965, however, the boundary dynamics that had defined postwar evangelicalism turned inward as new evangelicals of the first generation gradually and reluctantly lost control over the direction of their programs and various initiatives designed to revive Protestant orthodoxy. A new generation of evangelicals had begun to emerge from within the movement and with it a new agenda for evangelical effectiveness in the modern world. Interestingly, the issues that had brought conservative Protestants together as a greater evangelical coalition became the very issues that divided them: the new theological sophistication and cultural respectability, the quickened social conscience, and ecumenical revival.

During this time, the initial optimism with which many evangelicals greeted the 1960s rapidly faded as they watched the evangelical coalition slowly break up into a number of competing factions. As George Marsden observed, "by 1967 . . . it was becoming impossible to regard

American evangelicalism as a single coalition with a more or less unified and recognized leadership. In part the reason for this was negative, the result of internal crisis. The core ex-fundamentalist movement that the neo-evangelicals hoped to speak for was splitting apart" (1989:70).

Indeed, as Marsden further noted, "the transdenominational movement to reform fundamentalism was thus irreparably split over a combination of political and doctrinal issues. 'Neo-evangelicals' were so divided among themselves that the term lost its meaning. By the late 1970s, no one . . . could claim to stand at the center of so divided a coalition" (1989:71; cf., Marty 1977:196). Ironically, the unraveling of this coalition came just as the first generation of reforming evangelicals achieved its greatest and long-sought-for successes and established evangelical religion as a reputable force for orthodoxy in American religion. This final chapter will briefly examine the fragmentation of the new evangelical coalition in the 1960s and 1970s and the continuing definitional dilemmas it experienced into the 1990s.

FADING POSTWAR EVANGELICAL OPTIMISM

After the success of the 1966 World Congress on Evangelism, which was organized by the staff of *Christianity Today* in coordination with Billy Graham and held in West Berlin, Carl Henry wrote optimistically about evangelicalism's potential for further cooperative action in his ironically titled book, *Evangelicals at the Brink of Crisis* (1967). In this book, Henry outlined a number of ambitious initiatives that he believed evangelicals could put forward to great success in the wake of the Berlin Congress's revitalizing spirit. Caught up in the fervor of the Congress's impassioned message of far-ranging worldwide revival, Henry enthusiastically reported to his fellow conservatives: "Evangelical Christianity has not only received new prominence . . . but it has also gained new perspective and promise for the future" (Henry 1967:1). Henry could hardly contain his exuberance. "Not only is evangelical Christianity 'here to stay,'" he effused, "but [it] is obviously on the move again. It is making plans for winning men to Christ on a global basis. Its challenge speaks to modern man at every level, in this *intellectual* and *social* existence no less than his *religious* outlook" (1967:6, emphasis added).

But in little less than a decade, Henry was no longer as sanguine. The postwar evangelical coalition had come on hard times. Henry, who had been at the center of the postwar evangelical initiatives, found the new and even more socially and theologically progressive generation of "green edges" (as Henry called them), or "young evangelicals" (as Quebedeaux dubbed them in 1974), restless and, to some extent, unbridled in their enthusiasm for greater reform. Whereas some decades earlier Henry and his colleagues had criticized their elders for their theological stodginess, petty dogmatism, and religious fissiparousness, this new progressive generation now held *them* in contempt. The new evangelical coalition was itself "at the brink of crisis." The movement now seemed to be moving without the old guard, if not altogether beyond them.[1]

Indeed, Henry's little book, *Evangelicals in Search of Identity* (1976) captured the frustration and dismay of this earlier generation of new evangelical reformers, whose own coalition appeared to unravel before them even as they believed they had secured its success. As Henry noted, "the evangelical lion is nonetheless slowly succumbing to confusion about its own identity. The cohesion that American evangelicals had shown in the sixties has been fading in the seventies through multiplied internal disagreements and emerging counterforces" (1976:22). Henry discussed the connection of his works *At Brink of Crisis* and *In Search of Identity* in the foreword to the latter. In a great way, the spirit of these works differed so dramatically—as Henry's excitement about the future gave way to apprehension of the present—that *In Search of Identity* might well have bore the subtitle "Reflections of a Troubled Evangelical Soul." To quote Henry at length:

> In *Evangelicals at the Brink of Crisis* [1967] . . . I expressed the personal conviction that "the next ten years—the decade between now and the end of 1975—are critical ones for both conciliar ecumenism and evangelical Christianity. If conciliar ecumenism continues to repress the evangelical witness, and prevents it from coming to formative ecumenical influence, then conciliar ecumenism can only bog down into a retarded form of Christianity" [1967:110]. I think the adverse fortunes of conciliar ecumenism in the last decade supply an eloquent commentary on this warning. . . . But my observation did not stop there. "And," I continued, "if evangelical Christians do not join heart

to heart, will to will and mind to mind across their multitudinous fences, and do not deepen their loyalties to the Risen Lord of the Church, they may well become—by the year 2000—a wilderness cult in a secular society with no more public significance than the ancient Essenes in their Dead Sea caves" [1967:110-111]. This present series of Footnotes emerged because I think that both the Watergate era without and the *mounting evangelical dissension within* suggest that we are farther along the bleak road to those lonely caves than many evangelicals realize (1976:16, emphasis added).

Throughout *Evangelicals in Search of Identity,* a small collection of short essays that were originally conceived as "Footnotes" articles for *Christianity Today* (of which he was its first editor from 1956 to 1968), Henry recounted the grandness with which the new evangelicals broke onto the religious scene. "Twenty-five years ago," he mused, "there were signs that the long-caged lion would break its chains and roar upon the American scene with unsuspected power. The evangelical movement's mounting vitality baffled a secular press, beguiled by ecumenical spokesmen for liberal pluralism into regarding conservative Christianity as a fossil-cult destined to early extinction. While modernist disbelief and neoorthodox universalism scotched the indispensability of conversion, the Graham evangelistic crusades demonstrated anew the gospel's regenerating power" (1976:19).

Those had been heady days, Henry recalled. All seemed well as evangelical initiatives took the religious left by storm and gave testimony to the vitality of orthodox Protestant faith not witnessed to by separatist fundamentalists (see Fea 1994). Indeed, success fed success. But by the mid 1970s, a growing sense of discouragement, fed by cultural and political miscalculations as well as by internal wrangling over doctrinal points, overshadowed evangelicalism's earlier achievements. Evangelical initiative wavered. "While he is still on the loose, and still sounding his roar," Henry observed more wanly, "the evangelical lion is nonetheless slowly succumbing to an *identity crisis*. The noteworthy cohesion that American evangelicals gained in the sixties has been fading in the seventies through multiple internal disagreements and emerging counterforces" (1976:22, emphasis added).

Henry then set out "to assess the crumbling of evangelical unity" (1976:24), pulled as it was in many directions by various groups and individuals who claimed to represent or to speak for evangelical Protestantism. This changing dynamic, he pondered, was not all bad news, for "despite a slowdown in initiative and a crumbling of unity in the last ten years, American evangelicalism has nonetheless witnessed some noteworthy positive developments" (1976:33).

Henry's candid appraisal of evangelicalism was prefigured some-what obliquely in Yale Divinity professor Paul L. Holmer's essay on "Contemporary Evangelical Faith," published in David Wells and John Woodbridge's 1975 assessment of contemporary American evangeli-calism, *The Evangelicals*. As Holmer observed,

> In a peculiar but hearty way, most American evangelicals, amid their cantankerousness and splitting up over doctrine and practice, have also not quite succeeded in being respectable. They look marginal if you are very churchly; they appear intolerant if you are ecumenical; they seem antiintellecutal just when everything looks systematic and about to be settled. But my point is that they have kept the mood of conventicles, the mood of Christianity being a minority movement, alive amid their erstwhile success (1977:88).[2]

That said, evangelical disunity, returning once more to Henry's ap-praisal, was nothing to cheer about. "Notwithstanding the evidence of ongoing vitality," Henry remarked soberly, "the evangelical movement shows disturbing signs of dissipating its energies and of forfeiting its initiative" (1976:41).

Perhaps the most enervating of these concerns for the evangelical coalition was the increasingly open conflict over the inspiration and authority of the Bible. This dramatic episode came to be known as the "Battle for the Bible," after *Christianity Today* editor Harold Lindsell's 1976 best-selling bombshell exposé of liberal views in evangelical schools and among some of its most notable theologians.[3] Indeed, the fight among postwar evangelicals over biblical inerrancy, the centerpiece of postwar orthodox Protestant identity and the traditional dividing point between liberals and conservatives, vividly illustrates the breaking up of the new evangelical coalition. While during the 1940s and 1950s concerns over the inspiration and authority of the Bible were never far from the surface, this issue eventually erupted into the open in the 1960s. It emerged from among the ranks of the younger generation of evangelical scholars who were schooled in the methods of modern biblical criticism, who were poised to inherit the mantle of leadership, and who were positioned to define the evangelical social, political, and theological agenda well into the twenty-first century.

A PRELUDE TO WAR WITHIN THE EVANGELICAL COALITION

For some time, evangelicals had been seeking intellectual respectability by taking advanced degrees at more liberal schools. The usual route for evangelicals, typically of the Baptist and Reformed branches, was to take their first degree at an evangelical or fundamentalist college such as Westmont or Wheaton and then to go on to study at a more prestigious divinity school such as Harvard, Yale, or Boston, or to go overseas to Britain, Germany, or Switzerland. But advanced study at prestigious liberal seminaries and universities eventually took its toll on evangelical doctrinal cohesiveness as the new generation freely imbibed liberal theological assumptions and began to reframe distinctive doctrinal points from more progressive conservative categories. This shift was no better evident than in the way evangelicals dealt with the issue of higher criticism and the problems of the reliability of the Bible, most especially in the movement of many of the younger generation of faculty members of the Fuller Theological Seminary toward more theologically respectable and intellectually defensible positions. To be sure, the disruption this shift caused within the ranks of its faculty was by no means small as these differing biblical assumptions emerged during Fuller Seminary's search for a new president in 1962 and 1963 (see Marsden 1987:200-219). This episode, though seemingly an isolated event, provides a vivid example of the struggles evangelicals faced generally as they attempted to define the acceptable limits of theological diversity within their larger coalition.

For a number of years, Fuller Seminary had been defending itself against charges by fundamentalists such as Carl McIntire, John Rice, and John Walvoord that, in order to gain acceptance as peers at the theological round table with liberals, its faculty had willingly made doctrinal and ecclesiastical concessions to liberalism.[4] Indeed, many fundamentalists charged that Fuller's most recent president, Edward J. Carnell, showed contempt for fundamentalism in a published work that came perilously close to discarding the verbal inspiration of the Bible for the sake of theological dialogue (Rice 1959; cf., Carnell 1959:95-98, 121-128). But while one might expect that such concessions would naturally exacerbate the separation between evangelicals and fundamentalism, the doctrinal modifications these evangelicals offered, however modest, also set Fuller evangelicals at ideological odds with one another, effectively splitting its faculty into increasingly hostile cliques.

The issue came to a decisive and divisive point during the faculty's ten-year planning conference, held December 1-3, 1962, at which the faculty planned to select a new president.[5] Harold Lindsell, a founding faculty member and then–vice president of Fuller, and many of the older members of the faculty, pushed for stronger enforcement of the Seminary's statement on biblical inerrancy. Lindsell might well have become Fuller's next president had not the events of that weekend persuaded many of the more conservative members of the faculty to abandon Fuller for more biblically fundamental and doctrinally propitious places at which to pursue their teaching and research. In the end, the remaining faculty rallied around David A. Hubbard as its choice for president. Hubbard, a Fuller graduate who had studied at St. Andrews University, was at that time professor of Biblical Studies at Westmont College in Santa Barbara. In addition to his excellent credentials and irenic spirit, Hubbard also held a modified view of biblical inspiration (Marsden 1987:208-219). Throughout what would be a thirty-year tenure, Hubbard moved Fuller Seminary theologically to the center (Melton, et al., 1997:148-149).

While Fuller Seminary became the symbol of the new evangelicalism's more progressive direction, its detractors lost no time vilifying its remaining faculty as liberal and apostate. George Marsden pointed to the shifting alliances within the evangelical coalition that the turbulence of this transitional event signaled. "The episode," he wrote, "illustrated the way in which the doctrine of inerrancy was coming to be used in the new evangelical coalition. Having broken with fundamentalism, the conservative wing of the new evangelicals needed a meaningful test to limit how far reforms of fundamentalism might go. Inerrancy could play that role" (1987:227).

Beyond that, the Fuller episode also served as an indicator of the growing division within the new evangelical movement more gener-

ally.[6] For instance, only a few short years after this event, Harold
Ockenga, who had sat uncomfortably through the Fuller transition as
its interim president, convened an international conference of evangelical scholars at Gordon College in Wenham, Massachusetts, in June
1966. Ockenga held this conference largely because, as he put it, "it
[had become] evident that there were two views of Scripture held by
evangelicals," a "bifurcation that began to manifest itself" in earlier
conferences and meetings of evangelicals (Lindsell 1976:11, foreword). In the end, the conference proved disappointing as many
fundamentalists and evangelicals argued over the issue of inerrancy
without coming to any major points of agreement. The conference did
not bring the peace within the new evangelical coalition that Ockenga
had desired but revealed instead that the gulf between progressives
and conservatives was much greater than most evangelicals had
realized. Not long after this, these emerging oppositions coalesced into
two noticeable camps: moderate and progressive evangelicals, represented by Fuller Seminary and its constituents; and conservative
evangelicals, represented by the views of *Christianity Today* and
centered at Trinity Evangelical Divinity School in Chicago, where
many of the older Fuller faculty members had taken teaching positions
(Lindsell 1976 and Marsden 1987). Within the next ten years,
especially during 1976, the reputed "Year of the Evangelicals" (*Newsweek,* October 25, 1976:69), disagreements among progressive and
conservative evangelical scholars would erupt as the cause célèbre
within the evangelical world.

THE EVANGELICAL "BATTLE FOR THE BIBLE"

From 1966 to 1976, conservative evangelicals such as Harold Lindsell,
who had succeeded Carl Henry as editor of *Christianity Today* in 1968,
watched from the sidelines as the progressives took hold of the banner
of the new evangelical coalition and, as conservatives saw it, redefined
its mission and message. Then, in 1976, the first major barrage of
criticism from within came when Harold Lindsell published his
scathing broadside against the progressive evangelical positions in his
aptly titled pro-inerrancy diatribe, *The Battle for the Bible* (1976). Later
billed as "the book that rocked the evangelical world," *The Battle for*

the Bible, and its sequel, *The Bible in the Balance* (1979), set the acceptable limits of new evangelical reform as well as the boundaries of evangelicalism itself. In his initial chapter, Lindsell issued a call to arms that harkened back to the modernist controversies of half a century before: "A great battle rages today around biblical infallibility among evangelicals. To ignore the battle is perilous. To come to grips with it is necessary. To fail to speak is more than cowardice; it is sinful. There comes a time when Christians must not keep silent, when to do so is far worse than to speak and risk being misunderstood or disagreed with. If we Christians do not learn from history, we are bound to repeat its mistakes" (1976:26).

For Lindsell, evangelical faith is defined as that which holds firmly to an orthodox view of the divine origins of the Christian scriptures. The Bible is not simply a word from God but it is the very word of God in written form and is therefore without error and beyond human scrutiny. Every orthodox thought and every right action logically follows from this central and fundamental Christian tenet. Those who do not affirm biblical inerrancy, Lindsell argued pointedly, are no longer orthodox and can no longer legitimately claim to be fully "evangelical." As Lindsell put it, "It is my conviction that a host of evangelicals who no longer hold to inerrancy are still relatively evangelical. I do not for one moment concede, however, that in a technical sense anyone can claim the evangelical badge once he has abandoned inerrancy" (1976:210).

In addressing the issue of inerrancy, Lindsell not only appeared to be setting a boundary to prevent the further "leeward" drift of the evangelical coalition, but he also seemed to be separating out progressives who had already "gone over" from the main body of conservatives, so that they might not further influence the movement. As historian George Marsden reported, "Harold Lindsell and his confederates were determined that the party represented by Fuller would not take over evangelicalism as a whole." Marsden then continued, supplying helpful insight into Lindsell's motives for writing,

> The internal struggle at Fuller [during the 1960s] was thus extended
> to a wider struggle for dominance in the transdenominational move-
> ment. The party that hoped to control that movement, centered at
> *Christianity Today* and Trinity Evangelical Divinity School, was

deeply committed to inerrancy as the touchstone of the faith. They also saw that this doctrine could be used effectively both as a test by which to distinguish between two major parties of former fundamentalists and as a banner under which to rally wider conservative support (1987:279).

Historically, Lindsell pointed out, those who fell outside the limits of orthodox faith were excluded from the community of the faithful. Should this, he queried, be no less true for the so-called progressives? Despite this challenge, Lindsell, in the end, did not appear all that eager to exclude progressives over the issue of inerrancy but left some room for differences over the matter. "At least one other question must be decided also," he explained. "Is the term 'evangelical' broad enough in its meaning to include within it believers in inerrancy and believers in an inerrancy limited to matters of faith and practice? At this stage, no one is apt to argue that the refusal to accept inerrancy means that the person who does this is outside the Christian faith, i.e., saved" (1976:139). Although his book turned the evangelical camp into a doctrinal battleground, Lindsell, to change the metaphor, actually intended his exposé more as a diagnosis of a diseased body than as a prescription for radical surgery to remove an infectious growth. That is, though Lindsell asserted that those who believe in an errant Bible are an infection that grows and gradually spreads throughout the body of orthodoxy (1976:185), his aim was not to purge progressives from the evangelical camp but to reveal their dangerous error. In so doing, Lindsell hoped to win them back to orthodoxy.

However, the response by progressive evangelicals was predictably cool. Many believed Lindsell was overstating the issue in an effort to expose and expel progressives. In fact, a number of progressives believed that Lindsell's book was merely his declaration of war on his former colleagues and friends at Fuller Seminary whom he now believed to be in error. After all, had not the progressives eased him out of his position as vice president of Fuller Seminary in 1963, putting him on the outside of a movement of which he had once been a central figure? (see Marsden 1987:223).

By the late 1970s, Lindsell was fervently crusading against progressives within the evangelical coalition, but with little success. Indeed, much to the displeasure of conservative evangelicals, not only did the progressives refuse to mend their liberal-leaning ways, they were likewise gaining influence within the greater evangelical movement. Lindsell's first diatribe failed to bring the progressives to repentance. Their consciences, Lindsell might have argued, were "seared as with a hot iron" (1 Timothy 4:2).

Then, three years after his initial cannonade, Lindsell once again took careful aim at the progressives, sending another volley against their positions. In his next book, *The Bible in the Balance* (1979), Lindsell returned to the touchstone that was beginning to separate conservative evangelicals from progressives. "Today," Lindsell wrote, "an increasing number of evangelicals do not wish to make inerrancy a test of fellowship even though ordinary consistency requires an evangelical to believe in it" (1979:303). But, Lindsell observed, there are many who would prefer to drop inerrancy as a central defining characteristic of evangelical faith, believing that strict adherence to such an article of faith would be much too divisive. In fact, Lindsell noted, there are some who say that "one does not cease to be an evangelical so long as he retains belief in all the basic doctrines of the faith except inerrancy, provided he believes the Bible to be the infallible or inerrant rule of faith and practice [rather than inerrant in matters of history or science as well]" (1979:308). This subtle difference, Lindsell countered, was less than tolerable. An evangelical—whether conservative or progressive—cannot cease to believe what is central to historic evangelical faith and remain "evangelical." "It seems to me," Lindsell asserted, "that those who think the term *evangelical* can be applied to those who deny inerrancy in secondary matters [e.g., science and history] but affirm inerrancy in matters of faith and practice [e.g., beliefs and behavior] cannot honestly be called *evangelical*" (1979:308). As Lindsell charged further,

> some who think a man can be an inconsistent *evangelical* so long as he holds to inerrancy in matters of faith and practice, also think that Jesus taught that all the Bible is inerrant. Surely if the testimony of Jesus with respect to Jonah [who, by tradition, lived unharmed in the "belly of a whale" for three days] is not binding, why should not Jesus' testimony with regard to Scripture be disregarded too? So I must declare again that whoever denies inerrancy also denies the witness of Jesus Christ to the whole Bible. Those who deny the witness of

Jesus Christ entertain an erroneous Christology. How can they be considered evangelicals? (1979:309).[7]

So as not to be mistaken, Lindsell then reiterated his point with a rhetorical question: "Is he who denies inerrancy only an inconsistent evangelical or by this denial does he forfeit his right to the evangelical label?" (1979:311). He forfeits his right to the label, Lindsell answered, and for this reason:

Inerrancy does not stand by itself. It is inextricably linked to the person of Christ. To deny inerrancy is to deny what Jesus believed, taught, and practiced. It is a denial of the lordship of Jesus Christ. And I do not think that he who denies the lordship of Jesus can be an evangelical (1979:311).

But Lindsell was quick to emphasize that while these progressive scholars could not legitimately claim the mantle of evangelical orthodoxy, it did not necessarily mean that they should no longer be regarded as Christians, so long as they still "affirmed the other basics of evangelical faith" (1979:312).

This last comment might strike a person as curious because Lindsell seemed to be backing away just a little from his hard line on inerrancy. What could Lindsell have meant by implying that a person can deny the inerrancy of the Bible and remain a "Christian" but, at the same time, forfeit his or her claim to the "evangelical" label? It appears that, for Lindsell—and perhaps other evangelical spokespersons—the theological content of the word "evangelical" functioned as a sociological as well as a theological or ideological boundary between those inside and those outside the evangelical community. Lindsell's next point lends support to this observation and to this boundary interpretation of the inerrancy issue and of postwar evangelical history more generally: "There may be some who do not claim to be evangelicals who have saving faith in Christ. . . . But that is not what I am discussing here. I am talking about the proper use of the term *evangelical* both with respect to its meaning and to its application in the Christian Church" (1979:312).

In the end, this doctrinal dustup never became the theological donnybrook that it had threatened to become. Apart from a few picks and skirmishes, to change the metaphor, little else resulted from Lindsell's campaign against progressives within the ranks of the evangelical coalition. Still, there is a more important point to be gleaned from this episode, one that underscores the usefulness of reading the development of postwar evangelicalism in terms of its boundary defining dynamics. According to George Marsden's insightful history of Fuller Seminary, itself a microcosmic example of the evangelical boundary dilemma, the function of inerrancy was to curb reform among the more progressive wing of the evangelical coalition. As Marsden explained, while the inerrancy issue served the purpose of separating out conservatives from progressives at a theological level, "the doctrine also functioned [to define what is evangelical] at ecclesiastical and para-ecclesiastical institutional levels" (1987:227). In addition, the inerrancy issue "was logically connected with the crucial question of authority, which was central to the debates with liberals and secularists. Since fundamentalist evangelicals usually lacked authoritative church bodies, inerrancy was an effective tool for drawing a boundary for the movement. Nor was this boundary arbitrary: those who would not affirm the conservative version of inerrancy were usually progressive on the other issues as well" (1987:227).

While the inerrancy issue effectively drew a boundary between conservatives and progressives "theologically," a number of other concerns created further tensions within the new evangelical coalition that served to shatter the cohesiveness of the movement, eventually crippling its effectiveness. Indeed, at just the moment when conservative evangelicalism was making its presence known and its influence felt in American society, the postwar evangelical coalition fragmented, its various constituent parts dividing into numerous competing subgroups.[8]

THE EMERGING BOUNDARY WITHIN EVANGELICALISM

In November 1980, *The Christian Century* published a piece by Carl Henry in its "How My Mind Has Changed" series. In his article, Henry bared his soul to the broader Christian community. Though he did not air his grievances fully, Henry did reveal his frustration over the lost opportunities for greater evangelical influence in fostering spiritual revival and social reform due to its organizational division and ideological dissent. Wrote Henry, "during the 1960s I somewhat romanced the possibility that a vast evangelical alliance might arise in the United States to coordinate effectively a national impact in evangelism, education, publication and sociopolitical action. . . . By the early 1970s the prospect of a massive evangelical alliance seemed annually more remote, and by mid-decade it was gone" (1980:1060). Indeed, as Henry noted somewhat ruefully, "at the very time national newsmagazines spoke of 'the year of the evangelical', *Christianity Today* [the largest circulating Christian newsmagazine in the conservative Protestant world] turned more inward than outward by channeling all theological issues into the inerrancy debate" (1980:1061).

According to Henry, one reason for this lack of cohesion was the various new coalitions of evangelicals that emerged from the ruins of the new evangelicalism. As Henry observed, "Numerous crosscurrents now vex almost every effort at comprehensive evangelical liaison. At present no single leader or agency has the respect, magnetism or platform to summon all divergent elements to conference. Evangelical differences increasingly pose an *identity crisis*" (1980:1061, emphasis added). Indeed, Henry affirmed, though the debate over inerrancy and the authority of the Bible was but one example of evangelical coalitional disintegration writ large, it was not the only concern that disrupted united evangelical action. Henry noted that all the false starts, misdirected initiatives, and conflicting aims only aided in creating a "vacuum of missed opportunity" into which "many evangelical subgroups representing special interests stepped" (1980:1061). Division came as rival groups within the greater evangelical alliance took up one polarizing social or political issue after another.

Henry then adumbrated these various subgroups that, while appropriately addressing a number of critical social, political, and theological issues, were nevertheless threatening evangelical unity:

> Magazines like *Sojourners, The Other Side* and the *Reformed Journal* took antiestablishment positions; divergent Calvinistic and Arminian groups sought a revitalized influence; evangelical social-action groups arose with varying emphases. Additional movements came to the fore: World Vision's spectacular global ministry of evangelical

humanitarianism; the charismatic phenomenon; the flourishing electronic church; the new core of Roman Catholic evangelicals; the Fuller Theological Seminary's pro-ecumenical stance and alignment with critical views of the Bible; ecumenical alliances by left-wing evangelicals; politically right-wing groups like Moral Majority (1980:1061).

The battles that postwar evangelicals had waged against fundamentalists in the 1940s and 1950s seemed all but a distant memory as new conflicts emerged among evangelicals of varying stripes; yet there was one interesting twist. As George Marsden astutely pointed out, "A major difference between the prematurely passé neo-evangelicalism and the newer open or progressive evangelicalism was that while the former was preoccupied with its relation to fundamentalism, the latter had moved a step away from that connection." The progressive wing of the new evangelical coalition, while seeking to expand its alliances, likewise found itself caught in a dilemma over how to define itself on the left as well as the right. Ironically, Marsden observed further, "Some of the old guard of conservative neo-evangelicalism were now beginning to play the role that fundamentalism had played in the seminary's early days" (1987:256). The cycle seemed almost complete as the new evangelical coalition of the 1940s and 1950s was gradually becoming identified as the old evangelical establishment. Its once ambitious agenda now seemed relatively modest when compared to the far-reaching goals of the younger elements within the movement (see Quebedeaux 1974 and 1978). The future of evangelicalism lay increasingly in the hands of the progressives, who were moving well beyond the boundaries of acceptable diversity that the previous generation had painstakingly established.

EVANGELICAL AFFIRMATIONS

Carl Henry's musings at the beginning of the 1980s could easily have been repeated at the end of that turbulent decade. By 1990, evangelical disunity seemed the norm. Not only had evangelical Christians separated into competing organizations and voiced their differences in the pages of rival progressive and conservative journals and magazines, but highly publicized financial scandals and embarrassing revelations of sexual improprieties among the most visible televangelists had tarnished conservative Protestantism's image in the public mind. Who were the evangelicals, people now asked, if not these perverse, deceitful, avaricious, back-stabbing hypocrites?[9] Distressed by evangelicalism's lost reputation and by its further disintegrating unity, Henry joined Kenneth Kantzer, a former editor of *Christianity Today*, in convening the May 1989 Consultation on Evangelical Affirmations Conference, which was sponsored jointly by the National Association of Evangelicals and Trinity Evangelical Divinity School, where Henry and Kantzer had been teaching.[10]

The papers and responses presented at this conference, later edited by Kantzer and Henry and published in 1990 as *Evangelical Affirmations,* sought specifically "to clarify the character of the evangelical movement and to affirm certain truths critical to the advancement of the church of Christ" (1990:29). The aim of the conference was to gather recognized evangelical scholars and church leaders together in order to make a positive statement about conservative Protestantism and to put forth "a confession of what it means to be an evangelical" (1990:14). Implicitly, however, this statement separated genuine evangelicals from those, especially of the younger generation, who they felt had misappropriated the label. As the editors put it, "In a day when this term is used loosely to cover a broad variety of belief and unbelief, we trust that a clear statement of those common convictions that constitute our evangelical heritage will prove useful to the church" (1990:14-15). More explicitly, Kantzer wrote in the afterword, "the purpose was to state what doctrinal and ethical convictions mark one off as an evangelical. What are the boundaries of evangelical faith?" In short, Kantzer concluded, "'Evangelical Affirmations' seeks to be a statement of evangelical *identity.* . . . What are its boundaries? Who are in and who are out?"(1990:518, 513, emphasis added).

Interestingly, far from settling the question of identity, these Affirmations, and the collection of papers and responses that comment upon them, give further testimony to the persistent boundary dilemma of postwar evangelicalism, especially in its framers' attempts to draw not just external boundaries but also internal lines of separation and inclusion (cf., Douglas 1984:138 and Wuthnow 1988:9). For instance, as early as the introductory paragraph of the Affirmations statement itself, the problem of group boundary distinction becomes patently evident. "Evangelical Christianity is engaged in a broad conflict on many fronts," it read. "Internally, it is struggling over moral improprieties, doctrinal lapses, and problems of self-identity. Externally, it is carrying on a lingering battle with liberal Christianity and seeking to plug leaks in its doctrinal structure that still come from that source." The boundary is far from clear, the framers of the Affirmations statement complained. "Not only on the outside, but even within our own ranks, some confusion exists as to exactly who are evangelicals" (1990:27, 29). While most of the nine stated Affirmations that followed this preamble centered on issues of belief and practice (concluding with a section focusing on "Evangelical Identity"), what is of interest is not that these Affirmations attempted to set down the "distinguishing marks of all evangelicals" (1990:38), but that the pages and pages of commentary and discussion that followed reveal that even these identifying marks remained an issue of debate for most of the six to seven hundred evangelicals who had reportedly gathered there prayerfully to settle the matter.

The keynote address by Carl F. H. Henry and the response by Nathan O. Hatch are especially instructive on this point. In his address, Henry asked the same probing and penetrating question asked dozens of times in different ways since the 1940s: "Who are the Evangelicals?" It is not his answer that is of interest here (cast, as it was, in theological language), but rather the concern that prompted his question. For nearly fifty years after the founding of the NAE, Henry and other evangelicals were still asking the original question of boundary differentiation: How do we define ourselves?

The response Nathan O. Hatch gave to Henry's paper was in many ways more profound than Henry's carefully worded address. "I am not as sanguine as Mr. Henry in speaking about the evangelical movement," said Hatch. "In truth, there is no such thing as evangelicalism" (1990:97). As Hatch then explained,

> The vitality of conservative Protestantism in America, since the very early 19th century, has been directly related to its entrepreneurial quality, its populist and decentralized structure, and its penchant for splitting, forming, and reforming. Fundamentalism, the Holiness Movement, and Pentecostalism, the most immediate heirs of most of

us in this room, were generic names that easily mask the pluralism and decentralization of these movements. All were extremely diverse coalitions dominated by scores of self-appointed and independent-minded religious leaders (1990:97).

The era of Carl Henry (b. 1913), Harold Ockenga (1905-1985), E. J. Carnell (1919-1967), Billy Graham (b. 1918), and other new evangelicals was fast coming to an end, Hatch commented somewhat somberly. Far from the original ideal of a greater evangelical coalition united in faith and action, the movement of evangelicals was, by contrast, becoming increasingly fragmented. "The evangelical world," Hatch observed, "is decentralized, competitive, and driven by those who can build large successful organizations." While perhaps one cause of evangelical "centrifugal" acceleration was its rootlessness, according to Hatch, an obvious result of this outward movement was evangelical restlessness, a restlessness that seemed to drive evangelicals to form and reform ever new coalitions of interest and activity (cf., Rousseau 1984:111). As Hatch related to his fellow delegates, "So much of evangelical life is freshly minted new congregations, new publications, new seminaries. Few of us stand in a religious tradition which provides ballast and long-term orienta-tion" (1990:98; cf., Noll and Kellstedt 1995:146-147). It was there-fore no longer possible to speak definitively about what constituted evangelicalism or even who was and who was not a genuine evangelical.

In his lengthy essay "Evangelicals, Ecumenism, and the Church," Donald A. Carson, then professor of New Testament at Trinity Evangel-ical Divinity School, addressed the problem of evangelical self-identity and concluded that, since the evangelical label had been applied to almost every type of Protestant movement that had emerged in Church history, "inherent ambiguities generate numerous problems in self-definition" (1990:353). The trick, he concluded, was "to think of evangelicalism as a movement determined by its center, not its bound-ary." In this way, "contemporary evangelicalism embraces a wide range of people, but not all their theological opinions" (1990:354).

In response to Carson's lengthy address, Joseph Stowell, then president of Moody Bible Institute, asked pointedly, "What will become of a movement whose name is becoming more symbolic than substantive?" (1990:387). Can a person truly talk of evangelical Christianity and its identity apart from its core beliefs?, he wondered. Without establishing core beliefs, he asserted, and "without establishing our identity in a common belief system, there is little left except the hollow symbol of a name. Is it not then imperative that at some point soon, a clear *basic* confession be established that will reaffirm the priority of doctrinal assent as step one for the privilege of wearing the name?" (1990:391). Earlier, Stowell had questioned Carson's seeming support for ecumenical evangelism—unity of mission despite disunity over doctrine. In a set of rhetorical comments, Stowell challenged Carson and those who might agree with his views: "Should the evangelical turf be open to those who may be willing to share our call to world evangelism, even though they may not agree about what constitutes evangelization? . . . Of what good is the 'great commission' if we do not adhere to the authority of the inerrant Word that holds us accountable? . . . Any movement from core belief structures," he reasoned, "significantly weakens the fervor and impetus of our mission and, I fear, may plant the seed of the ultimate dismantling of the mission." Thus, he concluded, "Is it not imperative that we anchor our identity in what we affirm to be true? . . . The truth must not be diluted or polluted from within or without, and it cannot be risked for any reason, not even for the advance of missions or for cultural acceptance" (1990: 390, 392).

Although its aims were impressive, the convocation and subsequent statement on "Evangelical Affirmations" resulted in little more than the heavy tome its sessions produced. The conference's efforts to establish "core beliefs" by which to define evangelicalism and around which to unite its various factions failed to gain much success; evangelical identity became all the more contested. Contrary to Alister McGrath's later optimistic assessment of the Consultation on Evangelical Affirmations as "trendsetting" and "influential" (1995:166, 196), few leaders at the denominational level seemed convinced by its attempts to reduce evangelicalism to an informal set of creeds and convictions, especially ones drawn up by individuals who could no longer command authority to speak for the whole of evangelical Protestantism, let alone their own denominations. In the end, discussion of evangelical identity shifted from the popular level to the academic circles from whence it had originated. After 1990, such issues remained largely the province of evangelical scholars whose ruminations on "core beliefs" and essential traits found their way into academic books and journals published by evangelical presses.

With this shift to academic circles came a shift of emphasis. The burning questions no longer centered around "What constitutes evangelicalism?" or "Who are the evangelicals?," rather, the issue that now fueled evangelical intellectual fervor became one of power: "*Who* defines evangelicalism?"[11]

SUMMARY AND CONCLUDING REMARKS

Throughout this study on postwar American evangelicalism, the aim has been to examine the role group boundary dynamics came to play in defining the new evangelical coalition. Conscious not so much of who they were as of who they were not, the new evangelicals devoted much of their interests and energies defining and reinforcing their distinctiveness vis-à-vis fundamentalism and liberal Protestantism. It is primarily because of evangelicalism's preoccupation with differentiating itself from these two oppositional movements, therefore, that this study has argued for the efficacy of a boundary approach to understanding the emergence of the new evangelical coalition in the 1940s and 1950s, its modest successes in the 1950s and 1960s, and its diversification and eventual splintering in the 1970s and 1980s.

What is typical of most scholarly approaches to the study of twentieth-century American Protestantism, especially those of evangelical scholars, is the use of metaphorical language to describe the vast, almost indefinable, phenomena known collectively as "evangelical." The trouble with such metaphorical descriptions—even "thick" ones—is that rather than explain the how or why of evangelical unity and diversity, such pictures only provide momentary snapshots of it. As discussed in Chapter One, though Timothy Smith's "mosaic" and "kaleidoscope" metaphors are helpful aids to the mind's eye, such metaphors lead scholars no further to understanding the nature of evangelical diversity. Indeed, as sociologist Rodney Stark has emphasized, "metaphors, typologies and concepts are passive, they cast no light of their own" (1986:315). As for typologies, British sociologist Bryan R. Wilson has reminded us that types, even ideal ones, are only momentary pictures that draw together the essential elements present in a phenomenon or related phenomena at a given point in time (1970:23-24 and 1982:100-105). As with metaphors, their purposes are largely comparative.

Yet, a person cannot analyze a phenomenon without at least a conceptual understanding of what he or she is examining. It is for this reason that this study has offered as its working model the social structural dynamic of the "coalition" or "coalitional group" and has examined the internal and external tensions inherent to coalitional structures.

When applied to postwar American evangelicalism then, "coalition" is not simply a metaphor but an analytically useful model. Indeed, "coalition" suggests both the unity and diversity that typifies the ever-changing yet ever-remaining social world of American evangelicalism, a world preoccupied by two central questions: What is evangelicalism? and Who are the evangelicals? As such, these questions strike at the heart of group identity and the formation, transformation, and preservation of coalitional organizations. What is more, "coalition" points toward an explanation for the two opposing yet complementary dynamics of American evangelicalism: persistence despite change. But beyond this, while "coalition" allows us more analytic elbowroom than picturesque metaphors, it should be remembered that it is the dynamic inherent in coalitional organizations, not the image, that has guided the discussion throughout this study.

Since World War II, this study has argued, evangelicalism has been captivated by the issue of defining its boundaries. This is especially noticeable in the writings of postwar evangelicals whose flood of books and articles documents a sustained effort at defining the limits of evangelicalism by affirming and reaffirming its boundary differences with both liberalism and fundamentalism. While scholars have sometimes remarked upon the evangelical boundary concern, no one had yet explored the social structural dynamics of this dilemma in the detail presented in this study. Indeed, in this study I have argued that this boundary dynamic has been of central concern to evangelicals as they have attempted to build a discrete community around a distinct identity—a goal that continues to elude them.

Accordingly, the second chapter of this work addressed the notion of group boundaries more abstractly and outlined a boundary approach to the study of American Protestant religion. Departing from the tendency among scholars to separate American Protestants along liberal/conservative lines, it was suggested that as a theoretical model and an analytical tool a boundary approach takes into account the greater diversity within American Protestantism in that, beyond simply discussing boundary maintenance, it examines the intense interest conservative evangelicals have displayed over who is and who is not a part of the evangelical tradition and over where evangelicals should therefore draw their boundary lines.

But in order to understand the concerns of the new evangelical coalition, it was necessary to situate postwar evangelicalism within its historical context: the fundamentalist-modernist debates of the late nineteenth and early twentieth centuries. The third chapter sought to show more clearly the background of its emergence from the fundamentalist movement by briefly examining the major divisive encounters during this controversial period that shaped the sharp and sometimes acrimonious liberal/conservative split within Protestantism. Two consequences of the fundamentalist-modernist controversy, as suggested by Ferenc Szasz (1982) and George Marsden (1980), set the context for the rise of the new evangelical coalition. First, the sharp division between liberals and conservatives that came to characterize American Protestantism became a distinction that overshadowed denominational lines, often becoming more important than denominational loyalties themselves. Second, by the 1920s, conservative Protestantism, now largely identified as "fundamentalism," had moved away from the religious and cultural mainstream of American society—a move from center to periphery. The point of this chapter, then, was to provide reasons for the new evangelicalism's efforts to avoid perpetuating the bitter division between fundamentalists and liberals that resulted from these debates.

But to leave it there, as most researchers do, is to fail to consider the responses groups make to situations of social alienation or cultural marginalization. "Tension with society" is not an easy position for individuals or groups to sustain. Over time, tensions gradually weaken and defenses become more and more relaxed (Stark and Bainbridge 1985:23-24). Not surprisingly, then, during the 1930s, as the old fundamentalist coalition became increasingly more insular, alienating itself even further from mainstream culture, many of the more moderate fundamentalists began to rethink fundamentalism's relation to secular society, seeking to reduce fundamentalism's religious and cultural tensions with society. By the beginning of the 1940s, these renegade fundamentalists and other moderately conservative evangelicals were making initial efforts to minimize these two major consequences of the fundamentalist-modernist controversy. Among the many activities that commanded much of their time and energy were their efforts to revise and recast a number of conservative positions ranging from ecumenism and social uplift to major theological issues.

The reason for this moderating shift seems to have been an interest by evangelicals in effecting a general revival of biblical Christianity in America. Moderate fundamentalists believed that the stimulus for a revival would require their greater participation in American society and an effort on their part to address more directly and with greater relevance the religious and social concerns of the modern world. However, in order for these more moderate fundamentalists to reenter the religious and cultural mainstream, certain adjustments in their message and methods became necessary. First, moderates would have to band together and learn to cooperate with rather than separate from those with whom they disagreed. Additionally, recognizing the need to speak to the modern situation, moderates would have to develop a social agenda and design strategies for alleviating social ills. Third, moderate fundamentalists, who were seeking theological respectability for orthodoxy, would have to play down many of the more extreme fundamentalist doctrines, such as premillennial dispensationalism and biblical inerrancy.

But a curious thing happened along the way. In their attempts to soften the ecclesiastical, social, and theological excesses of fundamentalism—the very concerns that split liberals and conservatives a generation earlier—this growing coalition of "new" evangelicals slowly became aware of its own growing differences with fundamentalism. It was not long before evangelicals began to point out these differences and then reinforce the emerging boundary by founding their own cooperative agencies (such as the National Association of Evangelicals in 1942) and launching their own educational institutions (such as Fuller Seminary in 1947) and publications (such as *Christianity Today* in 1956) as rivals to those of the fundamentalists. Accordingly, the fourth chapter charted the mobilization of the new evangelical coalition and analyzed the boundary that emerged and that the evangelicals fostered between themselves and the fundamentalists.

In an interesting way, the movement of moderates away from fundamentalism and toward greater denominational cooperation, social involvement, and theological sophistication brought with it other, perhaps unforeseen, boundary crises for the new evangelical coalition. As argued above, in distancing themselves from the fundamentalist movement, the evangelicals drifted toward the liberal camp—too close, in fact, for their own comfort. This gradual "leftward" drift was menacing for conservatives precisely because it threatened to undermine evangelicalism's distinctiveness from liberalism and thus confuse the boundary between them. As suggested in Chapter Five, the new evangelical failure to bring orthodoxy back into the religious mainstream had something to do with its need to maintain its symbolic boundaries with liberal Protestantism. Because evangelicals could not fully embrace the modern secular world, the boundary between them and liberals grew sharper in importance as evangelical ecumenical, social, and theological concerns came uncomfortably close to the liberal mainline agenda. Indeed, evangelical literature and activities during the 1940s and 1950s revealed that, far from exhibiting resolve on these and other issues, evangelicals were instead quite preoccupied by their efforts to reinforce the distinctions between themselves and modernism or liberalism, especially with neoorthodoxy, a movement evangelical theologians briefly courted as a way of regaining theological prestige. Evangelicals, in short, though consciously *not* fundamentalists, were scrupulously *not* liberals. By the early 1960s, the leaders of the new evangelical coalition appeared to be at a decisive crossroads, or perhaps better, they were stopping precipitously before the banks of the intellectual "fiery brook" (Marx) that many of the more progressive evangelicals, though somewhat reluctantly, would eventually cross.[12]

During the 1960s and into the 1980s, division among evangelicals over the nature and origin of the Christian scriptures effectively ended evangelical social initiative. Throughout this period, it seemed that all their energies were being channeled toward the theological firefights within the boundaries of what remained of the postwar evangelical coalition. What is more, while by the 1990s most efforts aimed at united evangelical action were all but abandoned, a number of scholars and high-profile leaders began reaching out to mainline liberals, American Catholics, and Conservative and Reform Jews—groups long thought by evangelicals as apostate or hopelessly lost.

Thus, if theology were the *only* means by which evangelicals organized their symbolic universe and drew their boundaries of inclusion and exclusion, as most interpreters of American evangelicalism suppose, then such efforts by evangelicals would have been unthinkable. But, as this study has argued, the coalitional nature of evangelical Protestantism accounts for such ideologically (or theologically) dissonant actions. As Robert Wuthnow might put it, there is an underlying coherence to otherwise inconsistent and patently self-contradictory behavior. In this case, the coherence is located in evangelicalism's search for social and political avenues through which to effect change, especially in public morals, which has led to its desire to make common cause with other religious groups despite their non-evangelical beliefs.[13] Indeed, this curious ecumenical turn has resulted in the convocation of a number of conferences and the establishment of several interdenominational and interreligious organizations, some to good effect.[14]

As one might expect, these ecumenical dialogues were not warmly greeted by all evangelicals. However innocent and well-intentioned these dialogues might have been, a great number of wary conservatives offered pointed critiques of their colleagues for extending such unwelcome and potentially compromising overtures to such hated rivals.[15] While this topic is well beyond the scope of this present study, it is perhaps one new direction in contemporary American evangelicalism worthy of further exploration and scholarly analysis.[16]

Thus, when over half a century after the beginning of their movement evangelicals are still "in search of their identity," perhaps scholars should be wary of clever metaphors and simplistic typologies drawn only from the theological and ethical concerns of evangelical groups and give more, if not greater, consideration to the social structural boundaries by which evangelicals, in their attempts to come to terms with both modernity and rival religious communities, define themselves. While a boundary approach cannot answer the question, What constitutes evangelicalism? or, Who are the *real* evangelicals?, it can lend a measure of analytical insight into the social structural dilemmas and definitional ambiguities caused by evangelicalism's ambivalent approach to traditional faith and modern life, no less from its desire to reconcile the two. At the very least, then, this study has attempted to point evangelical scholarship in this new and relatively unexplored theoretical direction.

Notes

Chapter One

1. See, for example, Michaelsen and Roof 1986, Roof and McKinney 1987, Wuthnow 1988, Coalter, *et al.* 1990, Stone 1990, Finke and Stark 1992, Hoge, *et al.* 1994, McKinney 1994, and Demerath 1995.
2. See, for instance, Wuthnow 1989, Hunter 1991, Watt 1991, Jorstad 1993, Kepel 1994:100-139, and Shibley 1996.
3. See, for instance, Henry 1971, Bloesch 1973, Padilla 1976, Inch 1978, Bloesch 1983, Kantzer and Henry 1990, Horton 1991, Wells 1993, McGrath 1995, and Armstrong 1996.
4. See Carnell 1959a:13.
5. See, for example, the collection of essays in Kantzer 1978, Wells and Woodbridge 1977, Marsden 1984, Kantzer and Henry 1990, Dayton and Johnston 1991, Noll, *et al.* 1994, and Armstrong 1996; see also Marsden 1989.
6. See, for instance, Marsden 1984:viii and 1991:65, Dayton and Johnston 1991:12, and Wells 1994:390.
7. One of the least critical metaphors that evangelical scholars have offered has been Donald Bloesch's description of evangelicalism as a "mood" (1972:334 and 1973:41). By defining evangelicalism as a "mood," Bloesch not only divorced the term from its historic theological usage, however vague it may be, but almost completely removed the concept to the mysterious and impenetrable realm of private emotion and religious feeling, and hence away from any meaningful form of social scientific analysis.
8. Encountering these metaphors is somewhat akin to the frustration Socrates felt with Polus, who unknowingly confused description with definition. After Polus gave a series of metaphorically framed responses to the query, "What is the art of which Gorgias is master?", the impatient Socrates interrupted Polus and remarked, "But no one is asking what the art of Gorgias is *like,* but what it *is,* and what he should be called" (Plato's *Gorgias,* 1955, line 449). Still, one cannot fault evangelical scholars. The aim of most evangelicals is to describe their diversity and determine who is "in" and who is "out," not to explain why it exists.
9. Evangelical historians Joel A. Carpenter (1984a and 1989:115) and George M. Marsden (1987:287 and 1989:69-71) referred to fundamentalism in the 1930s and evangelicalism in the postwar period as religious "coalitions" and appear to organize their historical analyses of these movements with this dynamic somewhat in mind.
10. See Plato's *Phaedrus* 1973, section 265d-e and Plato's *Statesman* 1957, section

258b-268d.

11. In his broad-brush analysis of postwar Protestant America, Robert Wuthnow made a stronger separation between evangelicals and fundamentalists than the sources seem to warrant. The postwar separation of fundamentalists and evangelicals into two distinct categories was a slow, evolving process. I do not disagree with Wuthnow that "organizationally, these different points of view [fundamentalist and evangelical] were in fact consistent with the denominational positions of the two groups" (1988:179), but I would argue that the distinction between the two was not so clearly defined at first. While the distinction between fundamentalists and evangelicals did begin to appear in the early 1940s, taking organizational shape in the American Council of Christian Churches and the National Association of Evangelicals, this distinction did not become completely evident, and irreconcilable, until about 1956. Recognizing this fact, Carpenter (1984a) identified two types of fundamentalism in the 1930s and early 1940s: "progressive" and "separatist." Similarly, Marsden (1989) distinguished between "positive" and "negative" fundamentalists.

12. See Evans 1991.

13. George Marsden noted that the essential issue within fundamentalism during this period was the tension between separation and revivalistic evangelism: "Everywhere the leadership talked of a coming nationwide revival. Fundamentalists continually longed and prayed for such an awakening. Separatism, however, posed a dilemma. Although increasing numbers of fundamentalists favored ecclesiastical independence, often arguing that it was necessary if the gospel was to be freely proclaimed in its purity, most fundamentalists still remained in major denominations" (1987:47).

14. See Butler 1976:7-8; one such example of its theological obscurantism would be fundamentalism's overly literal reading of the apocalyptic sections of the Bible.

15. This complex picture will make conceptual clarity difficult to maintain. The boundaries between the new evangelicals, fundamentalists, liberals, and neo-orthodox groups are often blurred. One aspect of this boundary dynamic is that when this blurring of the boundaries occurs, boundary definitional activities become all the more evident. It must be made clear from the outset that this investigation into the boundary dynamics of postwar evangelicalism is *not* simply a study on boundary maintenance and should not be confused with or viewed as such.

16. These differing views and distinct responses to secular culture found their greatest and clearest expressions in the American Council of Christian Churches (ACCC), organized by separatist fundamentalists in 1941, and the National Association of Evangelicals, founded in 1942 by moderates, both "national, interdenominational, associations of conservative Protestants" (Watt 1991:42).

17. See Berger 1983 and Hunter 1983.

18. See McIntire 1944 and 1955; see also Lindsell 1976 and 1978. Evangelicalism's ambivalence toward secular society exemplifies the dilemma faced by Protestantism since the Reformation. Unlike the otherworldly outlook of the Roman Catholicism from which it separated, Protestantism laid great emphasis on this-worldly pursuits (Weber 1958). The Reformation thinkers (nota-

bly John Calvin) taught that how an individual lives in this world greatly affects his or her eternal destiny. That is, an individual's involvement with the world can either be spiritually beneficial or spiritually fatal; thus, individual choices have cosmic consequences. This socio-religious dynamic set in motion an interesting ethic that sought to balance believers' attitudes toward the material and spiritual realms. Old and New England Puritanism, for example, typified the challenge that orthodox Protestants continually faced: how to live in the world without becoming worldly (see Simpson 1955). The problem became acute when Puritans—individually and communally—had to determine at what point their engagement with the world would endanger salvation (see Morgan 1958). Consequently, the lines between the sacred and profane were sharply drawn and the boundaries between the two were clearly marked. Orthodoxy came to be characterized by its meticulous attention to the boundaries between the sacred and profane in the form of acceptable and unacceptable beliefs, behaviors, occupational aspirations, leisure activities, and the like. This attention to boundaries has been a powerful and pervasive theme in Protestant history.

19. While, to be sure, there are many Protestant groups that make up the highly diverse evangelical religious community in America—a spectrum that includes groups as different as Lutherans, Presbyterians, Pentecostals, Black Methodists, and Southern Baptists—it is not within the scope of this study to consider all of these varying types of evangelicalisms. Moreover, this study does not pretend to treat the evangelical movement *in toto* but only a smaller group forming an earlier defining coalition within that larger contemporary movement of American Protestants. "Evangelicalism," as understood in this study, also transcends those specific denominations whose names include the word evangelical, such as Evangelical Lutheran and Evangelical Brethren. While I will observe George Marsden's caveat "not to mistake a few prominent spokespersons for a movement" (1991:64), the focus of this study is on those who believed themselves to be speaking for a vast unrepresented and silent evangelical majority (see Ockenga 1942b and Marsden 1987:49-50).

20. See also Ramm 1981 and selected essays in Wells and Woodbridge 1977.

21. See also Hunter 1991.

22. See also Abraham 1984:15-20.

23. See also Marsden 1987.

24. Traditionally, the five points of fundamentalism are: (1) the inerrancy of the Bible, (2) the virgin birth of Christ, (3) the substitutionary atonement of Christ's death, (4) the bodily resurrection of Christ, and (5) the premillennial return of Christ. George Marsden noted that the famous "five points" were adopted by fundamentalists from the five-point declaration of essential doctrines approved by the Presbyterian General Assembly in 1910. As he pointed out, fundamentalists adopted only four of the General Assembly's "five points," replacing the fifth point with their own statement on Christ's second coming. The original fifth point of the 1910 declaration affirmed the authenticity of miracles (Marsden 1980:117).

25. See Watt 1991:42.

26. See also Kantzer and Henry 1990.

Chapter Two

1. See, for example, Henry 1957b, Jaberg 1960, Nash 1963, Shuy 1964, Lindsell 1965, Henry 1967, Inch 1978, Kantzer 1978, Webber 1978, Johnston 1979, Bloesch 1983, Smith 1986, Ellingsen 1988, Kantzer and Henry 1990, Dayton and Johnston 1991, Dayton 1993, McGrath 1995, and Armstrong 1996.
2. The use of the word "identity" in the context of this study is not meant to imply the type of psychic trauma suggested in Ericksonian psychology.
3. See also McGrath 1995:53.
4. Martin E. Marty made a similar observation about the dialectic of religious belief and behavior in his *Nation of Behavers* (1976).
5. Incidentally, Hunter's last phrase takes into consideration the Puritan, Pietistic, Confessional, and Revivalist streams that coalesced in the nineteenth century to form an evangelical coalition. His remarks also leave room for the Pentecostal and Holiness impulses that were denounced by the twentieth-century fundamentalists but were repatriated at the founding of the National Association of Evangelicals in 1942.
6. Dayton and Johnston (1991) identified a dozen traditions or "communities" that, while not all comfortable using the term evangelical to describe themselves, are typically listed under the general rubric of "evangelical." The most prominent of the traditions that they examined include the following: Premillennialism, Fundamentalism, Adventism, Pentecostal, Holiness, Restorationism, Black, Baptist, Pietistic, Mennonite, Reformed, and Lutheranism.
7. See Hughes 1988 and Hughes and Allen 1988.
8. See Quebedeaux 1974:18.
9. See also Carpenter 1984c:10. Joel Carpenter has likewise made this observation: "Fundamentalists are evangelicals, but not all evangelicals are fundamentalists" (quoted in Sweet 1984:260). One might add that though fundamentalists may be evangelical, many do not call themselves evangelical, believing that the term is simply another word for liberal.
10. It must be stressed that this study is not particularly concerned with how evangelicals or fundamentalists define themselves. The clearest picture that can be drawn is that both movements are *orthodox* Protestants. The primary focus of this section is not to define these groups or identify their differences but simply to point out that to these two types of Protestantisms the differences between them are important and that the boundaries that separate them are carefully observed. As before, scholars have noted this boundary activity but have tended to think of the separation between evangelical and fundamentalist communities as merely a consequence of theological quarrels.
11. See, for example, Feinberg 1957 and Walvoord 1957.
12. The controversy among Protestants—liberal, fundamentalist, and evangelical—over the Revised Standard Version of the Bible is a case in point. In his discussion, Quebedeaux seemed to anticipate the 1976 "Battle for the Bible" brouhaha over biblical inerrancy between fundamentalist Harold Lindsell and the new evangelicals. Ironically, this divisive battle was fought during the proclaimed "Year of the Evangelicals" (*Newsweek*, October 25, 1976:69).
13. Though Quebedeaux drew a distinction between "establishment" and "new" evangelicals—apparently to differentiate between the "old" new evangelicals

and the "new" new evangelicals, he created more confusion than is necessary. In this context, it might have been well for him to have left aside use of the term "new evangelical" altogether and adopt a term without traditional historical usage, such as "progressive" evangelical.

14. Indeed, the phrase "word of man" is indicative of the influence of Karl Barth and neo-orthodoxy.

15. See Quebedeaux 1976. Quebedeaux treated charismatic renewal, or neo-pentecostalism, as a different type of orthodoxy that is not so easily subsumed under either the fundamentalist or evangelical rubric.

16. See Dayton 1978:8.

17. See Edwards and Stott 1988, and Pinnock and Brown 1990.

18. See Meeking and Stott 1986, Ball 1992, and Colson and Neuhaus 1995.

19. See Tannenbaum, et al. 1978 and 1984, and Rudin and Wilson 1987.

20. Not surprisingly, Carnell's barbed attacks against fundamentalism—the most memorable being his definition of fundamentalism as "orthodoxy gone cultic" (1959a:113)—and his fraternization with liberal ideas did not endear him to fundamentalists. In addition, such inflammatory comments were interpreted by more conservative evangelicals as a ploy by Carnell to gain intellectual credibility for himself among liberal theologians and secular scholars.

21. By "conservative evangelical" William Abraham almost certainly must have meant the same as Quebedeaux's "Establishment Evangelicals," in contrast to his own pietistic tradition at Seattle Pacific University, where he then taught.

22. More recent studies have been no less indicative of the diversity that continues to characterize American evangelicalism and that plagues its interpreters. Gabriel Fackre (1993), for instance, identified six varieties of evangelicalism according to ideological and coalitional types, even as Dayton and Johnston (1991) discerned some twelve varieties according to denominational tradition. Fackre labeled his as follows: fundamentalists, old evangelicals, new evangelicals, justice and peace evangelicals, charismatic evangelicals, and ecumenical evangelicals (1993:22-23).

23. These methodological distinctions are adapted from McLoughlin (1967).

24. See, for example, Lofland and Skonovd 1981 and 1983, Robbins 1988, and Barker 1992:17-23.

25. Gordon Allport (1950), whose intrinsic/extrinsic model of religious orientation classifies liberals as religiously and psychologically balanced and conservatives as religiously maladjusted and psychologically unstable, is an example of psychological approaches that not only contrast liberal and conservative responses unnecessarily but also lend a pejorative air to the term conservative.

26. A noticeable exception is found in Dean R. Hoge's research in intrachurch conflict published in 1976 under the title *Division in the Protestant House,* a study that appears more theological than sociological. After presenting an elaborate historical and quantitative examination into the rise of the "two-party" division in Protestantism (cf., Marty 1970) in which he tested four theories that attempt to account for it, Hoge concluded that "the basic division among Protestants today is over certain specific theological beliefs" (1976:90). Indeed, Hoge has little to say about the social structural tensions that fuel intrachurch conflict other than the fact that liberals and conserva-

tives often conceal their class interests by speaking of their social and economic concerns in theological categories (see 1976:90 and 120-121). In one place, for instance, Hoge commented: "Our statistical comparisons confirmed the findings that theological causes account for more of the divisions than do any other factors, with the psychological 'social threat' factor as the next most important in certain areas" (1976:73). In another place he wrote: "The factors that test out as most fundamental are theological. What people believe about the nature of God and human nature and society—rather than age, economic class, clergy-laity differences, or psychological variations—underlies the formation of conflicting parties" (1976:74).

27. For further elaboration and modification of Niebuhr's model, see Stark and Bainbridge 1985, Roof and McKinney 1987, Finke and Stark 1992, Bainbridge 1997, and selected essays in Young 1997. Sociologists, following Niebuhr's lead (who followed Troelsch's), have offered numerous member "profiles" to distinguish "church," "sect," and "denomination." By the 1960s, these typologies had become quite complex. Benton Johnson (1963) swept away the conceptually burdensome church/sect typologies and offered a simple scheme: "A church is a religious group that accepts the social environment in which it exists. A sect is a religious group that rejects the social environment in which it exists" (1963:542; for a critical discussion on church/sect typologies, see Stark and Bainbridge 1985:19-37).

28. For an even fuller discussion, see McLoughlin 1978.

29. McLoughlin's historical frame of reference is essentially cyclic. Cyclical views of history posit a theory of recurrent cycles of social change and cultural development. In McLoughlin's scheme, American history is periodized, each period passing through more or less identical stages of development, each stage progressing in a somewhat similar fashion and passing the same developmental milestones. This historical model is often used to explain evangelical and fundamentalist resurgences of the 1970s and 1980s.

30. Although written from the perspective of a social anthropologist and ethnologist, Barth's insights clarify the nature of group boundaries generally. Though Barth's analysis of ethnic group boundaries is useful in analyzing postwar evangelicalism, this study does not argue, even implicitly, that evangelicalism is an ethnic group.

31. In his discussion of social differentiation, Georg Simmel noted that one aspect of group development is the tendency for group members to push out beyond their group's original boundaries. To Simmel, however, this dynamic is perceived as less unifying than it is to Barth. To quote Simmel at length: "After the process of social differentiation has led to a separation between high and low, the mere formal fact of occupying a particular social position creates among the similarly characterized members of the most diverse groups a sense of solidarity and, frequently, actual relationships. Accompanying such a differentiation of social groups, there arise a need and an inclination to reach out beyond the original spatial, economic, and mental boundaries of the group and, in connection with the increase in individualization and concomitant mutual repulsion of group elements, to supplement the original centripetal forces of the lone group with a centrifugal tendency that forms bridges with other groups" (Simmel 1971:253).

32. In her discussion of symbolic boundaries and rituals of purification, Douglas

posited four kinds of social pollution: "The first is danger pressing on external boundaries; the second, danger from transgressing the internal lines of the system; the third, danger in the margins of the lines. The fourth is danger from internal contradiction, when some of the basic postulates are denied by other postulates, so that at certain points the system seems to be at war with itself" (Douglas 1984:122).

33. Cohen argued that meaning can be found in modern as well as in traditional social relationships. In this way, Cohen creatively and effectively sidestepped the Gemeinschaft/Gesellschaft (Community/Society) impasse among secularization theorists (for a glimpse into this vast literature, see Greeley 1972, Niebuhr 1975, Wilson 1982 and 1985, Hammond 1985b and 1992, Stark and Bainbridge 1985, Michaelsen and Roof 1986, Roof and McKinney 1987, Beckford 1989, Bruce 1992, Demerath and Williams 1992, Finke and Stark 1992, and Barker, et al. 1993).

Chapter Three

1. See also Marsden 1980 and Szasz 1982. Marty's typology is reminiscent of Gordon Allport's (1950) "intrinsic" and "extrinsic" types of religious expression.
2. See Cauthen 1962, Hutchison 1976, and Hudson 1981.
3. In Pauline theology, the contrast drawn is between the "flesh" and the "spirit" (cf., Romans 8:1-17 and Galatians 5:13-25).
4. See Sandeen 1968 and 1970, and Marsden 1980.
5. According to Ernest Sandeen's account, the Prophecy conferences seem to have grown out of a series of informal meetings held first in New York City beginning in 1868 and later, formally, as the Believers' Meeting for Bible Study in Chicago beginning in 1875 (1970:132-140). In 1878 a formal creed was drafted and, according to Timothy Weber, the name of the meeting was changed to the Niagara Bible Conference (Weber 1987:26-28). The fact that there were many such conferences taking place during this period creates some confusion. It seems that the major prophetic conference was the Niagara Bible Conference ("the mother of them all—the Monte Cassino and Port Royal of the movement," Sandeen 1970:132). Its major meetings were held as follows: New York City, 1878; Chicago, 1886; Allegheny, Pennsylvania, 1895; Boston, 1901; Chicago, 1914; Philadelphia, 1918; and New York City, 1918. The proceedings from these conferences were reprinted in a four volume series edited by Donald W. Dayton (1988a).
6. See Weber 1987, Boyer 1992, and Stone 1993.
7. See Kraus 1958, Sandeen 1968 and 1970, Rausch 1979, Weber 1987, and Stone 1993.
8. See Sandeen 1970, Gaustad 1974, Numbers and Butler 1987, and Stone 1993.
9. For a brief biographical sketch, see Sandeen 1970:70-80.
10. See also Weber 1987.
11. For a more detailed discussion, see Bass 1978.
12. See, for example, Kellogg 1893 and Haldeman 1919.
13. See, for instance, Furniss 1954, Gatewood 1969, Ahlstrom 1975, Hutchison

1976, Marsden 1980, Hudson 1981, Szasz 1982, and Roberts 1988.

14. See also Sandeen 1970:235-237.

15. See also Longfield 1991.

16. During the early 1920s, fundamentalists urged state legislators to adopt laws banning the teaching of evolution and modern scientific theory in public educational institutions. Fundamentalists quickly organized to fight legislative battles at the state and local levels. Surprisingly, their political pressure on state legislators reaped many early gains for them in Oklahoma, Florida, North Carolina, and Texas, with Tennessee, Mississippi, and Arkansas following soon after (see Furniss 1954).

17. See also Ahlstrom 1975 and Szasz 1982.

18. Perhaps the most intriguing aspect of the anti-evolutionary crusades of Bryan and others was the ideological cast of their language. By and large, fundamentalists did not attack evolutionary theory on scientific but on ideological grounds, making their fight an enormously difficult one to win. For one thing, the idea of evolutionary development appealed to the American commonsense view of the world. Similarly, the belief that "evolution" might have actually been, as Lyman Abbott quipped, "God's way of doing things" had gained a measure of ideological acceptance among Protestant intellectuals by 1900 (Roberts 1988:145-161) and, to some extent, among their seminary students, who became influential clergymembers by the 1920s (see Longfield 1991).

19. See, for example, William Riley's address opening the 1919 World's Christian Fundamentals Association conference; for historical background, see Gasper 1981 and Carpenter 1984c.

20. As an incidental note, Machen's *Christianity and Liberalism* (1923) was still in print and available at many local Christian bookstores as recently as April 1996.

21. For a more detailed discussion, see Ahlstrom 1975, Hutchison 1976, and Longfield 1991.

22. See also Mathews 1924 and Burns 1926.

Chapter Four

1. See also Carpenter 1984a.

2. See Paine 1951, Butler 1976, Carpenter 1984c, and Marsden 1987.

3. For an early history of the American Council, see McIntire 1944; for early histories of the NAE, see *Evangelical Action!* 1942, *United . . . We Stand* 1943, Lindsell 1951:109-124, Murch 1956, Shelley 1967, and Evans 1991.

4. See *SST* editorial, June 20, 1942:494, and Butler 1976:18.

5. Because the focus of this chapter is on the symbolic boundary that the evangelicals drew to distinguish themselves from fundamentalists, the discussion will center on comments made by these new evangelicals. Even so, remarks by fundamentalists opposed to the new evangelical program will be included wherever necessary. Interestingly, their quarrel seems to have been over method more than over the orthodoxy of their group's doctrinal message. As Louis Gasper noted, "The National Association of Evangelicals proposed

to follow an inclusivist policy wherein its constituent members were not required to separate from denominations or churches affiliated with the Federal Council—a policy the American Council adamantly opposed. Furthermore the National Association of Evangelicals was opposed to the American Council's vitriolic attack upon the Federal Council, because they thought it might be more harmful than beneficial. The two fundamentalist groups agreed doctrinally, but were divided in method" (1981:26).

6. Of the various streams that came together to make up the postwar American evangelical coalition, this chapter focuses on the streams that were more central in the defining of the program of the National Association of Evangelicals, namely, the Reformed and Anabaptist traditions (see Noll and Kellstedt 1995:152, and Stackhouse 1995:157-158). The "Presbyterian-Baptist network," as George Marsden called it, believed that it represented and spoke for the concerns of the greater evangelical coalition. Wrote Marsden, "this group, having lost most of its denominational loyalties, was trying to take the lead in forging a new interdenominational alliance among conservative Protestants as diverse as Pentecostals and Missouri Synod Lutherans. This predominantly Calvinistic core group continually attempted to speak for evangelicalism as a whole. But because they themselves were a party within evangelicalism, they always had great difficulty getting other groups to follow their lead" (1987:49-50). Historically, the Pietistic-Arminian-Pentecostal-Holiness traditions—what Henry P. Van Dusen called the "Third Force" in American religion (McLoughlin 1967)—were excluded from the religious mainstream and did not play any key role in the modernist controversies or participate in the development of the fundamentalist movement in the 1920s and 1930s (for a fuller discussion of the Pentecostal-Holiness stream within American evangelicalism more broadly, see Synan 1977, Dayton 1978, Dayton 1988b, Dayton and Johnston 1991, and Dayton 1993). It is for these reasons, then, that the Pentecostal-Holiness groups are not included within the scope of this study on the emergence of the postwar new evangelical coalition.

7. Revival seems not only to have been on the minds of fundamentalists but also on the minds of liberals. In 1935, for instance, at the height of both the economic and religious depression in America (Handy 1960), the editors of *The Christian Century* asked the simple question, "Why No Revival?" (*CC* September 18, 1935:1168-1170). Their answer was not as optimistic as that of the fundamentalists, however. The editors wrote, "We might as well be frank about it. This depression has lasted too long for Christian leaders to continue to assert that because religion has always experienced revival in past depressions we are sure yet to witness a like phenomenon in this. That is merely wishful talk" (1168). A little further in the editorial, with an oblique reference to fundamentalism, the editors continued their assessment: "The better course is to admit candidly that there are as yet no clear signs of the kind of revival that grows out of the sympathetic contact of the church with the general community. Having made this admission, the candid mind will ask why it is so. The answer may be far more encouraging than mere blind whipping up of morale" (1168). Still, while the "conventional signs" of revival were not evident, the editors were not willing to give up on the possibility of a religious revival: "True, there is no outpouring as yet; no freshet of grace; no tidal movement. But far up in the creeks and inlets of the

church's devotion and intelligence there are gathering the waters of divine revival. At such an hour as we think not, the tide will turn, and come in— silent, irresistible, and full" (1170).

8. See also Carpenter 1984c:186-188 and Carpenter 1989.

9. Harold Ockenga defended the inclusion of Pentecostal and Holiness groups in the National Association of Evangelicals in a 1947 *UEA* editorial. His comments came in response to allegations by fundamentalists that the leadership of the NAE had been taken over by Pentecostals and that "tongue-speaking meetings" had been held under NAE auspices. Ockenga's response was direct: "I have known the Pentecostal brethren from the Assemblies of God, the Church of God, the Pentecostal Holiness Church, and other similar theological groups, which are in fellowship with the NAE. They are evangelical, Bible-believing, Christ-honoring, Spirit-filled brethren, who manifest in character and life the truths expressed in the statement of faith of the NAE. Set in ethical contrast with some of the fundamentalist brethren they shine brilliantly" (1947c:12).

10. See, for example, McIntire 1944, 1949, 1955, 1967a, and 1967b.

11. See also Ockenga 1943. If evangelicals sought united action, why, then, did they not unite with the American Council? One answer is because of the harshly negative approach of the American Council; another, noted above, is because of the American Council's separatist and exclusivist attitude toward what they deemed as liberal "apostasy," which they believed the Federal Council embodied. This helps explain in part why separatist fundamentalists, who would brook no fellowship with "apostate" Christians and unbelievers, similarly interpreted the NAE's inclusivist position—to achieve the broadest possible representation of evangelical orthodoxy in one organization—as acquiescence on the issue of apostasy. As Butler suggested, "Many of the men involved in the formation of the new group [NAE] were members of denominations which were part of the FCC and were not disposed to withdraw from their denominations" as McIntire and the member churches of the American Council had done. "Other procedural issues were involved, but the major difficulty was McIntire's insistence on complete separation from any connection with the FCC and from any denomination which was a member of the FCC" (Butler 1976:16). Another possible answer might be their diverging methodologies. The leaders of the NAE were not convinced that the American Council's approach could bring revival to America. In this case, then, the formation of the NAE might be best understood as a vote of "no confidence" in the American Council by moderate fundamentalists. An early editorial in the NAE's *United Evangelical Action* affirmed this sentiment: "Those active in developing the National Association do not consider either the organization of the American Council of Churches or the personnel engaged in its promotion fit and proper media for the achievement of the desires and hopes of evangelicals" (*UEA* Editorial 1943a:3).

12. For further background and historical discussion, see Butler 1976, and Carpenter 1984a and 1984c.

13. In an August 1943 editorial in the NAE's newsletter *United Evangelical Action,* J. Elwin Wright, appraising the situation of the national evangelical movement, bemoaned the lack of unity among conservative Protestants. In a passing comment, Wright seemed to distinguish between "evangelicals" and

"fundamentalists." Wright remarked, "I do not believe that the modernist movement has the vitality to successfully withstand such a movement as the National Association of Evangelicals may become. I also feel sure that any active opposition from within the ranks of *evangelicals* or *fundamentalists* will not be a deciding factor. Most of this opposition is based upon misinformation and is already waning" (1943:2, emphasis added). This differentiation, though subtle, might reveal an emerging distinction within his own thinking.

14. See the list of members and member churches in *Evangelical Action!* 1942:5-13 and Appendix; see also *United . . . We Stand* 1943.

15. See also Butler 1976:15-30.

16. Interestingly, though he differed with Henry on social issues, by 1956, because of his modified views on science and evolution, Ramm would be classed as one of the new evangelical theologians (see Butler 1976:109-115, and *CL* March 1956).

17. One example is separation from unbelief; see Paine 1951

18. "Jesus answered him, 'Truly, truly, I say to you, unless one is born again, he cannot see the kingdom of God'" (quoted from the *New American Standard Version*).

19. It was Charles Feinberg, a noted professor at the Biola Institute, who edited this lengthy point-by-point reply by fundamentalists to *Christian Life's* March 1956 feature on the evangelicals.

20. In his speech, William Ayer did not make the same qualitative distinction between evangelicals and fundamentalists that later evangelicals made. His comments implied that evangelical Christianity had the power to save America during these desperate times. Ayer's comments read in full: "It is not boasting to declare that evangelical Christianity has the America of our fathers to save. While our army and navy fight the enemy without, we have the enemy at home to battle, and he is in some ways more dangerous than the enemy abroad. We unhesitatingly declare that evangelicals have the 'keys of the kingdom.' Millions of evangelical Christians, if they had a common voice and a common meeting place, would exercise under God an influence that would save American democracy. The old slogan, 'United we stand; divided we fall,' is certainly applicable to the dangers of the fragmentized condition of evangelical Christianity in America" (1942:46).

21. See also Jaberg 1960 and Gangel 1962.

22. Bernard Ramm, who had earlier criticized Henry for being overly concerned with the social application of the Gospel, came to be identified with the new evangelical position (*CL* March 1956). His reply to a confused reader of an earlier article of his in *UEA* came close to defining modern fundamentalism as discontinuous with "historic fundamentalism." "In the last forty years," he wrote, "another movement has developed within historic fundamentalism that has given the term an odious connotation. Men with much zeal, enthusiasm and conviction, yet lacking frequently in education or cultural breadth, and many times highly individualistic, took to the stump to defend the faith. Many times they were dogmatic beyond evidence, or were intractable of disposition, or were obnoxiously anti-cultural, anti-scientific and anti-educational. Hence, the term came to mean one who was bigoted, and obscurantist, a fideist, a fighter and an anti-intellectual." (*UEA* October 15, 1951:2). In Ramm's interpretation, contemporary fundamentalism as a move-

ment grew away from historic fundamentalism and perverted its meaning. What Ramm seemed to be saying was that evangelicalism is, in fact, the true historic fundamentalism—thus conflating historic fundamentalism and evangelicalism. Admittedly, this is quite a shift in the way Ramm previously defined his position vis-à-vis the new evangelical coalition (see Ramm 1947).

Chapter Five

1. It must be remembered, however, that while the boundary with fundamentalism developed over a period of some twenty years, by contrast, the boundary between conservatives and the liberal mainstream had been firmly fixed since the controversies of the 1920s. Because of the changing relationship of evangelicals to both fundamentalism and liberalism, these social boundaries were subjected to a series of threats. This chapter examines the dilemma that the new evangelicals faced when their various initiatives threatened to blur the boundaries between themselves and the liberal mainstream.
2. Evangelicals were not so much trying to *draw* a boundary—as they had had to do with the fundamentalists—as they were trying to *maintain* an existing boundary with liberalism.
3. For example, one problem that evangelicals had was how to frame their doctrinal position in the "simplest possible terms" without compromising the "full-orbed" message of the Gospel. One might ask what the difference might be between unity achieved according to an orthodoxy defined in the "simplest possible terms" and an ecumenism based on Protestantism's "least common denominator" (Cairns 1955:4; see also Murch 1956). To evangelicalism's liberal and fundamentalist detractors, this was a glaring inconsistency. To evangelicals, however, this quandary represented the evangelical challenge to establish a unity that was neither separatist nor ecumenist.
4. See, for example, Murch 1950, Kaub 1951, and *UEA* January 1, 1951:2.
5. One might find it difficult to explain how new evangelicals could label liberal ecumenism as ecclesiastical "regimentation" (Lindsey 1956) and not see that their own insistence on a common creed (e.g., the NAE's seven-point statement of faith, Ford 1956) was itself a subtle form of religious regimentation. Moreover, given the Disciples of Christ's traditional abhorrence for creeds and associations, one might consider Murch (himself a staunch member of the Disciples of Christ) to have compromised himself not only by joining the NAE but also by subscribing to its creed. Murch had much more in common with his ecumenical arch-rival C. C. Morrison (longtime editor of *The Christian Century* and a Disciples minister) than he would have been willingly to admit.
6. It must be noted that liberal ecumenists of the Federal Council paid scant attention to the National Association of Evangelicals. They seemed to regard the NAE as simply another grouping of fundamentalists and therefore not to be taken seriously (see, for instance, Editorial 1943b:596). In the eyes of the liberals, the differences between Harold Ockenga of the NAF and Carl McIntire of the American Council were quite negligible.
7. See also Kik 1957a:17 and Petticord 1958:27.

8. See, for example, Gordon 1948, Murch 1950, and Lindsey 1956.
9. It should be pointed out that the apparent absurdity of the evangelical position on ecumenism can only make sense if it is explained social structurally, rather than theologically as most scholars suppose. Evangelicals were forced by the positions their religious rivals espoused to define their differences oppositionally, even if the positions marking those differences were both theologically untenable and logically inconsistent.
10. The phrase "Great Reversal" was adopted by David O. Moberg (1972) to describe the turn-of-the-century shift of emphasis within American Protestantism from social concern to social detachment. "Great Reversal" is a somewhat misleading phrase in that not only does it assume that the liberal/conservative division in evangelical Protestantism existed prior to 1870, with two noticeably distinct social agendas, but that liberals and conservatives changed positions on social issues. One would find it difficult to lump together abolitionists, prohibitionists, Sabbatarians, and labor organizers—many of whom were professed evangelicals—under a strictly conservative rubric.
11. See, for example, Ockenga 1947a and 1947b.
12. If the article topics published in the NAE's *United Evangelical Action* magazine are an accurate indicator of evangelical reading patterns, then even a casual glance at the tables of contents and indices from issues published between 1945 and 1960 suggests a diminishing interest in social concern. Few writers, in fact, were calling conservative Protestants to a renewed Christian social vision. Indeed, as decade passed into decade, Henry seems to have been the only evangelical speaking to this issue (see, for instance, Henry 1948, 1959, 1964, 1967, 1971, 1976, 1986a, and 1986b).
13. As discussed, many of the new evangelicals still thought of themselves as "fundamentalists" until sometime in the mid-1950s. In his study on Billy Graham and the fundamentalist-evangelical split, Farley Butler pinpointed this shift in thinking as occurring sometime in early 1956 (1976:122; for a more elaborate discussion see especially pp. 125-144). Before this point, the terms fundamentalist, evangelical, and conservative were often used interchangeably.
14. Interestingly, even into the 1960s and the 1970s, evangelical spokespersons such as Ockenga and Henry were still calling for organization and cooperation among conservative evangelicals in all areas, including social uplift. "Evangelicals need a plan of action," Ockenga urged his colleagues in 1960. "The pressing demand is for an overall strategy instead of piecemeal action by fragmentized groups" (1960:15). Even Henry, whose reputation as a socially conscious evangelical theologian was well established by the 1950s, found evangelical social involvement severely lacking organizational thrust. "The time is overdue," he wrote in his 1971 book, *A Plea for Evangelical Demonstration,* "for a dedicated vanguard to move evangelical witness to frontier involvement in the social crisis, an involvement to be followed, pray God, by universal engagement of the evangelical churches in social witness and betterment" (1971:22). Henry directed his call for "evangelical demonstration" at a Protestant orthodoxy that had as yet "produced no unified social ethic or program of evangelical social action" (1971:23). Indeed, Henry added, while evangelicals spoke urgently of such concern and began to sketch

out detailed plans that would translate "God's moral claim upon church and world into a framework of principles, policies, and programs," at every turn, evangelicals were "pre-empted" by the mainline liberals whose cultural influence and vast resources commanded greater respect by society at large (1971:23).

15. It was Carnell who, in fact, was among the first evangelicals to engage Swiss theologian Karl Barth, not because Carnell was neo-orthodox but because dialogue with Barth, who claimed to hold a modified "evangelical" position, lent credibility to the orthodox biblical position Carnell sought to reconstruct (see Nelson 1987). Though Barth would have disapproved of Carnell's preoccupation with apologetics, Barth appeared to have indirectly provided Carnell with the theological credibility that he so painfully desired (see Barr 1978:215). Additionally, while many evangelical theologians accused Barth of dishonesty for claiming to be orthodox and yet holding modernist presuppositions, Carnell argued that Barth was confused in his loyalties more than he was dishonest or insincere. "I am convinced," wrote Carnell after his encounter with Barth during Barth's lecture series "An Introduction to Evangelical Theology" at the University of Chicago in May 1962 (see "Introduction to Theology" 1963), "that Barth is an inconsistent evangelical rather than an inconsistent liberal" (Carnell 1969:156; see also Carnell 1961).

16. Gregory Bolich saw the evangelical news journal, *Christianity Today*, which was launched in the fall of 1956, as lending a clearer sense of "cohesiveness" to the evangelical cause. As Bolich noted, "All these varied expressions had in common the desire to avoid the pitfalls that befell fundamentalism" (1980:45).

17. Incidentally, this distinction became one of the sticking points for the new evangelicals, who later lashed out at Barth in the pages of *Christianity Today*. Among evangelicals, Geoffrey Bromiley, who translated many of Barth's works into English, became the most sympathetic interpreter of Barth's theology, distilling it into fairly digestible form.

18. See also Van Til 1962 and 1964.

19. See especially Van Til 1964:378. In his biography of Carl F. H. Henry, Bob Patterson suggested that the primary reason why evangelicals could not embrace neo-orthodoxy was its non-orthodox view of the Bible. This difference did not prevent all contact among evangelicals and neo-orthodoxy, however. As Patterson observed, "In spite of important differences with neo-orthodoxy, many evangelicals (including Henry) have drunk deeply at the neo-orthodox well. They have learned from Reinhold Niebuhr, who said that justice is the social expression of Christian love. They have learned from Karl Barth, probably the most profound and influential Christian theologian of our age. Some evangelicals dismissed Barth as a 'new modernist' [e.g., Van Til 1946] . . ., but others have valued his contribution" (Patterson 1983:49; cf., Carnell 1960b and 1969).

20. See also Van Til 1964 and Marsden 1987:110-111.

21. Evangelicals often discredited their rivals by negating their apostolic and Reformation heritage. "Who are the inheritors of the Reformation?," asked a *Christianity Today* editorial. "The inheritors of the Reformation are evangelical Christians" was the unequivocal reply. "They stand with the Reformers in preaching the Bible as the Word of God and against those who would invoke

some way of knowledge and of salvation other than that revealed" (*CT* October 26, 1959:21; cf., Henry 1986b:26, 32). Although neo-orthodox theologians claimed they were seeking to recover the Reformation heritage that had been discarded by modernists, the evangelical view eventually excluded them from this heritage, along with liberals and modernists.

22. Though reporting on the North American Conference on Faith and Order (held at Oberlin College and attended by representatives from most major Protestant denominations), theologian G. Aiken Taylor, then minister of the First Presbyterian Church in Alexandria, Louisiana, expressed a similar concern over the blurring of boundaries between evangelicals and liberals when he wrote, "No greater time of danger has come upon the Christian Church than the present. For today Faith cannot be distinguished from Doubt by the language it uses or the confession it makes. . . . This is the situation which has driven Christians of every faith to a re-alignment of their loyalties. A new evangelical ecumenism is rising to meet the vapid ecumenism of radical theology. . . . When opposing armies become hard to tell apart by the uniform they wear, increasing alertness is indicated. There comes a time when some 'shibboleth' may be the only way to distinguish a man of Ephraim from a friend. Thus, instead of fading into disuse, such tests as the so-called five points of fundamentalism may loom in increasing importance. But even here the possibility of confusion remains" (1958:17).

Chapter Six

1. In *The Young Evangelicals* (1974), Quebedeaux discussed the advent of this new evangelical configuration. In two later works, *The New Charismatics* (1976) and *The Worldly Evangelicals* (1978), he documented various new expressions of evangelical religion and projected the religious consequences of the new evangelical push toward greater cultural and political participation in secular society (cf., Jorstad 1993; for a contemporaneous critique of evangelical political conservatism by one of these "young" evangelicals, see Pierard 1970. As Pierard prefaced his comments, "It is my sincere conviction that, if the trend toward political, economic, and social conservatism is not reversed, evangelical Christianity will soon be facing a crisis of disastrous proportions. In fact, its very survival in the 1970's may well depend on whether it can escape from the Unequal Yoke. If nothing is done, evangelicalism in the 1980's will be relegated to the status of a small and insignificant sect"; 1970:10).

2. It is interesting to compare Holmer's comments, which seem curiously out of place in an evangelical publication, with David Wells's recent critique of evangelical theology in his book *No Place for Truth* (1993). In the final chapter, titled "The Reform of Evangelicalism," Wells warned that "Unless the evangelical Church can recover the knowledge of what it means to live before a holy God, unless in its worship it can relearn humility, wonder, love, and praise, unless it can find again a moral purpose in the world that resonates with the holiness of God and that is accordingly deep and unyielding—unless the evangelical Church can do all of these things, theology will have no place

in its life. But the reverse is also true." The irony of evangelical success, Wells told his readers, rested in its ability to be simultaneously inside the world while it remained outside of it, to be both morally and culturally relevant and alien to it. As he put it: "Those who are most relevant to the modern world are irrelevant to the moral purpose of God, but those who are irrelevant in the world by virtue of their relevance to God actually have the most to say to the world. They are, in fact, the only ones who hav[e] anything to say to it" (1993:301). This, as Martin Marty might say, is the "irony of it all"—the irony of evangelical moral (ir)relevance, the irony of its cultural (ir)relevance.

3. For a more detailed and dispassionate theological discussion of the inerrancy crisis in American evangelicalism, see Johnston 1979:15-47. For a more general exposition on the continuing evangelical controversy over the inspiration and authority of the Bible, see Noll 1984 and 1986.

4. See McIntire 1951 and 1955, Walvoord 1957, and Rice 1959; see also Pickering 1959, and Lightner 1962:115-143.

5. For a detailed reporting of these events, see Marsden 1987:200-233.

6. It was Harold J. Ockenga who, as past president of Fuller Theological Seminary, spoke at the inauguration of Edward J. Carnell as its second president in 1954, declaring that "The new evangelicalism has its main fountain in Fuller Theological Seminary" (1954c:4).

7. E. J. Carnell once accused Karl Barth of being an "inconsistent evangelical," a phrase Lindsell may have borrowed from the late Carnell as an oblique reference to Carnell's crusade for a defensible orthodox evangelical theology (see Carnell 1961 and 1969:156).

8. Recall the fourteen subcultural types of evangelicalism that Robert Webber (1978) discerned.

9. As Henry reflected, somewhat wistfully, in his keynote address at the 1989 Evangelical Affirmations conference, "the evangelical movement has squandered much of its moral and spiritual initiative, and secular society has placed a large question mark over its motives, its goals, and even its integrity" (Kantzer and Henry 1990:69).

10. For additional background, see Kantzer and Henry 1990:513-518, and Carson and Woodbridge 1993:391. Some of the more notable evangelicals who attended, presented papers, or indicated wholehearted support for the "Consultation on Evangelical Affirmations" by serving on one of its coordinating committees included Billy Graham, Jerry Falwell, Charles Colson, Thomas Zimmerman, John White of the NAE, Vernon Grounds, Harold O. J. Brown, John Ankerberg, J. I. Packer, Nathan Hatch, David F. Wells, and John Woodbridge (Kantzer and Henry 1990:527-535).

11. See, for instance, Dayton and Johnston 1991, Horton 1991, Sweeney 1991a and 1991b, Carpenter 1993, Dayton 1993, Marsden 1993, Sweeney 1993, and Mohler 1993 and 1996; see also Sweet 1988. The cordial but pointed dialogues between Dayton and Marsden, who offer rival interpretations of American evangelical history and of its bounded constituencies, are especially instructive of this point. In its September 1993 "Special Issue," *Christian Scholar's Review,* an influential evangelical journal, published extended replies by Dayton and Marsden to the question "Who is an Evangelical?," as well as a lopsided panel of responses by such evangelical luminaries as Clark Pinnock, Joel Carpenter, and Daniel Fuller, son of the late pioneer radio

evangelist Charles Fuller. As this symposium proved, the impasse between Reformed (Marsden) and Wesleyan (Dayton) interpretations—what Albert Mohler referred to as the "Doctrine Party" and the "Experience Party" (1996:32)—remained nearly irresolvable. Indeed, Douglas Sweeney's youthful appeal for synthesis, reminiscent of the naively visionary "ecumenical evangelism" of the 1950s, went largely ignored by his Reformed evangelical colleagues on the panel.

12. One question that readily comes to mind is this: If boundaries function to define the group and thus structure its relationship to other groups (Barth 1969 and Cohen 1985), why, then, have the new evangelicals had such a difficult time defining themselves? The answer, it seems, has something to do with the quandary of how evangelicals should relate to the modern world, an issue to which evangelical spokespersons have almost uniformly responded with troubling uncertainty. Their indecisive response is not at all surprising, given evangelicalism's determination to make orthodoxy both respectable and responsive to contemporary society by occupying the territory between fundamentalism and liberalism.

13. Since the advent of the modern urban industrial age, American Protestants of all stripes have been caught up with the soul-searching question of how to live faithfully in an ever-modernizing, ever-secularizing world. What, Protestants have pondered, is the proper Christian response to the demands of an increasingly non-Christian culture? In general, the American Protestant response to modernism has been either to adapt to it or attack it (James Davison Hunter, 1983, contrasts liberal "accommodation" with conservative Protestant "resistance"). In contradistinction to liberal adaptation and fundamentalist attack, one might best describe the evangelical response to modernity as an ambivalent mixture of both. One consequence of this ambivalence is seen in the "unsettledness" of their position vis-à-vis the modern world. Evangelicals have found it constantly necessary to define and redefine themselves and make adjustments in their responses to secular society, sometimes with obsessive regularity. But because their positions are defined less by the content of the debate than by their relationship to their rivals on the right and on the left, evangelicals have found themselves often vacillating between withdrawal from secular society and engagement with it. This situation makes their responses quite inconsistent from one issue to the next, that is, predictably unpredictable.

14. How else might one account for the openness of Colson and Neuhaus's book, *Evangelicals and Catholics Together* (1995)? While the aim is not union but cooperation, the social forces that seem to draw representative Catholics and evangelicals into common cause certainly harken back to the new evangelical coalition's call for "Cooperation Without Compromise" (Paine 1949 and Murch 1956). Notice, for instance, the language in the essay by George Weigel, president of the Ethics and Public Policy Center, Washington, D.C., and protegé of Neuhaus, language that broadens the dialogue within American Christianity even as it draws a boundary between the evangelical-Catholic coalition and mainline liberal Protestantism: "Evangelicals and Catholics share a common affection for the American democratic experiment. Unlike many in the leadership of mainline/old-line Protestantism, evangelicals and Catholics do not regard America as an ill-fated republic, born in injustice and

dedicated to the rape of first North America and then the world. Rather, evangelicals and Catholics tend to think, *together,* that America remains a providentially guided experiment in religious freedom, religious tolerance, and the possibility of constructing political community amidst luxuriant diversity" (1995:49, emphasis added). Another example of the redrawing of coalitional boundaries is found in a book by the respected evangelical writer Norman L. Geisler and co-author Ralph E. MacKenzie, entitled *Roman Catholics and Evangelicals: Agreements and Disagreements* (1995). Their work, which seeks "to examine some of our common spiritual roots and see if we have any theological or moral bridges upon which we can both travel" (1995:15), concludes with a curiously charitable and ecumenical observation by the authors, one, it might be added, that evinces the coalitional dynamic that explains both the emergence of the new evangelicalism in the 1940s and its broadening diversity and changing alliances since that time. To quote Geisler and MacKenzie at length: "Since evangelicals and Roman Catholics have so much in common doctrinally and morally . . ., and, in spite of our significant intramural doctrinal differences . . . we believe that there are, nonetheless, many areas of common spiritual heritage and practical social and moral cooperation possible. This includes fighting our common enemies of Secularism and occultism that have infiltrated our culture and public schools. In addition to this there are root moral issues that have emerged in the political arena, such as abortion, pornography, immortality, and special rights for homosexuals, that call for our common cooperation" (1995:357; see also Ball 1992).

15. See, for instance, Tannenbaum, *et al.* 1978 and 1984, Rudin and Wilson 1987, Edwards and Stott 1988, Fournier 1990, Pinnock and Brown 1990, Ball 1992, Fackre 1993, Charles 1994, Fournier 1994, Colson and Neuhaus 1995, and Olson 1995.

16. See, for instance, the critical and cautionary comments in Yarbrough 1989, Armstrong 1994, Anderson 1995, Ankerberg and Weldon 1995, and Armstrong 1996.

17. It is certainly far too early to comment definitively on this curious emerging alliance of historically mortal "theological" enemies. At this juncture, success of the evangelical/Catholic dialogues may well be predicated on the ability of their respective representatives to mobilize their constituencies and fuse them into an effective theologically tolerant socio-political Christian coalition.

References and Sources

Abraham, William J. 1984. *The Coming Great Revival: Recovering the Full Evangelical Tradition*. San Francisco: Harper & Row Publishers.

Ahlstrom, Sydney E. 1975. *A Religious History of the American People* (vol. 2). Garden City, NY: Image Books.

———. 1977. "From Puritanism to Evangelicalism: A Critical Perspective." Pp. 289-309 in *The* Evangelicals, edited by David F. Wells and John D. Woodbridge. Grand Rapids, MI: Baker Book House.

Albanese, Catherine L. 1992. *America: Religions and Religion* (2nd edition). Belmont, CA: Wadsworth Publishing Co.

Allport, Gordon W. 1950. *The Individual and His Religion*. New York: Macmillan.

Ammerman, Nancy T. 1982. "Operationalizing Evangelicalism: An Amendment." *Sociological Analysis* 43 (170-171).

Anderson, Mary Jo. 1995. "Evangelicals vs. Catholics." *Crisis* 13 (October 1: 25-28).

Ankerberg, John and John Weldon. 1995. *Protestants and Catholics: Do They Now Agree?* Eugene, OR: Harvest House Publishers.

Armstrong, John H. (ed.). 1994. *Roman Catholicism: Evangelical Protestants Analyze What Divides and Unites Us*. Chicago: Moody Press.

———(ed.). 1996. *The Coming Evangelical Crisis: Current Challenges to the Authority of Scripture and the Gospel*. Chicago: Moody Press.

Ashbrook, William E. 1963. *Evangelicalism: The New Neutralism*. Columbus, OH: published by author.

Ayer, William W. 1942. "Evangelical Christianity Endangered by Its Fragmentized Condition." Pp. 41-46 in *Evangelical Action!* Boston: United Action Press.

Bainbridge, William Sims. 1997. *The Sociology of Religious Movements*. New York: Routledge.

Ball, William Bentley (ed.). 1992. *In Search of a National Morality: A Manifesto for Evangelicals and Catholics*. Grand Rapids, MI: Baker Books.

Barker, Eileen. 1992. *New Religious Movements: A Practical Introduction*. London: HMSO.

Barker, Eileen, James A. Beckford, and Karel Dobbelaere (eds.). 1993. *Secularization, Rationalism, and Sectarianism*. Oxford: Clarendon Press.

Barr, James. 1978. *Fundamentalism*. Philadelphia: The Westminster Press.

Barth, Fredrik (ed.). 1969. *Ethnic Groups and Boundaries*. London: George Allen and Unwin.

Bass, Clarence B. 1978. *Backgrounds to Dispensationalism* (Reprinted). Grand Rapids, MI: Baker Book House.

Baxter, David. 1964. "Does Extremism Erode Historical Christianity?" *United Evangelical Action* 23 (May: 5-6).

Bebbington, David. 1994. "Evangelicalism in Its Settings: The British and American Movements since 1940." Pp. 365-388 in *Evangelicalism: Comparative*

    Studies of Popular Protestantism in North America, the British Isles, and Beyond, 1700-1990, edited by Mark A. Noll, David W. Bebbington, and George A. Rawlyk. New York: Oxford University Press.

Beckford, James A. 1989. *Religion and Advanced Industrial Society.* London: Unwin Hyman.

Bellah, Robert N. and Frederick Greenspahn (eds.). 1987. *Uncivil Religion.* New York: Crossroad.

Bellah, Robert N., Robert Madsen, William M. Sullivan, Ann Swidler and Steven M. Tipton. 1985. *Habits of the Heart.* New York: Harper & Row.

Berger, Peter L. 1969. *The Sacred Canopy.* Garden City, NY: Anchor Books.

———. 1983. "From the Crisis of Religion to the Crisis of Secularity." Pp. 14-24 in *Religion and America: Spirituality in a Secular Age,* edited by Mary Douglas and Steven M. Tipton. Boston: Beacon Press.

Berger, Peter L. and Thomas Luckmann. 1967. *The Social Construction of Reality.* Garden City, NY: Anchor Books.

Berkhof, Louis. 1950. "'Liberalism' Attacked by Barthian Movement." *United Evangelical Action* 9 (March 1: 7).

Bloesch, Donald G. 1972. "The New Evangelicalism." *Religion in Life* 41 (327-339).

———. 1973. *The Evangelical Renaissance.* Grand Rapids, MI: Eerdmans.

———. 1983. *The Future of Evangelical Christianity.* Garden City, NY: Doubleday & Co.

Bolich, Gregory G. 1980. *Karl Barth and Evangelicalism.* Downers Grove, IL: InterVarsity Press.

Boone, Kathleen C. 1989. *The Bible Tells Them So: The Discourse of Protestant Fundamentalism.* Albany: SUNY Press.

Boyer, Paul. 1992. *When Time Shall Be No More: Prophecy Belief in Modern American Culture.* Cambridge, MA: Belknap/Harvard.

Bradbury, John W. 1948. "Evangelical Unity." *United Evangelical Action* 7 (February 15: 7).

Bromiley, Geoffrey W. 1957. "Fundamentalism-Modernism: A First Step in the Controversy." *Christianity Today* 2 (November 11: 3-5).

———. 1958. *The Unity and Disunity of the Church.* Grand Rapids, MI: Eerdmans Publishing Co.

———. 1959. "Barth: A Contemporary Appraisal." *Christianity Today* 3 (February 2: 9-10).

Bromley, David G. and Anson Shupe (eds.). 1984. *The New Christian Politics.* Macon, GA: Mercer University Press.

Bruce, Steve. 1988. *The Rise and Fall of the New Christian Right: Conservative Protestant Politics in America, 1978-1988.* Oxford: Clarendon Press.

———. 1990. *Pray T.V.: Televangelism in America.* London: Routledge.

———(ed.). 1992. *Religion and Modernization.* Oxford: Clarendon Press.

Bruce, Steve, Peter Kivisto, and William H. Swatos, Jr. (eds.). 1995. *The Rapture of Politics: The Christian Right as the United States Approaches the Year 2000.* New Brunswick, NJ: Transaction Books.

Burns, Vincent Godfrey. 1926. *Fosdick and the Fundamentalists.* New York: The League for Public Defense.

Buswell, J. Oliver, Jr. 1949. "'Here I Stand. . . .'" *United Evangelical Action* 8 (December 1: 4).

Butler, Farley P., Jr. 1976. "Billy Graham and the End of Evangelical Unity." Unpublished doctoral dissertation, University of Florida.

Cairns, Earle E. 1955. "A New Era in Evangelical Cooperation." *United Evangelical Action* 14 (August 15: 3-4, 6, 15-16).

Carnell, Edward John. 1958. "Orthodoxy and Ecumenism." *Christianity Today* 2 (September 1: 15-18, 24).

———. 1959a. *The Case for Orthodox Theology*. Philadelphia: The Westminster Press.

———. 1959b. "Post-Fundamentalist Faith." *The Christian Century* 76 (August 26: 971).

———. 1960a. "Orthodoxy: Cultic vs. Classical" ("How My Mind Has Changed" series). *The Christian Century* 77 (March 30: 377-379).

———. 1960b. *The Theology of Reinhold Niebuhr* (Revised ed.). Grand Rapids, MI: Eerdmans Publishing Co.

———. 1961. "Barth as Inconsistent Evangelical." *The Christian Century* 78 (June 6: 713-714).

———. 1969. *The Case for Biblical Christianity* (Ronald H. Nash, ed.). Grand Rapids, MI: Eerdmans Publishing Co.

Carpenter, Joel A. 1980. "A Shelter in the Time of Storm: Fundamentalist Institutions and the Rise of Evangelical Protestantism, 1929-1942." *Church History* 49 (62-75).

———. 1984a. "From Fundamentalism to the New Evangelical Coalition." Pp. 3-16 in *Evangelicalism and Modern America*, edited by George M. Marsden. Grand Rapids, MI: Eerdmans Publishing Co.

———. 1984b. "The Fundamentalist Leaven and the Rise of an Evangelical United Front." Pp. 257-288 in *The Evangelical Tradition in America*, edited by Leonard I. Sweet. Macon, GA: Mercer University Press.

———. 1984c. "The Renewal of American Fundamentalism, 1930-1945." Unpublished doctoral dissertation. The Johns Hopkins University.

———. 1989. "Revive Us Again: Alienation, Hope, and the Resurgence of Fundamentalism, 1930-1950." Pp. 105-125 in *Transforming Faith*, edited by M. L. Bradbury and James B. Gilbert. New York: Greenwood Press.

———. 1993. "The Scope of American Evangelicalism: Some Comments on the Dayton-Marsden Exchange." *Christian Scholar's Review* 23 (September: 53-61).

Carson, Donald A. 1990. "Evangelicals, Ecumenism and the Church." Pp. 347-385 in *Evangelical Affirmations*, edited by Kenneth S. Kantzer and Carl F. H. Henry. Grand Rapids, MI: Zondervan Publishing Co.

Carson, D. A. and John D. Woodbridge (eds.). 1993. *God and Culture: Essays in Honor of Carl F. H. Henry*. Grand Rapids, MI: Eerdmans.

Case, Shirley Jackson. 1918. *The Millennial Hope*. Chicago: University of Chicago Press.

Cauthen, Kenneth. 1962. *The Impact of American Religious Liberalism*. New York: Harper & Row.

Charles, J. Daryl. 1994. "Evangelical-Catholic Dialogue: Basis, Boundaries, Benefits." *Pro Ecclesia* 3 (Summer: 289-305).

Cherry, Conrad (ed.). 1971. *God's New Israel: Religious Interpretations of American Destiny*. Englewood Cliffs, NJ: Prentice-Hall.

Clabaugh, Gary K. 1974. *Thunder on the Right: The Protestant Fundamentalists*. Chicago: Nelson-Hall.

Clark, Gordon H. 1962. "Special Report: Encountering Barth in Chicago." *Christianity Today* 6 (May 11: 35-36).

Coalter, Milton J., John M. Mulder, and Lewis B. Weeks (eds.). 1990. *The Mainline Protestant 'Decline': The Presbyterian Pattern*. Louisville: Westminster/John Knox Press.

Cohen, Anthony P. 1985. *The Symbolic Construction of Community*. London: Tavistock Publications.

Colson, Charles and Richard John Neuhaus (eds.). 1995. *Evangelicals and Catholics Together: Working Toward a Common Mission*. Dallas, TX: Word Publishing.

Cowie, David. 1957. "What is Christian Separation?" *Christianity Today* 2 (November 11: 12-15).

Crunkilton, Willard. 1952. "The 'One Church' Idea." *United Evangelical Action* 10 (February 1: 7-8).

Dayton, Donald W. 1974. "An American Revival of Karl Barth?" (2 parts) *The Reformed Journal* 24 (October: 17-21; November: 24-26).

———. 1978. *Discovering an Evangelical Heritage*. New York: Harper & Row.

———(ed.). 1988a. *The Prophecy Conference Movement* (4 vols). New York: Garland Publishing Co.

———. 1988b. "Yet Another Layer of the Onion: Or Opening the Ecumenical Door to Let the Riffraff In." *The Ecumenical Review* 40 (January: 87-110).

———. 1993. "'The Search for the Historical Evangelicalism': George Marsden's History of Fuller Seminary as a Case Study." *Christian Scholar's Review* 23 (September: 12-33).

Dayton, Donald W. and Robert K. Johnston (eds.). 1991. *The Variety of American Evangelicalism*. Downers Grove, IL: InterVarsity Press.

Demerath, N. J., III. 1995. "Cultural Victory and Organizational Defeat in the Paradoxical Decline of Liberal Protestantism." *Journal for the Scientific Study of Religion* 34, 4 (December: 458-469).

Demerath, N. J., III and Rhys H. Williams. 1992. *A Bridging of Faiths: Religion and Politics in a New England City*. Princeton: Princeton University Press.

DeWolf, L. Harold. 1959. *The Case for Theology in Liberal Perspective*. Philadelphia: The Westminster Press.

Dollar, George W. 1973. *A History of Fundamentalism in America*. Greenville, SC: Bob Jones University Press.

Dormon, James H. 1980. "Ethnic Groups and Ethnicity: Some Theoretical Considerations." *Journal of Ethnic Studies* 7, 4 (23-36).

Douglas, Mary. 1984. *Purity and Danger* (Reprinted). London: Ark Paperbacks.

Douglas, Mary and Steven M. Tipton (eds.). 1983. *Religion and America: Spirituality in a Secular Age*. Boston: Beacon Press.

Editorial. 1940a. "An Unfair Test of Fellowship." *Baptist and Reflector* 106 (February 8: 2-3).

Editorial. 1940b. "'Essentials' and 'Non-Essentials.'" *Baptist and Reflector* 106 (May 9: 2).

Editorial. 1942a. "A Temporary Committee that Should Never Be Permanent." *The Presbyterian Guardian* 11 (March 25: 87-88).

Editorial. 1942b. "Facts Versus Whips." *United Evangelical Action* 1 (December: 2).

Editorial. 1943a. "A Question Answered." *United Evangelical Action* 1 (January: 3).

Editorial. 1943b. "Sectarianism Receives New Lease on Life." *Christian Century* 60 (May 19: 596).

Edman, V. Raymond. 1956. "From Luther to Barth." *Moody Monthly* 56 (April: 20-23, 37).

Edwards, David L. and John Stott. 1988. *Essentials: A Liberal-Evangelical Dialogue.* Downers Grove, IL: InterVasity Press.

Ellingsen, Mark. 1988. *The Evangelical Movement: Growth, Impact, Controversy, Dialog.* Minneapolis: Augsburg Publishing House.

Evangelical Action!: A Report of the Organization of the National Association of Evangelicals for United Action. 1942. Boston: United Action Press.

Evans, Elizabeth. 1991. *The Wright Vision: The Story of the New England Fellowship.* Lanham, MD: University Press of America.

Evans, Mike. 1986. *The Return.* Nashville: Thomas Nelson Publishers.

Fackre, Gabriel. 1993. *Ecumenical Faith in Evangelical Perspective.* Grand Rapids, MI: William B. Eerdmans Publishing Co.

Fea, John. 1994. "Understanding the Changing Facade of Twentieth-Century American Protestant Fundamentalism: Toward a Historical Definition." *Trinity Journal* 15 (Fall: 181-199).

Feinberg, Charles L. (ed.). 1957. "An Answer to 'Is Evangelical Christianity Changing?'" *King's Business* 48 (January: 23-28).

Finke, Roger and Rodney Stark. 1992. *The Churching of America, 1776-1990: Winners and Losers in Our Religious Economy.* New Brunswick, NJ: Rutgers University Press.

Ford, George L. 1956. "Why the NAE is Succeeding." *United Evangelical Action* 15 (March 15: 5, 29-30).

Fournier, Keith A. 1990. *Evangelical Catholics: A Call for Christian Cooperation to Penetrate the Darkness with the Light of the Gospel.* Nashville, TN: Thomas Nelson.

———(with William D. Watkins). 1994. *A House United?: Evangelicals and Catholics Together.* Colorado Springs, CO: Navpress.

Frank, Douglas, W. 1986. *Less than Conquerors: How Evangelicalism Entered the Twentieth Century.* Grand Rapids, MI: Eerdmans.

Fuller, Daniel P. 1972. *Give the Winds a Mighty Voice: The Story of Charles E. Fuller.* Waco, TX: Word Books.

———. 1993. "Response to Donald W. Dayton." *Christian Scholar's Review* 23 (September: 41-43).

Furniss, Norman F. 1954. *The Fundamentalist Controversy, 1918-1931.* New Haven, CT: Yale University Press.

Gaebelein, Arno C. 1914. "The Present-day Apostasy: A Proof of the Inspiration of the Bible and the Near Coming of Our Lord." Pp. 148-155 in *The Coming and Kingdom of Christ,* edited by James M. Gray. Chicago: The Bible Institute Colportage Association.

Gangel, Kenneth O. 1962. "What's Wrong With Being a Fundamentalist?" *United Evangelical Action* 21 (November: 16-17).

Garrett, James L., Jr., E. Glenn Hinson, and James E. Tull. 1983. *Are Southern Baptists "Evangelicals"?* Macon, GA: Mercer University Press.

Gasper, Louis. 1981. *The Fundamentalist Movement, 1930-1956* (Reprinted). Grand Rapids, MI: Baker Book House.

Gatewood, Willard B., Jr. (ed.). 1969. *Controversy in the Twenties.* Nashville, TN: Vanderbilt University Press.

Gaustad, Edwin S. (ed.). 1974. *The Rise of Adventism: Religion and Society in Mid-Nineteenth-Century America.* New York: Harper & Row.

Geisler, Norman L. and Ralph MacKenzie. 1995. *Roman Catholics and Evangelicals: Agreements and Differences.* Grand Rapids, MI: Baker Book House.

Gier, Nicholas F. 1987. *God, Reason, and the Evangelicals.* Lanham, MD: University Press of America.

Gordon, Ernest. "Ecclesiastical Octopus" (a digest of *An Ecclesiastical Octopus* in six parts). *United Evangelical Action* 7, 14-19 (September 1-November 15).

Graham, Billy. 1960. "What Ten Years Have Taught Me." *The Christian Century* 77 (February 17: 186-189).

Greeley, Andrew M. 1972. *The Denominational Society.* Glenview, IL: Scott, Foresman and Co.

Grounds, Vernon. 1956. "The Nature of Evangelicalism." *Eternity* (February: 12-13, 42-43).

———. 1961. "Fundamentalism Needs a Reformation." *Eternity* 12 (December: 21-24, 29).

Hadden, Jeffrey K. and Charles E. Swann. 1981. *Prime Time Preachers: The Rising Power of Televangelism.* Reading, MA: Addison-Wesley Publishing Co.

Haldeman, I. M. 1919. *The Signs of the Times.* Philadelphia: Philadelphia School of the Bible.

Hammond, Phillip E. 1983. "In Search of a Protestant Twentieth Century: American Religion and Power Since 1900." *Review of Religious Research* 24, 4 (281-294).

———. 1985a. "Evangelical Politics: Generalizations and Implications." *Review of Religious Research* 27, 2 (189-192).

———(ed.). 1985b. *The Sacred in a Secular Age.* Berkeley: University of California Press.

———. 1992. *Religion and Personal Autonomy: The Third Disestablishment in America.* Columbia: University of South Carolina Press.

Hammond, Phillip E. and James D. Hunter. 1984. "On Maintaining Plausibility: The Worldview of Evangelical College Students." *Journal for the Scientific Study of Religion* 23, 3 (221-238).

Handy, Robert T. 1960. "The American Religious Depression, 1925-1935." *Church History* 29 (3-16).

Harden, Margaret G. c.1966. *A Brief History of the Bible Presbyterian Church and Its Agencies.* Cape May, NJ: Bible Presbyterian Church.

Harrell, David E., Jr. (ed.). *Varieties of Southern Evangelicalism.* Macon, GA: Mercer University Press.

Harrison, Everett F. 1958. "Criteria of Biblical Inerrancy." *Christianity Today* 2 (January 20: 16-18).

Hart, D. G. 1994. *Defender of the Faith: J. Gresham Machen and the Crisis of American Protestantism in Modern America.* Baltimore, MD: The Johns Hopkins University Press.

Hedstrom, James A. 1982. "Evangelical Program in the United States, 1945-1980: The Morphology of Establishment, Progressive, and Radical Platforms." Unpublished doctoral dissertation, Vanderbilt University.

Henry, Carl F. H. 1947. *The Uneasy Conscience of Modern Fundamentalism.* Grand Rapids, MI: Eerdmans.

———. 1948a. "The Vigor of the New Evangelicalism" (pt. 1). *Christian Life* (January: 30-32).

———. 1948b. "The Vigor of the New Evangelicalism" (pt. 2). *Christian Life* (March: 35-38, 85).

———. 1949. "Conservative or Liberal—What Is the Difference?" *United Evangelical Action* 7 (January 15: 3-4).

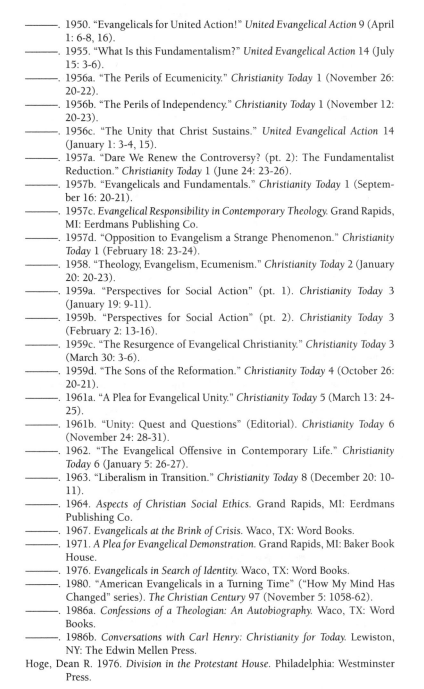

―――. 1950. "Evangelicals for United Action!" *United Evangelical Action* 9 (April 1: 6-8, 16).

―――. 1955. "What Is this Fundamentalism?" *United Evangelical Action* 14 (July 15: 3-6).

―――. 1956a. "The Perils of Ecumenicity." *Christianity Today* 1 (November 26: 20-22).

―――. 1956b. "The Perils of Independency." *Christianity Today* 1 (November 12: 20-23).

―――. 1956c. "The Unity that Christ Sustains." *United Evangelical Action* 14 (January 1: 3-4, 15).

―――. 1957a. "Dare We Renew the Controversy? (pt. 2): The Fundamentalist Reduction." *Christianity Today* 1 (June 24: 23-26).

―――. 1957b. "Evangelicals and Fundamentals." *Christianity Today* 1 (September 16: 20-21).

―――. 1957c. *Evangelical Responsibility in Contemporary Theology.* Grand Rapids, MI: Eerdmans Publishing Co.

―――. 1957d. "Opposition to Evangelism a Strange Phenomenon." *Christianity Today* 1 (February 18: 23-24).

―――. 1958. "Theology, Evangelism, Ecumenism." *Christianity Today* 2 (January 20: 20-23).

―――. 1959a. "Perspectives for Social Action" (pt. 1). *Christianity Today* 3 (January 19: 9-11).

―――. 1959b. "Perspectives for Social Action" (pt. 2). *Christianity Today* 3 (February 2: 13-16).

―――. 1959c. "The Resurgence of Evangelical Christianity." *Christianity Today* 3 (March 30: 3-6).

―――. 1959d. "The Sons of the Reformation." *Christianity Today* 4 (October 26: 20-21).

―――. 1961a. "A Plea for Evangelical Unity." *Christianity Today* 5 (March 13: 24-25).

―――. 1961b. "Unity: Quest and Questions" (Editorial). *Christianity Today* 6 (November 24: 28-31).

―――. 1962. "The Evangelical Offensive in Contemporary Life." *Christianity Today* 6 (January 5: 26-27).

―――. 1963. "Liberalism in Transition." *Christianity Today* 8 (December 20: 10-11).

―――. 1964. *Aspects of Christian Social Ethics.* Grand Rapids, MI: Eerdmans Publishing Co.

―――. 1967. *Evangelicals at the Brink of Crisis.* Waco, TX: Word Books.

―――. 1971. *A Plea for Evangelical Demonstration.* Grand Rapids, MI: Baker Book House.

―――. 1976. *Evangelicals in Search of Identity.* Waco, TX: Word Books.

―――. 1980. "American Evangelicals in a Turning Time" ("How My Mind Has Changed" series). *The Christian Century* 97 (November 5: 1058-62).

―――. 1986a. *Confessions of a Theologian: An Autobiography.* Waco, TX: Word Books.

―――. 1986b. *Conversations with Carl Henry: Christianity for Today.* Lewiston, NY: The Edwin Mellen Press.

Hoge, Dean R. 1976. *Division in the Protestant House.* Philadelphia: Westminster Press.

Hoge, Dean R., Benton Johnson, and Donald A. Luidens. 1994. *Vanishing Boundaries: The Religion of Mainline Protestant Baby Boomers.* Louisville: Westminster/John Knox Press.

Holmer, Paul L. 1977. "Contemporary Evangelical Faith: An Assessment and Critique." Pp. 88-115 in *The Evangelicals,* edited by David F. Wells and John D. Woodbridge. Grand Rapids, MI: Baker Book House.

Hoover, Stewart M. 1988. *Mass Media Religion: The Social Sources of the Electronic Church.* Newbury Park, CA: Sage Publications.

Hordern, William E. 1959. *The Case for a New Reformation.* Philadelphia: Westminster Press.

———. 1962. *A Layman's Guide to Protestant Theology* (Revised edition). New York: Macmillan Publishing Co.

Horton, Michael Scott. 1991. *Made in America: The Shaping of Modern American Evangelicalism.* Grand Rapids, MI: Baker Book House.

Howard, David M. 1986. *The Dream that Would Not Die: The Birth and Growth of the World Evangelical Fellowship, 1846-1986.* Exeter: The Paternoster Press, LTD.

Hudson, Winthrop S. 1981. *Religion in America* (3rd edition). New York: Charles Scribner's Sons.

Hughes, Richard T. (ed.). 1988. *The American Quest for the Primitive Church.* Urbana and Chicago: University of Illinois Press.

Hughes, Richard T. and C. Leonard Allen. 1988. *Illusions of Innocence: Protestant Primitivism in America, 1630-1875.* Chicago: University of Chicago Press.

Hunter, J. H. 1957. "Billy Graham and His Critics." *The Evangelical Christian* 55 (June: 268).

Hunter, James Davison. 1982. "Operationalizing Evangelicalism: A Review, Critique and Proposal." *Sociological Analysis* 42 (363-372).

———. 1983. *American Evangelicalism: Conservative Religion and the Quandary of Modernity.* New Brunswick, NJ: Rutgers University Press.

———. 1987. *Evangelicalism: The Coming Generation.* Chicago: University of Chicago Press.

———. 1991. *Culture Wars: The Struggle to Define America.* New York: Basic Books.

Hutchison, William R. 1976. *The Modernist Impulse in American Protestantism.* Cambridge, MA: Harvard University Press.

———(ed.). 1985. *American Protestant Thought in the Liberal Era* (Reprinted). Lanham, MD: University Press of America.

Inch, Morris A. 1978. *The Evangelical Challenge.* Philadelphia: The Westminster Press.

"Introduction to Theology: Questions to and Discussion with Dr. Karl Barth." 1963. *Criterion* 2 (Winter: 3-11, 18-24).

"Is Doctor Henry Right?" 1947. *United Evangelical Action* 6 (July 15: 5, 15-16).

"Is Evangelical Theology Changing?" 1956. *Christian Life* 17 (March: 16-19).

Jaberg, Russell L. 1960. "Is There Room for Fundamentalism?" *Christianity Today* 4 (July 18: 6-7).

Jelen, Ted G. 1991. *The Political Mobilization of Religious Beliefs.* New York: Praeger.

Johnson, Benton. 1963. "On Church and Sect." *American Sociological Review* 28 (539-549).

Johnson, Terry, Christopher Dandeker, and Clive Ashworth. 1984. *The Structure of Social Theory.* New York: St. Martin's Press.

Johnston, Robert K. 1979. *Evangelicals at an Impasse.* Atlanta: John Knox Press.

Jorstad, Erling. 1970. *The Politics of Doomsday: Fundamentalists of the Far Right.* Nashville: Abingdon Press.

———. 1981. *Evangelicals in the White House: The Cultural Maturation of Born Again Christianity 1960-1981.* New York: The Edwin Mellen Press.

———. 1987. *The New Christian Right 1981-1988: Prospects for the Post-Reagan Decade.* Lewiston, NY: The Edwin Mellen Press.

———. 1993. *Popular Religion in America: The Evangelical Voice.* Westport, CT: Greenwood Press.

Kantzer, Kenneth S. 1977. "Unity and Diversity in Evangelical Faith." Pp. 58-87 in *The Evangelicals,* edited by David F. Wells and John D. Woodbridge. Grand Rapids, MI: Baker Books House.

———. 1978. "Evangelicals and the Inerrancy Question." Pp. 83-100 in *Evangelical Roots,* edited by Kenneth S. Kantzer. Nashville, TN: Thomas Nelson.

Kantzer, Kenneth S. and Carl F. H. Henry (eds.). 1990. *Evangelical Affirmations.* Grand Rapids, MI: Zondervan Publishing Co.

Kaub, Verne P. 1951. "Super-Church is Born." *United Evangelical Action* 9 (January 1: 3-4, 6, 8).

Kellogg, Samuel H. 1893. *The Jews: Prediction & Fulfillment.* London: James Nisbet & Co.

Kepel, Gilles. 1994. *The Revenge of God: The Resurgence of Islam, Christianity, and Judaism in the Modern World* (Alan Braley, trans.). University Park, PA: The Pennsylvania State University Press.

Kik, J. Marcellus. 1956. "Are Evangelicals Literalists?" *Christianity Today* 1 (November 12: 26-27, 33).

———. 1957a. "That They May Be One." *Christianity Today* 1 (January 21: 16-17).

———. 1957b. "Unity of the Spirit." *Christianity Today* 1 (June 22: 7-8, 22).

———. 1958. *Ecumenism and the Evangelical.* Grand Rapids, MI: Baker Book House.

King, Rachel H. 1963. "My Pilgrimage from Liberalism to Orthodoxy." *Christianity Today* 8 (December 6: 7-10).

Knauss, Elizabeth. 1923. *The Conflict: A Narrative Based on the Fundamentalist Movement.* Los Angeles: Bible Institute of Los Angeles.

Kraus, C. Norman. 1958. *Dispensationalism in America: Its Rise and Development.* Richmond, VA: John Knox Press.

Kuklick, Bruce. 1985. *Churchmen and Philosophers: From Jonathan Edwards to John Dewey.* New Haven: Yale University Press.

Ladd, George E. 1962. "The Evangelical Dilemma: Doctrinal Purity vs. Visible Unity." *Eternity* 13 (June: 7-9, 33).

Liebman, Robert and Robert Wuthnow (eds.). 1983. *The New Christian Right: Mobilization and Legitimation.* New York: Aldine Publishing Co.

Lightner, Robert P. 1962. *Neo-evangelicalism.* Findlay, OH: Dunham Publishing Co.

Lindsell, Harold. 1951. *Park Street Prophet: A Life of Harold John Ockenga.* Wheaton, IL: Van Kampen Press.

———. 1965. "Who Are the Evangelicals?" *Christianity Today* 9 (June 18: 3-6).

———. 1976. *The Battle for the Bible.* Grand Rapids, MI: Zondervan Publishing House.

———. 1978. "Another Battle About the Bible." Pp. 75-82 in *Evangelical Roots,* edited by Kenneth S. Kantzer. Nashville TN: Thomas Nelson.

———. 1979. *The Bible in the Balance.* Grand Rapids, MI: Zondervan Publishing House.

Lindsey, Albert J. 1956. "Ecumenicity and Church Regimentation." *United Evangelical Action* 15 (August 15: 3-4).

Lofland, John and Norman Skonovd. 1981. "Conversion Motifs." *Journal for the Scientific Study of Religion* 20, 4 (December: 373-385).

———. 1983. "Patterns of Conversion." Pp. 1-24 in *Of Gods and Men: New Religious Movements in the West,* edited by Eileen Barker. Macon, GA: Mercer University Press.

Longfield, Bradley J. 1991. *The Presbyterian Controversy: Fundamentalists, Modernists, and Moderates.* New York: Oxford University Press.

Machen, J. Gresham. 1922. "Liberalism or Christianity?" *Princeton Theological Review* 20 (93-117).

———. 1923. *Christianity and Liberalism.* Grand Rapids, MI: William B. Eerdmans Publishing Co.

———. 1933. "The Responsibility of the Church in Our New Age." *The Annals of the American Academy of Political and Social Science* 165 (January: 38-47).

Markus, R. A. 1980. "The Problem of Self-Definition: From Sect to Church." Pp. 1-15 in *Jewish and Christian Self-Definition* (vol. 1), edited by E. P. Sanders. Philadelphia: Fortress Press.

Marsden, George M. 1977. "From Fundamentalism to Evangelicalism: A Historical Analysis." Pp. 142-162 in *The Evangelicals,* edited by David F. Wells and John D. Woodbridge. Grand Rapids, MI: Baker Book House.

———. 1980. *Fundamentalism and American Culture.* New York: Oxford University Press.

———. 1983. "Preachers of Paradox: The Religious New Right in Historical Perspective." Pp. 150-168 in *Religion and America: Spirituality in a Secular Age,* edited by Mary Douglas and Steven M. Tipton. Boston: Beacon Press.

———(ed.). 1984. *Evangelicalism and Modern America.* Grand Rapids, MI: Eerdmans Publishing Co.

———. 1987. *Reforming Fundamentalism: Fuller Seminary and the New Evangelicalism.* Grand Rapids, MI: Eerdmans Publishing Co.

———. 1989. "Unity and Diversity in the Evangelical Resurgence." Pp. 61-76 in *Altered Landscapes: Christianity in America, 1935-1985,* edited by David W. Lotz. Grand Rapids, MI: Eerdmans.

———. 1991. *Understanding Fundamentalism and Evangelicalism.* Grand Rapids, MI: Eerdmans Publishing Co.

———. 1993. "Response to Don Dayton." *Christian Scholar's Review* 23 (September: 34-40).

Marty, Martin E. 1970. *Righteous Empire: The Protestant Experience in America.* New York: Harper Torchbooks.

———. 1976. *Nation of Behavers.* Chicago: University of Chicago Press.

———. 1977. "Tensions Within Contemporary Evangelicalism: A Critical Appraisal." Pp. 190-208 in *The Evangelicals,* edited by David F. Wells and John D. Woodbridge. Grand Rapids, MI: Baker Book House.

———. 1981. "The Revival of Evangelicalism and Southern Religion." Pp. 7-21 in *Varieties of Southern Evangelicalism,* edited by David E. Harrell, Jr. Macon, GA: Mercer University of Press.

Massee, J. C. 1954. "The Thirty Years' War." *The Chronicle* 17 (April: 106-116).

Masters, D. C. 1960. "The Rise of Evangelicalism" (pt. 1). *The Evangelical Christian* (December: 26-28, 30-33).

———. 1961. "The Rise of Evangelicalism" (pt. 2). *The Evangelical Christian* (January: 18-20, 21, 23-24).

————. 1961. "The Rise of Evangelicalism" (pt. 3). *The Evangelical Christian* (February: 22-24, 26).

Mathews, Shailer. 1924. *The Faith of Modernism*. New York: The Macmillan Company.

May, Henry F. 1949. *Protestant Churches and Industrial America*. New York: Harper & Brothers.

McCall, Duke K. 1953. "Northern Fundamentalism." *Baptist and Reflector* 119 (September 3: 12).

McCowan, Kenneth. 1963. "Historic Contemporary Fundamentalism." *Christianity Today* 7 (July 5: 12).

McGrath, Alister. 1995. *Evangelicalism and the Future of Christianity*. Downers Grove, IL: InterVarsity Press.

McGuire, Meredith B. 1987. *Religion: The Social Context* (2nd edition). Belmont, CA: Wadsworth Publishing Co.

McIntire, Carl. 1944. *Twentieth Century Reformation*. Collingswood, NJ: Christian Beacon Press.

————. 1949. *Modern Tower of Babel*. Collingswood, NJ: Christian Beacon Press.

————. 1951. "N.A.E., Fuller Seminary, Championed by Ockenga." *Christian Beacon* 16 (May 10: 1, 4-5, 8).

————. 1955. *Servants of Apostasy*. Collingswood, NJ: Christian Beacon Press.

————. 1967a. *Outside the Gate*. Collingswood, NJ: Christian Beacon Press.

————. 1967b. *The Protestant Revolt: Road to Freedom for American Churches*. Arlington, VA: Crestwood Books.

McKinney, William (ed.). 1994. *The Responsibility People: Eighteen Senior Leaders of Protestant Churches and National Ecumenical Agencies Reflect on Church Leadership*. Grand Rapids, MI: Eerdmans Publishing Co.

McLoughlin, William G. 1955. *Billy Sunday Was His Real Name*. Chicago: University of Chicago Press.

————. 1967. "Is There a Third Force in Christendom?" *Daedalus* 96 (Winter: 43-68).

————(ed.). 1968. *The American Evangelicals: 1800-1900*. New York: Harper Torchbooks.

————. 1978. *Revivals, Awakenings, and Reform*. Chicago: University of Chicago Press.

Mead, Sidney E. 1963. *The Lively Experiment*. New York: Harper & Row.

Meeking, Basil and John Stott (eds.). 1986. *The Evangelical-Roman Catholic Dialogue on Mission,1977-1984*. Grand Rapids, MI: Eerdmans Publishing Co.

Melton, J. Gordon, Phillip Charles Lucas, and Jon R. Stone. 1997. *Prime-Time Religion: An Encyclopedia of Religious Broadcasting*. Phoenix, AZ: The Oryx Press.

Merrill, William P. 1925. *Liberal Christianity*. New York: The Macmillan Company.

Meyer, Donald B. 1960. *The Protestant Search for Political Realism: 1919-1941*. Berkeley: University of California Press.

Michaelsen, Robert S. and Wade Clark Roof (eds.). 1986. *Liberal Protestantism: Realities and Possibilities*. New York: The Pilgrim Press.

Moen, Matthew C. 1989. *The Christian Right and Congress*. Tuscaloosa, AL: University of Alabama Press.

Mohler, R. Albert, Jr. 1993. "Southern Baptists and American Evangelicals: A Common Quest for Identity." Pp. 224-239 in *Southern Baptists and American Evangelicals*, edited by David S. Dockery. Nashville, TN: Broadman & Holman.

————. 1996. "'Evangelical': What's in a Name?" Pp. 29-44 in *The Coming Evangelical Crisis: Current Challenges to the Authority of Scripture and the Gospel*, edited by John H. Armstrong. Chicago: Moody Press.

Moore, R. Laurence. 1986. *Religious Outsiders and the Making of Americans*. New York: Oxford University Press.

Morgan, Edmund S. 1958. *The Puritan Dilemma: The Story of John Winthrop*. Boston: Little, Brown and Company.

Morrison, C. C. 1924. "Fundamentalism and Modernism: Two Religions." *The Christian Century* 41 (January 3: 5-6).

Mouw, Richard J. 1995. "Evangelical and Roman Catholics in Dialogue." *The Catholic World* 238 (November: 259-264).

Mueller, J. Theodore. 1957. "Back to the Reformers." *Christianity Today* 2 (October 28: 7-10).

Murch, James DeForest. 1946. "Belligerent Orthodoxy." *United Evangelical Action* 4 (February 1: 12).

————. 1949. "Amsterdam, 1948: United Evangelical Action Imperative." *United Evangelical Action* 8 (May 15: 3-5).

————. 1950a. "Is the WCC Building a Super-Church?" *United Evangelical Action* 9 (December 1: 8-9).

————. 1950b. "National Super Church to Be Born in Cleveland." *United Evangelical Action* 9 (August 1: 3-4, 6).

————. 1950c. "The Defeat of Liberalism." *United Evangelical Action* 9 (July 15: 7).

————. 1956. *Cooperation Without Compromise: A History of the National Association of Evangelicals*. Grand Rapids, MI: Eerdmans.

Murphy, Cullen. 1981. "Protestantism and the Evangelicals." *The Wilson Quarterly* 5 (Autumn: 105-119).

Nash, Ronald. 1963. *The New Evangelicalism*. Grand Rapids, MI: Zondervan.

————. 1987. *Evangelicals in America: Who They Are, What They Believe*. Nashville, TN: Abingdon Press.

Nelson, Rudolph. 1987. *The Making and Unmaking of an Evangelical Mind: The Case of Edward Carnell*. New York: Cambridge University Press.

Niebuhr, H. Richard. 1975. *The Social Sources of Denominationalism* (reprint of 1929 edition). New York: Meridian Books.

Noll, Mark A. 1984. "Evangelicals and the Study of the Bible." Pp. 103-121 in *Evangelicalism and Modern America*, edited by George M. Marsden. Grand Rapids, MI: Eerdmans Publishing Co.

————. 1986. *Between Faith & Criticism*. San Francisco: Harper & Row.

Noll, Mark A., David W. Bebbington, and George A. Rawlyk (eds.). 1994. *Evangelicalism: Comparative Studies of Popular Protestantism in North America, the Bristish Isles, and Beyond, 1700-1990*. New York: Oxford University Press.

Noll, Mark A., Nathan O. Hatch, George M. Marsden, David F. Wells, and John D. Woodbridge (eds.). 1983. *Eerdman's Handbook to Christianity in America*. Grand Rapids, MI: Eerdmans Publishing Co.

Noll, Mark and Lyman Kellstedt. 1995. "The Changing Face of Evangelicalism." *Pro Ecclesia* 4 (Spring: 146-164).

Numbers, Ronald L. and Jonathan M. Butler (eds.). 1987. *The Disappointed: Millerism and Millenarianism in the Nineteenth Century*. Bloomington, IN: Indiana University Press.

Ockenga, Harold John. 1942a "Contentious Versus Evangelical Christianity."
       United Evangelical Action 1 (August 1: 2).
———. 1942b. "The Unvoiced Multitudes." Pp. 19-39 in *Evangelical Action!*
       Boston: United Action Press.
———. 1943. "Christ for America." *United Evangelical Action* 2 (May 4: 3-4, 6).
———. 1946a. "This is Liberalism." *United Evangelical Action* 5 (September 15:
       12-13).
———. 1946b. "This is Orthodoxy." *United Evangelical Action* 5 (October 1: 12-
       13).
———. 1946c. "We Get Slapped." *United Evangelical Action* 5 (February 15: 2).
———. 1947a. "Can Fundamentalism Win America?" *Christian Life And Times* 2
       (June: 13-15).
———. 1947b. "The Last Word." *Christian Life And Times* 2 (October: 52-54).
———. 1947c. "The 'Pentecostal' Bogey." *United Evangelical Action* 6 (February
       15: 12-13).
———. 1954a. "Religiously Speaking—What is Liberalism?" *United Evangelical
       Action* 12 (January 15: 5-6, 8) (Reprinted version of 1946a).
———. 1954b. "Religiously Speaking—What is Orthodoxy?" *United Evangelical
       Action* 12 (February 1: 5-6) (Reprinted version of 1946b).
———. 1954c. "Theological Education," *Bulletin of the Fuller Theological Semi-
       nary* 4, 4 (October, November, December: 4-5, 7-8).
———. 1955. "Vanguard of the Evangelical Movement." *United Evangelical Action*
       14 (June 1: 3-6).
———. 1956. "The Reality of Church Unity." *United Evangelical Action* 15 (March
       1: 3-4, 6).
———. 1958. "The New Evangelicalism." *The Park Street Spire* (February: 2-7).
———. 1960. "Resurgent Evangelical Leadership." *Christianity Today* 5 (October
       10: 11-15).
———. 1978. "From Fundamentalism, Through New Evangelicalism, to Evangel-
       icalism." Pp. 35-46 in *Evangelical Roots,* edited by Kenneth S. Kantzer.
       Nashville, TN: Thomas Nelson.
Olson, Roger E. 1995. "Whales and Elephants, Both God's Creatures but Can They
       Meet?: Evangelicals and Liberals in Dialogue." *Pro Ecclesia* 4 (Spring: 165-
       189).
Orr, J. Edwin. 1949. "The Tide is Rising in Southern California." *United Evangelical
       Action* 8 (December 1: 3-4, 12).
Otto, Rudolph. 1958. *The Idea of the Holy* (John W. Harvey, trans.). New York:
       Oxford University Press.
Packer, J. I. 1959. *Fundamentalism and the Word of God.* Grand Rapids, MI:
       Eerdmans Publishing Co.
Padilla, C. René (ed.). 1976. *The New Face of Evangelicalism: An International
       Symposium on the Lausanne Covenant.* Downers Grove, IL: InterVarsity
       Press.
Paine, Stephen W. 1942. "The Possibility of United Action." Pp. 49-61 in
       Evangelical Action! Boston: United Action Press.
———. 1949. "Cooperation Without Compromise." *United Evangelical Action* 8
       (May 1: 9-13, 26-31).
———. 1950. "God's Word for God's World." *United Evangelical Action* 9 (May 1:
       9-13, 26).
———. 1951. *"Separation"—Is Separating Evangelicals.* Boston: Fellowship Press.
Patterson, Bob E. 1983. *Carl F. H. Henry.* Waco, TX: Word Books.

Petticord, Paul P. 1958. "True Ecumenicity." *United Evangelical Action* 17 (May 15: 6-8, 10-11, 13, 27).

Phillips, Timothy R. and Dennis L. Okholm. 1996. *The Nature of Confession: Evangelicals and Postliberals in Conversation.* Downers Grove, IL: InterVarsity Press.

Pickering, Ernest. 1959. "New Evangelicalism: Its Present Status." *The Sword of the Lord* 25 (April 24: 1, 4).

Pierard, Richard V. 1970. *The Unequal Yoke: Evangelical Christianity and Political Conservatism.* Philadelphia: J. B. Lippincott, Co.

Pinnock, Clark H. 1993. "Fuller Theological Seminary and the Nature of Evangelicalism." *Christian Scholar's Review* 23 (September: 44-47).

Pinnock, Clark H. and Delwin Brown. 1990. *Theological Crossfire: An Evangelical-Liberal Dialogue.* Grand Rapids, MI: Zondervan Publishing House.

Plato. 1955. *Gorgias.* New York: Bobbs-Merrill.

———. 1957. *Statesman.* New York: Bobbs-Merrill.

———. 1973. *Phaedrus.* New York: Penguin Classics.

Provenzo, Eugene F., Jr. 1990. *Fundamentalism and American Education: The Battle for the Public Schools.* Albany, NY: SUNY Press.

Quebedeaux, Richard. 1974. *The Young Evangelicals.* New York: Harper & Row.

———. 1976. *The New Charismatics.* New York: Doubleday.

———. 1978. *The Worldly Evangelicals.* San Francisco: Harper & Row.

Ramm, Bernard. 1947. "Is Doctor Henry Right?—No!" *United Evangelical Action* 6 (July 15: 5, 16).

———. 1957. "Are We Obscurantists?" *Christianity Today* 1 (February 18: 14-15).

———. 1965. "The Continental Divide in Contemporary Theology." *Christianity Today* 10 (October 8: 14-17).

———. 1981. *The Evangelical Heritage* (Reprinted). Grand Rapids, MI: Baker Book House.

Rausch, David A. 1979. *Zionism Within Early American Fundamentalism, 1878-1918.* New York: The Edwin Mellen Press.

Rawlyk, George A. and Mark A. Noll (eds.). 1993. *Amazing Grace: Evangelicalism in Australia, Britain, Canada, and the United States.* Grand Rapids, MI: Baker Books.

Rees, Paul. 1955. "The Nature of the Unity We Seek." *United Evangelical Action* 14 (December 1: 9-10).

———. 1957. "What About the Criticism?" *Christian Life* 18 (April: 14-16).

Reid, W. Stanford. 1962. "Areas of Neglect: Evangelical Defeat by Default." *Christianity Today* 6 (January 5: 27-28).

Rice, John R. 1957. "Billy Graham Openly Repudiates Fundamentalism." *The Sword of The Lord* 23 (May 17: 2, 10-12).

———. 1959. "Fuller Seminary's Carnell Sneers at Fundamentalism." *The Sword of The Lord* 25 (October 30: 1, 7, 11).

Riley, William B. 1919. "The Great Divide or Christianity and the Present Crisis." *Watchman-Examiner* 7 (June 26: 997-999).

Robbins, Thomas. 1988. *Cults, Converts, & Charisma: The Sociology of New Religious Movements.* Newbury Park, CA: Sage Publications.

Roberson, Jesse J. 1964. "Liberalism's Fatal Weakness." *Christianity Today* 8 (April 24: 5-7).

Roberts, Jon H. 1988. *Darwinism and the Divine in America: Protestant Intellectuals and Organic Evolution, 1859-1900.* Madison: The University of Wisconsin Press.

Roddy, Sherman. 1958. "Fundamentalists and Ecumenicity." *The Christian Century* 75 (October 1: 1109-1110).

Roof, Wade Clark and William McKinney. 1987. *American Mainline Religion: Its Changing Shape and Future*. New Brunswick, NJ: Rutgers University Press.

Rosell, Garth M. 1996. *The Evangelical Landscape*. Grand Rapids, MI: Baker Books.

Rousseau, Jean-Jacques. 1984. *A Discourse on Inequality*. New York: Penguin Classics.

Roy, Ralph L. 1953. *Apostles of Discord*. Boston: Beacon Press.

Rudin, A. James and Marvin R. Wilson (eds.). 1987. *A Time to Speak: The Evangelical-Jewish Encounter*. Grand Rapids, MI: Eerdmans.

Russell, C. Allyn. 1976. *Voices of American Fundamentalism*. Philadelphia: The Westminster Press.

Ryrie, Charles C. 1956. *Neo-Orthodoxy: What it Is and What it Does*. Chicago: Moody Press.

Sandeen, Ernest R. 1968. *The Origins of Fundamentalism*. Philadelphia: Fortress Press.

————. 1970. *The Roots of Fundamentalism*. Chicago: University of Chicago Press.

Scarborough, L. R. 1922. "Southern Baptists Concerned About Fundamentalist Invasion." *The Baptist* 3 (October 7: 1111-1112).

Scofield, C. I. 1896. *Rightly Dividing the Word of Truth*. New York: Loizeaux Brothers.

Shelley, Bruce L. 1967. *Evangelicalism in America*. Grand Rapids, MI: Eerdmans Publishing Co.

Shuy, Roger W. 1964. "What Do We Call Ourselves?" *United Evangelical Action* 23 (May: 3, 11).

Silk, Mark. 1988. *Spiritual Politics: Religion and America Since World War II*. New York: Simon and Schuster.

————. 1989. "The Rise of the 'New Evangelicalism': Shock and Adjustment." Pp. 278-299 in *Between the Times: The Travail of the Protestant Establishment in America 1900-1960,* edited by William R. Hutchison. New York: Cambridge University Press.

Simmel, Georg. 1971. *On Individuality and Social Forms: Selected Writings* (Donald N. Levine, ed.). Chicago: University of Chicago Press.

Simpson, Alan. 1955. *Puritanism in Old and New England*. Chicago: University of Chicago Press.

Smart, Ninian. 1983. *Worldviews: Crosscultural Explorations of Human Beliefs*. New York: Charles Scribner's Sons.

Smidt, Corwin E. (ed.). 1989. *Contemporary Evangelical Political Involvement*. Lanham, MD: University Press of America.

Smith, Timothy L. 1957. *Revivalism and Social Reform: American Protestantism on the Eve of the Civil War*. New York: Harper Torchbooks.

————. 1986. "The Evangelical Kaleidoscope and the Call to Unity." *Christian Scholar's Review* 15, 2 (125-40).

Smith, Wilbur. 1971. *Before I Forget*. Chicago: Moody Press.

Stackhouse, John G. 1995. "The National Association of Evangelicals, the Evangelical Fellowship of Canada, and the Limits of Evangelical Cooperation." *Christian Scholar's Review* 25 (December: 157-179).

Stark, Rodney. 1986. "Jewish Conversion and the Rise of Christianity: Rethinking the Received Wisdom." Pp. 314-329 in the *Published Proceedings of the Annual Meeting of the Society for Biblical Literature*.

Stark, Rodney and William Sims Bainbridge. 1980. "Towards a Theory of Religion: Religious Commitment." *Journal for the Scientific Study of Religion* 19 (114-128).

———. 1985. *The Future of Religion: Secularization, Revival, and Cult Formation.* Berkeley: University of California Press.

———. 1987. *A Theory of Religion.* New York: Peter Lang.

Stevick, Daniel B. 1964. *Beyond Fundamentalism.* Richmond, VA: John Knox Press.

Stinchcombe, Arthur L. 1968. *Constructing Social Theories.* Berkeley: University of California Press.

Stone, Jon R. 1990. "The New Voluntarism and Presbyterian Affiliation." Pp. 122-149 in *The Mainline Protestant 'Decline': The Presbyterian Pattern*, edited by Milton J. Coalter, John M. Mulder, and Lewis B. Weeks. Louisville: Westminster/ John Knox Press.

———. 1991. "Messianic Judaism: A Redefinition of the Boundary Between Christian and Jew?" *Research in the Social Scientific Study of Religion* 3 (237-252).

———. 1993. *A Guide to the End of the World: Popular Eschatology in America.* New York: Garland Publishing, Inc.

Stowell, Joseph M., III. 1990. "Response to Donald A. Carson." Pp. 387-396 in *Evangelical Affirmations*, edited by Kenneth S. Kantzer and Carl F. H. Henry. Grand Rapids, MI: Zondervan Publishing Co.

Streiker, Lowell D. and Gerald S. Strober. 1972. *Religion and the New Majority.* New York: Association Press.

Sumner, Robert L. 1959. *Man Sent from God.* Murfreesburo, TN: Sword of the Lord Publishers.

Sweeney, Douglas A. 1991a. "The Essential Evangelicalism Dialectic: The Historiography of the Early Neo-Evangelical Movement and the Observer-Participant Dilemma." *Church History* 60 (March: 70-84).

———. 1991b. "The 'Strange Schizophrenia' of Neo-Evangelicalism: A Bibliography." *Evangelical Studies Bulletin* 8 (Spring: 6-8).

———. 1993. "Historiographical Dialectics: On Marsden, Dayton, and the Inner Logic of Evangelical History." *Christian Scholar's Review* 23 (September: 48-52).

Sweet, Leonard I. 1984. "The Evangelical Tradition in America." Pp. 1-86 in *The Evangelical Tradition in America*, edited by Leonard I. Sweet. Macon, GA: Mercer University Press.

———. 1988. "Wise as Serpents, Innocent as Doves: The New Evangelical Historiography." *Journal of the American Academy of Religion* 56 (397-416).

Synan, Vinson. 1977. "Theological Boundaries: The Arminian Tradition." Pp. 38-57 in *The Evangelicals*, edited by David F. Wells and John D. Woodbridge. Grand Rapids, MI: Baker Books House.

Szasz, Ferenc M. 1982. *The Divided Mind of Protestant America, 1880-1930.* University, AL: University of Alabama Press.

Tanenbaum, Marc H., Marvin R. Wilson, and A. James Rudin (eds.). 1978. *Evangelicals and Jews in Conversation on Scripture, Theology, and History.* Grand Rapids, MI: Baker Book House.

———. 1984. *Evangelicals and Jews in an Age of Pluralism.* Grand Rapids, MI: Baker Book House.

Taylor, G. Aiken. 1950. "Issues that Unite and Divide." *Christianity Today* 2 (January 6: 16-17).

Thurston, Burton. 1956. "The Nature of the Unity We Seek." *United Evangelical Action* 14 (February 1: 4-6).

United . . . We Stand: A Report of the Constitutional Convention of the National Association of Evangelicals. 1943. Boston: National Association of Evangelicals.

Vanderlaan, Eldred C. (ed.). 1925. *Fundamentalism Versus Modernism*. New York: The H. W. Wilson Co.

Van Til, Cornelius. 1962. *Christianity and Barthianism*. Philadelphia: The Presbyterian and Reformed Publishing Co.

———. 1964. *Karl Barth and Evangelicalism*. Philadelphia: Presbyterian and Reformed Publishing Co.

Van Til, Henry R. 1961. "In Defense of Orthodoxy." *Christianity Today* 5 (March 27: 10-12).

Walhout, Edwin. 1963. "The Liberal-Fundamentalist Debate." *Christianity Today* 7 (March 1: 3-4).

Walvoord, John F. 1957. "What's Right About Fundamentalism?" *Eternity* 8 (June: 6-7, 34-35).

Warner, R. Stephen. 1979. "Theoretical Barriers to the Understanding of Evangelical Christianity." *Sociological Analysis* 40, 1 (1-9).

Watt, David Harrington. 1991. *A Transforming Faith: Explorations of Twentieth-Century American Evangelicalism*. New Brunswick, NJ: Rutgers University Press.

Webber, Robert E. 1978. *Common Roots: A Call to Evangelical Maturity*. Grand Rapids, MI: Zondervan Publishing House.

Weber, Max. 1958. *The Protestant Ethic and the Spirit of Capitalism* (Talcott Parsons, trans). New York: Charles Scribner's Sons.

———. 1963. *The Sociology of Religion* (Ephraim Fischoff, trans). Boston: Beacon Press.

Weber, Timothy. 1987. *Living in the Shadow of the Second Coming* (2nd edition). Chicago: University of Chicago Press.

Wells, David F. 1993. *No Place for Truth: or What Happened to Evangelical Theology?* Grand Rapids, MI: William B. Eerdmans Publishing Co.

———. 1994. "Evangelicalism in Its Settings: The British and American Movements since 1940." Pp. 389-410 in *Evangelicalism: Comparative Studies of Popular Protestantism in North America, the Bristish Isles, and Beyond, 1700-1990,* edited by Mark A. Noll, David W. Bebbington, and George A. Rawlyk. New York: Oxford University Press.

Wells, David F. and John D. Woodbridge (eds.). 1977. *The Evangelicals*. Grand Rapids, MI: Baker Book House.

Willard, W. Wyeth. 1950. *Fire on the Prairie: The Story of Wheaton College*. Wheaton, IL: Van Kampen Press.

Wilson, Bryan R. 1970. *Religious Sects*. London: Weidenfeld & Nicolson.

———. 1982. *Religion in Sociological Perspective*. New York: Oxford University Press.

———. 1985. "Secularization: The Inherited Model." Pp. 9-20 in *The Sacred in a Secular Age,* edited by Phillip E. Hammond. Berkeley: University of California Press.

Woodbridge, Charles. 1969. *The New Evangelicalism*. Greenville, SC: Bob Jones University Press.

Wright, J. Elwin. 1942. "An Historical Statement of Events Leading up to the National Conference at St. Louis." Pp. 3-16 in *Evangelical Action!* Boston: United Action Press.

———. 1943. "An Appraisal of Our Situation." *United Evangelical Action* 2 (August: 2-3).

———. 1947. "Can Fundamentalism Win?" *United Evangelical Action* 6 (September 15: 12-13).

Wurth, G. Brillenburg. 1957. "Theological Climate in America." *Christianity Today* 1 (February 18: 10-13).

Wuthnow, Robert. 1988. *The Restructuring of American Religion.* Princeton, NJ: Princeton University Press.

———. 1989. *The Struggle for America's Soul: Evangelicals, Liberals, and Secularism.* Grand Rapids, MI: Eerdmans Publishing Co.

Yarbrough, Robert W. 1989. "Retreating Authority: Evangelical-Liberal Rapprochement?" *Christian Scholar's Review* 19 (December: 149-162).

Young, Lawrence A. (ed.). 1997. *Rational Choice Theory and Religion: Summary and Assessment.* New York: Routledge.

List of Referenced Christian Periodicals

Baptist and Reflector
Christian Century
Christian Life (and Times)
Christianity Today
Eternity
King's Business
Moody Monthly
The Presbyterian Guardian
Sunday School Times
United Evangelical Action

Index

Abbott, Lyman 192 n18
Abraham, William
    evangelical reform 16-17
    evangelical orthodoxy 17,
    37-8
    typologies 26, 35-6, 189
    n21
Adventists 58, 188 n6
Allport, Gordon 189 n25
American Civil Liberties Union
    (ACLU) 65
American Council of Christian
    Churches 18, 31, 74, 75,
    77-9, 81-2, 85, 92, 94, 107,
    119-21, 186 n11, 192 n3
Ammerman, Nancy 26, 29
Anabaptist tradition 26-7
Ankerberg, John 200 n10
anti-Christ 123
anti-intellectualism 105, 118,
    163, 195 n22
apocalypticism 10, 33, 63, 186
    n14
apostasy 67, 78-9, 81, 84, 92,
    113, 124, 165, 183, 194
    n11
apostles 107-10, 131, 144, 154
apostolic
    church 90, 106-7, 120,
    198 n21
    gospel 140
Arnold, Paul L. 88-90
Assemblies of God 194 n9

Augustine 110
Ayer, William Ward 87, 108,
    121-3, 144, 195 n20

Baptist Bible Union 67
Baptist tradition 24, 26-27
Barr, James 150
Barth, Fredrik 44-45, 190 n30
    "Ethnic Groups and
    Boundaries" 44
Barth, Karl 20, 34, 61, 119,
    145-57, 189 n14, 198 n15
Bauman, Louis S. 77
Beecher, Henry Ward 55
Bennett, John C. 147
Berger, Peter 46
Bible
    authority of 3, 28, 32, 54-
    6, 64, 83, 108, 114, 125,
    163
    and Christian service 89
    historical-critical method
    32, 55, 149, 164
    infallibility of 26, 31, 33,
    39, 55, 57, 61, 124, 153,
    163-71, 177, 181, 187 n24,
    200 n3
    inspiration of 28, 34, 146,
    151, 153, 164, 168, 200 n3
    literalism 52, 115
    as Word of God 136, 167,
    198 n21
Bible Presbyterian Church 67

Bible Institute of Los Angeles
     (Biola)   63, 88, 103-4, 195
     n19
Black Methodists   24, 187 n19
Bloesch, Donald   185 n7
Bob Jones University   31
Bolich, Gregory   28, 148, 198
     n16
Boston University   146, 164
Brethren   24
Briggs, Charles   62
Bromiley, Geoffrey   132, 137,
     198 n17
Brown, Harold O.J.   200 n10
Brownville, C. Gordon   85
Brunner, Emil   148, 156
Bryan, Willian Jennings   64-6,
     70, 192 n18
Butler Act   65
Butler, Farley P.   16, 100-1,
     105, 147, 152, 194 n11,
     197 n13

Cairns, Earle E.   130
Calvinism   27, 129. 187 n18,
     193 n6
Carnell, Edward J.   29-30, 34,
     113-6, 146, 164-5
     *The Case for Orthodox
     Theology*   114
     on fundamentalism   189
     n20
     on neo-orthodoxy   153,
     198 n15
     "Orthodoxy: Cultic vs.
     Classic"   114
     "Orthodoxy and Ecu-
     menism"   135-6
     "Post-Fundamentalist
     Faith"   113-14
     and theological scholar-
     ship   147

Carpenter, Joel A.   8-9, 74, 76,
     77, 79, 185 n9, 186 n11,
     188 n9, 200 n11
Carson, Donald A.   177
     "Evangelicals, Ecu-
     menism, and the Church"
     176
Case, Shirley Jackson   63
charismatics   173, 189 n15
Christian Century   69, 105, 111,
     113-15, 171, 193 n7
Christian Life (and Times)   93-
     4, 98, 100-3, 141, 195 n19
     "Is Evangelical Theology
     Changing?"   100
Christian Reformed   24
Christianity Today   98, 105-6,
     108, 109, 117, 135, 148,
     154, 160, 162, 163, 166,
     167, 172, 174, 181, 198
     n16
Church of God   194 n9
Churches of Christ   24
civil rights   34
Clarke, William Newton   56
coalitions   6-7, 179
Cohen, Anthony   44, 47-8, 191
     n33
Colson, Charles   200 n10
     *Evangelicals and Catholics
     Together*   201 n14
communism   124
Conant, Judson E.   68
Confessionalism   188 n5
Conservative Baptist Church
     67
conversion   27
Crunkilton, Willard   127

Daniel, Book of   92
Darby, John Nelson   58-60
     "secret rapture"   59
Darrow, Clarence   65-6

Darwinism   54, 56, 64-6, 101,
    192 n16
Dayton, Donald W.   24, 35, 189
    n22, 200 n11
Disciples of Christ   196 n5
dispensationalism   33, 53, 58-
    63, 89, 103, 115, 181
Dormon, James H.   45
Douglas, Mary   44, 46-7, 190
    n32
    Purity and Danger   46
Durkheim, Émile   47
Dutch Reformed Church   24

ecumenism   20, 106-7, 119,
    122-7, 132, 135, 153, 159,
    161
Erdman, Charles   70
eschatology   103
Eternity magazine 98
Evangelical Affirmations Con-
    ference   173-8
Evangelical Brethren   187 n19
evangelical "kaleidoscope" 5-6,
    24, 45, 178
Evangelical Lutheran Church
    39, 187 n19
evangelical "mosaic" 4, 6, 178
evangelicalism
    broadening boundaries 8,
        113, 117, 149
    as coalition 6-8, 10-13, 16,
        53, 74, 76-7, 84, 93, 98,
        105, 117-18, 123, 129,
        159, 165, 173, 178, 180,
        181-2, 185 n9
    definitions of 3, 110, 168-
        73
    diversity within   23-4,
        132, 136-8, 162-4
    and ecumenism   121-33,
        183

fragmentation of   159,
    163-71
metaphors for   4-5, 178-9
and neo-orthodoxy   156
and orthodoxy   16, 84, 87,
    89, 105, 114, 119, 137,
    147, 160, 171
and science   102
and secularism   12
and social conscience   27,
    33-4, 52, 80-1, 87-97, 101,
    103, 118-19
as "subculture" 9
typologies   31-3

Fackre, Gabriel   189 n22
faith
    boundaries of   14, 27, 75,
        83, 93, 131
    orthodox   78, 167
    and salvation   26
Falwell, Jerry   200 n10
"family resemblances" 5-6, 37
Federal Council of Churches
    (FCC)   18, 77-9, 81-2, 85,
    119-23, 125, 196 n6
Feinberg, Charles   195 n19
Fletcher, William   156
    The Moderns   156-7
Ford, George L.   131-2, 135
    "Why the NAE is Succeed-
        ing" 131, 135
Foreign Mission Society   77
Fosdick, Harry Emerson   68-9,
    144, 153
    "Shall the Fundamentalists
        Win?" 69
Free Methodists   24
Friends   24
Fuller, Charles   91, 200 n11
Fuller, Daniel   200 n11
Fuller Theological Seminary
    17, 29, 32, 86, 91, 105,

147, 164-8, 171, 173, 181,
200 n6
fundamentalism
and ecumenism 91, 111
growth of 9
marginalization of 10, 53-
4, 62, 66, 70-1, 73-5, 180
and obscurantism 145,
149, 195 n22
progressive 11, 186 n11
reform of 95
rejection of 95, 97
and secularism 2
and separatism 12, 15, 31,
115, 120, 186 n11
as subculture 8
typologies 30-1, 188 n6
Fundamentalist Fellowship 67

Gaebelein, Arno 60
Gasper, Louis 17-18, 151, 192
n5
The Fundamentalist Move-
ment, 1930-1956 17-18
Geisler, Norman L.
Roman Catholics and Evan-
gelicals 202 n14
General Association of Regular
Baptists 67
Gospel 110, 121, 125, 136,
139-44, 196 n3
Graham, Billy 16, 32, 37, 109,
147, 160, 162, 197 n13,
200 n10
and Christianity Today
105
Grounds, Vernon G. 98-101,
116, 200 n10
"The Nature of Evangeli-
calism" 98

Hargis, Billy James 31
Harvard University 146, 164

Hatch, Nathan O. 175-6, 200
n10
Henry, Carl F.H. 32, 116, 117,
134, 145, 146, 173-5
biography of 198 n19
and Christianity Today
105-7, 143
"Dare We Renew the Con-
troversy?" 108
and ecumenism 107, 122,
125, 129, 197 n14
on evangelical social conscience 86, 88, 91, 138-41,
144, 197 n12
on evangelicalism 117-18,
128, 133, 142, 147, 163,
172
"Evangelicals and Funda-
mentals" 109-10
Evangelicals at the Brink of
Crisis 160-2
Evangelicals in Search of
Identity 161-2
on fundamentalism 108-9
on neo-orthodoxy 154-5,
162
"Perspectives for Social
Action" 143
A Plea for Evangelical
Demonstration 197 n14
The Uneasy Conscience of
Modern Fundamentalism
86, 89, 138-9, 141
"The Vigor of the New
Evangelicalism" 141
heresy 62, 131-2
Himes, Joshua V. 58
Hodge, Charles 55
Hodgman, S.A. 64
Hoge, Dean R. 189 n26
Division in the Protestant
House 189 n26

Holiness groups   24, 26-7, 77, 175, 188 n5, 188 n6, 194 n9
Holmer, Paul L.   163, 199 n2
   "Contemporary Evangelical Faith" 163
Holy Rollers   101
Holy Spirit   33, 103, 129
Hordern, William   150
Hubbard, David A.   165
Hudson, Winthrop   56, 63
Hunter, James Davison   14-15, 26, 32, 37, 188 n5
   on evangelical traditions 26-9

intellectualism   75, 105, 112, 118, 146-7, 160, 164, 182

Jaarsma, Cornelius   96
Jesus   129, 144
   faith in   137, 170
   Headship of   129
   incarnation of   87
   inerrant witness of   169
   redemption by   139, 141, 143-4
   resurrection of   187 n24
   Second Advent   57, 90, 155
   vicarious atonement of 125, 143, 187 n24
   virgin birth of   68, 101, 187 n24
   as Word of God   150-1
Johnson, Benton   190 n27
Johnston, Robert K.   5-6, 35
Jonah   169
Judaism   33, 183

Kamm, S.R.   95
Kantzer, Kenneth   174

   Evangelical Affirmations 174
Kellogg, Samuel   61
Kik, J. Marcellus   125, 129, 131, 134-5
   Ecumenism and the Evangelical   129
King's Business   63, 104
Kuhn, Thomas   41

Ladd, George Eldon   146
Laws, Curtis Lee   54
Lindsell, Harold   13, 165-8, 171
   The Battle for the Bible 163, 188 n12
   The Bible in the Balance 167-170
Lindsey, Hal   31
Longfield, Bradley J.   66
Luckmann, Thomas   46
Lutherans   24, 187 n19, 188 n6

Machen, J. Gresham   55, 67-70, 78, 82, 110, 117
   Christianity and Liberalism 67, 82, 192 n20
marginalization (of fundamentalism)   10, 53-4, 62, 66, 70-1, 73-5, 180
Marsden, George M.
   on evangelicalism   16-17, 62, 85, 159-60, 165, 167, 173, 180, 185 n9, 200 n11
   on fundamentalism   9, 53, 71, 185 n9, 186 n13
   on neo-orthodoxy   148
   typologies   26, 28, 187 n19
Marston, Leslie R.   96
Marty, Martin E.   13-14, 51-2, 200 n2
   Nation of Behavers   188 n4
Massee, J.C.   67
McClain, Alva   104

McGrath, Alister 177

McIntire, Carl 164
    on apostasy 78
    on evangelical concessions
        13
    as separatist fundamental-
        ist 31, 194 n11

McLoughlin, William 41-3,
    190 n29
    "Is There a Third Force in
    Christendom?" 41

Mencken, H.L. 66

Mennonites 24, 188 n6

Merrill, William P. 70
    Liberal Christianity 70

metaphors 4-5, 18, 35, 87, 88,
    178, 183

method
    historical 41-2
    phenomenological 26
    psychological 39-40
    social structural 3, 15, 17-
        19, 25, 43, 179, 197 n9
    sociological (institutional)
        40
    theological 39

Miller, William 58

Moberg, David O. 197 n9

Mohler, Albert 201 n11

Moody, Dwight 52, 110

Moral Majority 173

Mormons 101

Morrison, C.C. 69-70, 196 n5
    "Fundamentalism and
    Modernism: Two Reli-
    gions" 69

Moses 144

Murch, James Deforest 79, 124,
    196 n5

mysticism 40

National Association of Evan-
    gelicals (NAE)

    as coalition 74-85, 93,
        122, 126, 131, 192 n3
    as ecumenical 126, 128,
        130
    founding of 74, 119, 175,
        181, 188 n5
    and Gospel 125
    as moderating force 18,
        32, 76, 79, 83, 96, 105-8,
        120, 124, 159, 186 n11,
        193 n5
    and separatism 75, 103
    and social engagement 80,
        85, 93
    and unity 130-1, 134-5

National Council of Churches
    (NCC) 18, 107, 124-5,
        146

Nazarenes 23

Nelson, Frank 95-6

Nelson, Rudolph 147

neo-orthodoxy 17, 20, 99, 119,
    145-57

New Testament 129, 133, 155

Niebuhr, H. Richard 40-1, 190
    n27
    *The Social Sources of De-
    nominationalism* 40

Niebuhr, Reinhold 198 n19

Northern Baptist Convention
    67, 94

Northern Presbyterians 67

Ockenga, Harold J. 117, 139,
    148, 194 n9
    "Can Fundamentalism
    Win America?" 91
    on ecumenism 121, 123
    on evangelical unity 126,
        129, 132, 134, 166, 197
        n14
    on fundamentalism 81-2,
        91-4

on neo-orthodoxy   152-3
on orthodoxy   77-9, 116,
    144
Orthodox Presbyterian Church
    67, 68
orthodoxy
    and Barth   151
    "classic"   30, 114-16
    "cultic"   30, 114-16, 189
        n20
    evangelical   16, 84, 87, 89,
        105, 114, 119, 137, 147,
        160, 181, 196 n3
    and fundamentalism   20,
        37, 42, 75, 88, 92, 101-2,
        104, 109
    historic   96, 98-100, 108,
        110, 124, 187 n18
    revival of   76-7, 91, 103,
        113, 120
    rival versions of   18, 28,
        52, 83, 117, 130
    and tensions   14, 82, 107,
        122
    theological   15, 17
orthopraxy   15
The Other Side   172
Otto, Rudolf   40
    The Idea of the Holy   40

Packer, J. I.   200 n10
Paine, Stephen W.   81-3, 121-
    2, 153
    "The Possibility of United
        Action"   82
Patterson, Bob   198 n19
Pentecost   89
Pentecostals   24, 26, 33, 77,
    175, 187 n19, 188 n5, 188
    n6, 194 n9
Pharisees (Pharisaism)   87,
    106, 113
Pierard, Richard V.   199 n1

Pietism   188 n5, 188 n6
Pinnock, Clark   200 n11
Plato   7, 185 n8, 185 n10
Plymouth Brethren   58
premillennialism   57-63, 181,
    187 n24, 188 n6
Presbyterians   24, 187 n19, 187
    n24
Price, George McCready   64
primitivism   28
Princeton Theology   55
prophecy   61
Prophecy conferences   57, 60,
    191 n5
Puritanism   187 n18, 188 n5

Quebedeaux, Richard   26, 29,
    37, 188 n12, 189 n15
    Evangelical/Fundamental-
        ist continuum   30-4
    The New Charismatics   199
        n1
    The Worldly Evangelicals
        199 n1
    The Young Evangelicals
        199 n1

racism   140, 145
Ramm, Bernard   88-9, 155-6,
    195 n16, 195 n22
    "The Continental Divide in
        Contemporary Theology"
        155
Rees, Paul   128, 132
    "The Nature of the Unity
        We Seek"   128
Reformation   106, 110, 154-5,
    186 n18, 198 n21
Reformed-Confessional tradi-
    tion   26-8, 188 n6
Reformed Journal   172
relativism   75
Restorationism   188 n6

revival 3, 9, 12, 75-6, 81, 118,
    140, 172, 181, 193 n7
Rice, John R. 103, 164
    Sword of the Lord 103
Riley, William Bell 64, 65, 67,
    94, 192 n19
Roddy, Clarence 111
Roddy, Sherman 111-13
    "Fundamentalists and Ec-
    umenicity" 111
Roman Catholicism 33, 92, 99,
    123-4, 126, 133, 173, 183,
    186 n18, 201 n14
Rousseau, Jean-Jacques 6

St. John 123, 129
St. Paul 126, 150
St. Peter 89
sanctification 27, 33
Sandeen, Ernest R. 60, 191 n5
Satan 83, 121, 134
Schleiermacher, Friedrich 144
Scofield Bible 60
Scofield, C. I. 60-1
Scopes "monkey" trial 62, 64-
    6, 101
secularism 12-13, 92, 140
separatism 59-60, 75, 81, 85,
    88, 91-2, 101, 103, 120,
    139-140, 148, 186 n13,
    194 n11
Seventh-day Adventists 24
Simmel, Georg 190 n31
social action 80, 81, 89, 94,
    139-140, 143, 172, 182
social ethic 33, 52, 85-6, 88,
    90, 96-7, 101, 103, 119,
    145, 159, 160, 197 n12
social gospel 20, 52, 138, 143-4
social reform 27, 34, 87, 90,
    141, 172
Sojourners 172
Smith, Timothy L. 4-6, 24, 178

Southern Baptists 187 n19
Spina, Frank 37
Stark, Rodney 5, 178
Stoll, John H. 103
Stowell, Joseph 176-7
Straton, John Roach 67
Sunday, Billy 67, 68
Sunday School Times 78
super-orthodoxy 83
Sutherland, S.H. 104
Sweet, Leonard 23-4
Szasz, Ferenc 53, 180

Taylor, G. Aiken 199 n22
televangelism 174
theology
    as symbolic boundary 15-
    18, 35
Tillich, Paul 147
Trinity Evangelical Divinity
    School 166, 167, 174, 176
Troeltsch, Ernst 40
"two-party" system 19, 25, 38,
    51, 156

United Evangelical Action 88,
    96, 125, 127-8, 197 n12
unity
    spiritual 125-7, 129, 133,
    137

Van Dusen, Henry P. 193 n6

Walvoord, John F. 31, 110, 164
Warfield, B.B. 55, 117
Watt, David Harrington 8-9
Webber, Robert E. 26, 34-5
Weber, Max 40
Weber, Timothy 191 n5
Weigel, George 201 n14
Wells, David F. 71, 73, 200 n10
    The Evangelicals 163
    No Place for Truth 199 n2

Wesleyans 24
Westmont College 164, 165
Wheaton College 32, 146, 164
White, John 200 n10
Wilson, Bryan R. 178
Wittgenstein, Ludwig 5-6
Woodbridge, John D. 71, 73, 200 n10
World Congress on Evangelism 160
World Council of Churches (WCC) 124, 128, 146
World Vision 172

World War I 62-3, 67, 115, 150
World War II 93, 102, 156, 179
World's Christian Fundamentals Association 65, 67, 192 n19
Wright, J. Elwin 77, 79, 84, 120-1, 194 n13
Wurth, G. Brillenburg 143-4, 153-4
Wuthnow, Robert 46, 183, 186 n11

Zimmerman, Thomas 200 n10